Items Worth Noting

AF704226

Taxpayer Refund and Relief Act of 1999

Didn't have a chance. It was vetoed as expected. A much smaller tax bill will extend some credits and fix some important items. The Taxpayer Relief Act of 1997, being a maze of beginning dates, ending dates, income thresholds and special conditions, has many provisions that took effect in 1998 and have built in increases in 1999 and future years.

Sale of principal residence exclusion for sales after May 6, 1997: Allows homeowners to exclude tax on gain of up to $250,000 if single and up to $500,000 if married and filing jointly. In the 5-year period before the current sale, you must have used the property as your home for a total of two years. You do not have to buy replacement property and you can take advantage of the exclusion as many times as you can meet the two-year ownership and residency rule. See Chapter Two for more complete discussion.

Capital gains rate reduction after May 6, 1997: When stocks, land, collectibles, business property and other capital assets are sold, the profit is a capital gain. The time the asset is held determines if it is short-term or long-term. Since January 1, 1998, the holding period for long term is 12 months.

Short-term gains are taxed as ordinary income—15% to 39.6%

Long-term gains are taxed at lower rates—10% to 20% (For taxpayers in the 15% bracket—**10%**; For taxpayers in the 28% thru 39.6% brackets—**20%**)

Because mutual fund vendors provide shareholders with the holding period breakdown, be sure to give this information to your tax preparer.

Child Tax Credit began in 1998: In addition to the 1999 exemption of $2,750 for each dependent child, the Child Tax Credit is a non-refundable credit against federal taxes. The 1999 credit is $500 per child. An eligible child must be under the age of 17 by the close of the year in which the credit is claimed. The child must also be your dependent child, grandchild, stepchild, or foster child. The phaseout threshold of modified adjusted gross income for joint filers is $110,000; single or head of household filers is $75,000; married separate filers is $55,000. Low income families with three or more qualifying children may qualify for a refundable supplemental child credit under some rather complex rules.

At enactment Congress knowingly allowed the alternative minimum tax computation to not be reduced by the new child tax credit. This can result in no credit being available for an estimated 800,000 middle income parents! In 1998's budget bill a one year reprieve was passed. For 1998 returns, the new child tax credit **was allowed** as an offset against alternative minimum tax. The Taxpayer Refund and Relief Act of 1999 contained a permanent remedy to the AMT tax problem. It was vetoed as expected and Congress promises to deal with the Child Tax Credit problem and extend some credits yet this fall.

Contribution Mileage Rate: The mileage rate for volunteer workers is 14¢ per mile.

Foreign Earned Income Exclusion Increasing $2,000 each year: The 1999 foreign earned income exclusion of $74,000 will increase to $76,000 in 2000, $78,000 in 2001 and $80,000 in 2002 and later years.

Estimated Income Tax Threshold Has Increased: No underpayment penalty will be imposed if the tax due, reduced by withholding taxes, is less than $1,000.

IRAs Change: Effective for tax year 1997, the maximum IRA deduction for a married couple filing jointly increased from $2,250 to $4,000, up to $2,000 each, as long as their combined compensation is at least that much. Effective for tax year **1998**, more people can make deductible contributions to regular IRAs. For active participants in employer's plans the phaseout threshold of income raised in 1998 and increases annually until 2007. The 1999 range for single taxpayers is $31,000 to $41,000, for married taxpayers filing joint is $51,000 to $61,000. An active participant spouse does not keep the non-active participant spouse from making a deductible contribution. Distributions from an IRA for up to $10,000 of first time home buyer expenses and for higher education costs will not be subject to the 10% early withdrawal penalty.

Roth IRAs Began in 1998: Contributions to a Roth IRA are not deductible, but distributions of money held in the account for five years or longer, in addition to other requirements, are tax free.

Paying For Education: Education tax-planning is very important. New tax law provides many ways to help pay for you, your spouse or your children's college education. Among the provisions are the HOPE and Lifetime Learning credits that allow a credit for tuition and related expenses, Education IRAs, rules for qualified tuition programs, penalty-free withdrawals from regular IRAs for education expenses, extension of the exclusion for employer-provided assistance, and deductions for interest on education loans. The complex rules prevent simultaneous use of these new provisions and each have their own phaseout thresholds of income. See "Education," in Chapter Three for a more complete discussion.

Other Miscellaneous Items

MSSP audit guide for ministers: Market Segment Specialization Program audit guides help IRS examiners gain insight into the particular market segments in order to perform more competent audits.

Contribution Substantiation: Any donor who makes a contribution of **$250** or more after 1993 must obtain substantiation of the contribution from the donee to obtain a deduction. Each contribution is viewed separately. All contributions made on the same date, however, should be combined for purposes of determining if the donor has exceeded the $250 level. The taxpayer must be given the statement by the donee the **earlier** of the date his tax return is filed or the due date of the return (including extensions). For contributions made in 1994, the taxpayer was given until October 16, 1995 to obtain the statement.

Include on the statement: (1) Date gift was given, (2) Name of donor, (3) Name and address of donee organization, (4) The $ amount if cash or a simple description if property (5) One of these statements: "Only intangible religious benefits were received by the donor."**or** "Value of tangible benefit donor received was $________."

WORTH TAX & FINANCIAL SERVICE
Box 725 ● Winona Lake, Indiana 46590
(219) 267-4687

FOREWORD

My name is B.J. Worth, founder and owner of Worth Tax & Financial Service. My staff and I are excited to be celebrating the 27th anniversary of doing taxes in Winona Lake/Warsaw, IN area this spring of 2000! We are happy to introduce you to a new product. Many of you asked for recordkeeping book for your auto log and expenses. The exciting event of becoming owner of "Bugzy", a 1998 VW Beetle, prompted the "Auto Log" pictured on page 129 for $3.99. It contains the two auto sections from the "Professional Tax Record Book."

I am blessed with a very experienced staff of tax consultants and customer service specialists. One of the most sought after designations for a tax consultant is that of becoming an EA. To become "enrolled to practice before the IRS" one must sit for a two-day exam administered annually by the IRS and meet continuing education requirements. Worth Tax & Financial Service is privileged to have four tax accountants who have the designation of EA.

Having published **"Income Tax Guide for Ministers & Religious Workers"** since 1973, the **"Professional Tax Record Book"** since 1982, we have a large clientele of ministers from all over the world! We can assist our tax clients with IRAs, 403(b)s mutual funds, lump-sum distributions, etc. In 1991, my husband Jack, an ordained minister, and I became licensed representatives.

Taxpayers need us and we need taxpayers. Our two-fold goal is to keep our clients' taxes to a minimum and to maximize their earning power. When congress passes "so-called" tax cuts, the "revenue neutral gurus" in the bowels of congress hunt for ways to create offsetting tax increases. The resulting complex tax language makes it imperative that you as a taxpayer let my professional preparers help you through the maze.

You will find references to Internal Revenue Code Sections, Revenue Rulings, court cases, etc. throughout this publication. Quotations of important portions of tax law and regulations are included to give you confidence in what you read and learn.

It is necessary for us to update "Income Tax Guide for Ministers and Religious Workers" each year. So we must strongly encourage you to READ EACH NEW EDITION carefully, in order for you to be able to apply the law changes to your situation.

A minister quite often has difficulty teaching and communicating to the church officials how they, the employer, can assist him in paying the least amount of tax legally possible. A one hour tape presentation of **"Minister's Compensation Package, Tax & Financial Planning,"** is available to share the basic information with your financial committee. We encourage you to take advantage of our "Tax Preparation by Mail" service and our comprehensive payroll service. Detailed information is given at the end of the book.

We want to be your tax professional! We would love to meet you in person at one of our seminars.

- B.J. Worth, EA, ATA, CTP

Table of Contents

CHAPTER ONE

Income and Fringe Benefits

Employees of churches and integral agencies of churches are divided into two classifications; the dual-status minister and the lay employee. **Dual-status means** that the minister is an **employee** for income reporting, fringe benefit and expense deducting purposes, and **self-employed** for social security purposes. A dual-status minister is one who has been given the authority by a church to perform substantially all of the ministerial duties. These duties include preaching, teaching, evangelism, conduct of worship, administration, baptisms, weddings, funerals, and communions. Commissioned, licensed or employed ministers of a church or an integral agency of a church that provides for ordination of ministers are considered **as if** they were ordained or "the equivalent thereof" if they are performing ministerial duties. Employees of churches and integral agencies of churches who do not perform ministerial duties are lay employees. Generally, employees of non-integral agencies are lay employees, even if they are officially ordained, licensed or commissioned. There are definite tax advantages to being a dual-status minister. It is important to determine the proper status of each employee when they are employed. A close examination of court cases and letter rulings reflect a very liberal and friendly definition of who is a dual-status minister. Chapter Two gives full discussion concerning this definition.

Where to Report Income

Dual-Status Minister

Ministers employed by churches and integral agencies of churches have a dual-status treatment in the Internal Revenue Code. They are to be treated as employees for income tax reporting according to "common law rules" in Reg.31.3401(c)-1; and as self-employed for social security reporting Sec. 1402(a)(8). On a dual-status minister's Form W-2, Box 3, for social security wages and Box 5, for medicare wages should be left blank. The **chart shown in Chapter Six, page 95,** is a good guide as to what is considered taxable income and entered in Box 1 and what is considered non-taxable and not shown.

Withholding of income tax for the dual-status minister is not required according to Sec. 3401(a)(9), it is optional. If the dual-status minister did not file Form 4361, it is necessary for social security to be computed on Schedule SE. If a minister has filed Form 4361, "Application for Exemption from Self-Employment Tax for Ministers," and has received an approved copy, he is exempt from social security on earnings from the ministry, and needs only to indicate that by writing "Exempt---Form 4361" on the self-employment line of Form 1040, page 2.

Ministers are considered employees for income reporting, expense deducting and fringe benefit eligibility. Unreimbursed or reimbursed without "an accountable plan," automobile, travel, and professional expenses are allowed only as miscellaneous itemized deductions on Schedule A. They are also subject to limitations: (1) meals & entertainment are reduced by 50%, then combined with other miscellaneous deductions, (2) only the percentage of unreimbursed expenses spent in earning the taxable salary are allowable, and (3) they are further reduced by 2% of the Adjusted Gross Income.

Lay Employees

Lay Employees are employees for both income and social security purposes. On a lay employee's Form W-2, Box 1 will show his salary, Box 3 will show the social security wage, and Box 5 will show the medicare wage. Until the end of 1983, a not-for-profit organization or church was exempt from withholding and matching social security on their lay employees, unless they chose to cover them by filing Form SS-15. As a part of the Social Security Amendments Act of 1983, social security coverage was extended on a **mandatory** basis to all lay employees of not-for-profit organizations as of January 1, 1984. The Tax Reform Act of 1984 provided for an election by a church or qualified church-controlled organization that is opposed for religious reasons to the payment of social security taxes, not to be subject to such taxes. (Form 8274) Lay employees of churches that make the election **are liable for paying social security** on their personal returns on Schedule SE, Section B. Electing church employers are responsible for withholding income tax, filing quarterly reports, and a W-2 for each employee. (See complete discussion in Chapter Four.)

Unreimbursed or reimbursed without "an accountable plan," automobile, travel, and professional expenses are allowed only as miscellaneous itemized deductions on Schedule A. They are also subject to limitations: (1) meals & entertainment are reduced by 50%, then combined with other miscellaneous deductions, and (2) they are further reduced by 2% of the Adjusted Gross Income.

Employed Ministers Are Not to Use Schedule C For Reporting Salary

Employed ministers are definitely self-employed for social security purposes. However, for income reporting, expense deducting, and fringe benefit provision purposes, the Internal Revenue Code speaks clearly about their status being that of an employee. IRS publications on the issue have historically presented the dual-status treatment for ministers performing services for a church or an integral agency of a church. To ignore the historic IRS position and report a minister's salary and deduct their professional expenses on Schedule C will often cause an audit and an assessment of additional tax liability. Thousands of ministers have suffered this traumatic and costly experience.

"Income Tax Guide for Ministers & Religious Workers" is happy to have clearly focused our efforts on educating church employers and their ministers on how to establish an accountable reimbursement plan for employee business expenses to produce the **desired lower tax liability without conflicting with existing IRS code & regulations.** Ministers who have prepared their returns or permitted our service to prepare their returns as dual-status ministers have experienced a much lower audit risk. If their return is audited they will not be assessed an additional tax liability because of how they reported their ministry income and expenses.

● ***Historic IRS Position***

The IRS's position that an employed minister is an employee for income reporting purposes is well defined in the following quote from IRS Publication 517, page 2:

> *"EMPLOYMENT STATUS FOR OTHER TAX PURPOSES*
>
> *Even though you are considered a self-employed individual in performing your ministerial services for social security tax purposes, you may be considered an employee for income or retirement plan tax purposes. Some of your income may be considered income from self-employment and other income may be considered income from wages.*
>
> ***Common-law employee.*** *Under common law rules, you are considered an employee or a self-employed person depending on all the facts and circumstances. Generally, you are an employee if your employer has the legal right to control both what you do and how you do it, even if you have considerable discretion and freedom of action.*
>
> *If you are employed by a congregation for a salary, you are generally a common-law employee and income from the exercise of your ministry is considered income from wages for income tax purposes. However, amounts received directly from members of the congregation, such as fees for performing marriages, baptisms, or other personal services, are considered income from self-employment.*
>
> ***Example.*** *A church hires and pays you a salary to perform ministerial services subject to its control. Under the common law rules, you are an employee of the church while performing those services.*
>
> *If you are not certain whether you are an employee or a self-employed person, you can get a determination from the IRS by filing Form SS-8..."*

Before requesting a determination from the IRS, get and study a copy of the full text of Revenue Ruling 87-41. It states, "If the relationship of employer and employee exists, the designation or description of the relationship by the parties as anything other than that of employer and employee **is immaterial**." To draft a contract or an agreement that states that an independent contractor relationship exists when facts and circumstances indicate an employer/employee relationship actually exists is an exercise of futility. It also does not matter how payments are measured or paid, what they are called, or whether the employee works full or part time.

Your wages as an employed minister are to be reported on Form W-2, Wage and Tax Statement, for income tax purposes, but no social security taxes are withheld. This is because you are treated as self-employed for social security purposes. You must pay self-employment tax on those wages yourself unless you request and receive an exemption from self-employment tax. **On your Form W-2, Box 3 for social security wages and Box 5 for medicare wages should be blank.**

The 20 Common Law Rules

As an aid to determining whether an individual is an employee under the common law rules, twenty factors have been developed based on an examination of cases and rulings considering whether an individual is an employee. In applying the IRS twenty-factor test, there is no set number of factors that make the payee an employee. Each case is evaluated on its own merits. Some of the factors that indicate the presence of **"the right to control"** weigh more in importance on the scale of determining if an employer/employee relationship exists. The threshold level of control necessary to find employee status is generally lower when applied to professional services than when applied to nonprofessional services. Ministers are professionals. If enough of the factors indicate there is an employer/employee relationship and the employer does not treat the employee correctly, the IRS penalties are substantial.

In Revenue Ruling 87-41,CB 1987-1, 296, we find a list of **THE TWENTY COMMON LAW FACTORS.** This list, along with our explanations, is as follows:

(1) *Compliance with instructions;* A payee who MUST OBEY the payor's instructions about when, where and how he is to do the work is apt to be an employee. Even if no instructions are given, the control factor is present if the employer has the right to control how the work results are achieved. A minister paid by a church or organization is generally required to hold a certain theological position and maintain an honorable lifestyle and hold worship services at set times, teach classes, etc.

(2) *Training required;* The use of an employee handbook or staff meetings would be a factor of control and indicative of employee status. A payee who is an independent contractor ordinarily receives no training from the payor.

(3) *Integration of services into business operations;* How closely related to the work of the payor is the work of the payee? It would seem rather difficult to prove a church or organization's purpose and ministry is not closely integrated with the purpose and ministry of the minister hired to perform ministerial duties. A minister has the responsibility to lead a local church in conformance with the beliefs of the church. This is another factor that indicates control. A payee who is an independent contractor would have a separate line of business from the payor.

(4) *Services rendered personally;* If the payor requires a payee to physically perform the services himself, then this shows control by the payor over the payee. An independent contractor would have the right to hire a substitute without getting the payor's consent.

(5) *Hiring, supervising, and paying assistants;* When the payor hires, trains and pays the staff working with the payee it indicates control by the payor and employee status. Independent contractors must have the right to hire staff or assistants at their own discretion, regardless of payor's wishes.

(6) *Continuing relationship;* An ongoing long term relationship between the payor and the payee indicates an employee status. A continuing relationship may exist even if work is performed at recurring, although irregular, intervals. An independent contractor will finish an assignment and work for several payors.

(7) *Set hours of work;* A payee's ability to schedule his activities according to his own desire merely demonstrates that less supervision is necessary in connection with a professional. When the payor sets regular hours of work it is a definite indication of control and an employee status. An independent contractor will schedule a job and have the right to change the date and time and give scheduling priority to other jobs.

(8) *Full time required;* When a payee must work full time for one payor, it indicates control and the employee status. An independent contractor is free to work when and for whom he wishes.

(9) *Work done on premises;* When the payor provides the premises for a payee to perform the work to be done it indicates an employee status. When the employing church or organization owns the worship location or office in which the professional minister performs most of his duties it indicates the factor of control.

(10) *Services performed in order or sequence set;* When the payor has the right to establish the schedule and routines of the payee an employer/employee relationship exists. A church employer has regular worship services, committee meetings, etc., that a minister must plan for and lead as scheduled. A minister does not have the ability to unilaterally discontinue the regular services of a local church. An independent contractor evangelist schedules meetings any day or evening of the week he may choose.

(11) *Oral or written reports;* An employee is usually required to give reports or an accounting of his time and accomplishments. An independent contractor submits invoices to the payor.

(12) *Payment by hour, week, month;* When a payee is paid by the hour, week, month, mile etc., this is an indication of employee status. An independent contractor estimates his cost of labor and materials and invoices the payor by the job.

(13) *Payment of business and/or traveling expenses;* This factor weighs as light as a feather. It is good tax planning for either an employee or an independent contractor to "adequately account" to the employer or payor and be reimbursed for job related expenses. An employee who does not establish an accountable plan with his employer can only deduct the expenses on Schedule A if he itemizes his deductions. An independent contractor is able to deduct his job related expenses on Schedule C.

(14) *Furnishing of tools and materials;* When the payor provides the necessary tools and materials for a payee to carry out their duties, an employer/employee relationship is indicated. An independent contractor owns, repairs and takes with him from job to job the tools necessary for his trade.

(15) *Significant investment;* When the payor provides the work facilities and the payee performing the services is not required to make an investment, an employer/employee relationship is indicated. A church provides the church building for holding services and an office in which to perform administrative services and often buys religious materials for the minister. To voluntarily purchase books, tapes, computer equipment, furnishings for a home office, etc., does not count as required significant investment.

(16) *Realization of profit or loss;* An employee is shielded from risk of loss. If a payee is subject to a real risk of economic loss due to significant investments and bonafide liabilities it indicates an independent contractor status. An independent contractor evangelist could incur travel and advertising expenses and experience economic loss if he failed to secure adequate engagements.

(17) *Working for more than one firm at a time;* A payee who performs services for more than one firm at a time could be a part-time employee of each firm. However if a payee works or consults with many clients and customers simultaneously it would be a strong indicator of an independent contractor status.

(18) *Making service available to general public;* To the extent of honorariums received from individuals for ministerial services (weddings, funerals, etc.), outside speaking engagements, writing, etc., a minister does receive independent contractor income to be reported on Schedule C. There are many ways of holding one's self out to the public such as: business cards, a business name at the top of an invoice, a business listing in a phone book, distribution of a brochure, advertisements in a newspaper or trade journal, placement of business name on key chains or jackets, etc.

(19) *Right to discharge;* An employer has the ability to fire an employee. A payee serving as a minister of a church or organization is accountable to the payor to maintain certain theological positions, an acceptable lifestyle and an acceptable performance of their duties. This is true in a denominational connectional church polity as well as in an independent autonomous church polity. That in connectional church polity a bishop or overseer appoints the minister to a church and the church usually pays the minister for services rendered indicates more control and is a substantial indication of a co-employer/employee relationship. While the congregation of a connectional church cannot fire a minister, they can certainly seek dismissal for just cause through the bishop or overseer. Independent contractor agreements that are being fulfilled are not able to be terminated without loss to the payor.

(20) *Right to terminate relationship without incurring liability.* When a payee has the right to terminate his relationship with the payor at any time he wishes without incurring liability, that fact indicates an employer/employee relationship. An independent contractor agrees to complete a specific job and is responsible for its satisfactory completion or is legally obligated to make good for failure to complete the job.

● *Additional Factors to Consider*

To be eligible for "Tax Free" fringe benefits such as group medical insurance, group term life insurance, etc., an individual must be a common law employee. If a minister could be considered as an independent contractor and use Schedule C for reporting income and expenses, **he would have to report as taxable income** the value of any fringe benefits provided by a payor.

To be eligible to make contributions to a Sec. 403(b) Tax Sheltered Account, prior to 1997, an individual had to be a common law employee of a not-for-profit organization according to Revenue Ruling 66-274. A provision in the Small Business Job Protection Act of 1996 permits participation in tax-sheltered accounts by a minister or chaplain, who in connection with the exercise of his ministry is a self-employed individual or is working for an employer that is not a qualified tax-exempt organization.

When the source of income is from a not-for-profit organization: Payment for services performed on a regular and continuous basis is to be treated as salary, not independent contractor income. To be a not-for-profit corporation, it is important that individuals do not personally benefit from funds and assets acquired. If a minister actually had complete control of funds and assets of a church, it would no longer be a not-for-profit organization or church. Even a payee who creates a for-profit corporation becomes its employee when paid for services rendered. Revenue Ruling 71-86 states that a president, sole shareholder, who sets his own hours, duties, salary and was not responsible to anyone else, was an employee for income tax withholding, social security and federal unemployment tax purposes. Similarly, Revenue Ruling 73-361 treats an officer performing substantial services as an employee.

When the source of income is from individuals for whom a service was performed, reporting the income on Schedule C is correct. Honorariums received for performing weddings, funerals, baptisms and counseling are correctly reported as self-employment income on Schedule C.

Preparer penalties: Tax preparers are subject to negligence penalties if they knowingly prepare a return incorrectly. After a careful study of the citations just presented, a tax preparer who disregards the position of the IRS by not preparing an employed minister's tax return as dual-status would be guilty of negligently understating the minister's tax liability. Sec. 6694 provides for a penalty of $1,000 per return prepared with an intentional disregard of rules or regulations.

Churches who fail to prepare W-2's for their employees are subject to many penalties. Providing a Form 1099 to an employed minister rather than a W-2 can result in a $50 penalty, as **it is necessary to prepare "correct" informational returns to avoid penalties.** It is very important to learn what the law requires and carefully meet those obligations. Chapter Six discusses the rules and shows filled out examples of payroll reporting and informational returns.

Statutory employee status can not be used by ministers: It is a status limited to four occupational groups. Statutory employees receive a W-2 and are able to deduct their business expenses on Schedule C. Because of this ability, some ministers have attempted to claim this status.

The four specific occupational groups deemed to be statutory employees regardless of whether they are employees under the usual common law guidelines are: (1) agent-drivers and commission drivers engaged in the distribution of various products; (2) full-time life insurance salespersons; (3) home workers; and (4) traveling or city salespersons other than those acting as agent-drivers or commission drivers.

- ***WHY all the Confusion over Status and Contention with the IRS?***

Often a church treasurer or board will ask their minister what tax status they prefer as if it is an optional decision. Our theological colleges and seminaries do a very poor job teaching ministerial students about tax law and how it applies to them. Due to inadequate knowledge of tax law, many wrong decisions have been made.

Many clergy tax advisors, accountants, and publications have continued to recommend or show examples of using Schedule C for **employed ministers**. The "fight for the right to use Schedule C" that has caused thousands of ministers to be audited and assessed additional tax liabilities is inexcusable.

Call the IRS and only those with considerable experience who answer the inquiries give correct answers to questions regarding the correct tax status of a minister.

It is unfortunate that some of the confusion concerning the minister's correct status has been caused by uninformed IRS employees and the courts. Going against the historic position stated in IRS publications results in taxable fringe benefits and **increases the IRS audit exposure.** Most ministers claiming to be independent contractors can not afford legal representation to pursue their case through the courts.

- ***An Important District Court Case - Weber v. Commissioner, 103 T.C. 378, 386 (1994)***

A few years ago, in North Carolina, IRS audited several hundred United Methodist ministers' tax returns that reported their salary income and professional expenses spent to earn that income on Schedule C. A tax liability was assessed when the professional expenses were changed from Schedule C to Schedule A, itemized deductions. These audits resulted in a District Court Case in North Carolina, Weber v. Commissioner, in January, 1993. The case was well represented by Rev. Weber's denomination and the written result was released on August 25, 1994. An appeal was filed and the final decision was received on July 31, 1995. The IRS position stands. This case was a test case for the United Methodist ministers as to the issues it contains. Petitioners in many of the pending cases agreed to be bound by the final decision in this case.

Special Trial Judge John J. Pajak, seems to have carefully read the Book of Discipline of the United Methodist Church. He decided that the "right to control" test was of primary importance and found that Weber was subject to significant control. The court stated, "generally a lower level of control applies to professionals. Petitioner is a professional minister." He was required to work at the church to which he was assigned and was required to attend meetings. He had to explain the position of the Discipline on any topic he chose to present in his sermons. He did not have the authority to unilaterally discontinue the regular services of a local church. Though the church did not give him a Form W-2, the court gave that factor little weight. The Court found that Reverend Weber's position was intended to be permanent as opposed to transitory, and that the benefits provided by the Church indicated an employment relationship.

Methodist ministers, spouses, and dependents are covered by life insurance and contributions are made to the General Board of Pensions of the United Methodist Church that provides payments upon retirement. Ministers are expected to make voluntary contributions to the pension plan equal to 3 percent of their salary. As an employee, Rev. Weber is entitled to tax free treatment of these fringe benefits.

A more recent U.S. Tax Court decision in Radde v. Commissioner, T.C. Memo 1997-490 upholds the Weber decision that as a minister Rev. Radde was an employee. In Private Letter Ruling 9825002, a minister **was denied his request** to be considered an independent contractor.

- ***Other Tax Court Cases have Resulted in Conflicting Decisions.***

The tax courts have added to the confusion by giving conflicting decisions. On the same day that Rev. Weber's District Court Case was released, in Florida, another judge gave a conflicting opinion in Shelley v. Commissioner, T.C. Memo 1994-432. The church Rev. Shelley pastored was a member of the International Pentecostal Holiness Church. The judge's opinion that Rev. Shelley was an independent contractor is a decision by a small Tax Court that the IRS will not follow.

Weber v. Commissioner was a decision of a District Court that was agreed to be a precedent setting case.

On December 2, 1996, Greene v. Commissioner, T.C. Memo 1996-531 it was determined that an Assembly of God missionary to Bangladesh was an independent contractor rather than an employee. On June 20, 1997, Alford v. United States, U.S. Court of Appeals for the eighth circuit, No. 96-3287 also determined that an Assembly of God pastor was an independent contractor rather than an employee. Both IRS and the District Court determined that Alford was an employee. The District Court concluded that Alford was an employee of not only the local church but also of the district and national organizations. If this decision had not been appealed it would have exposed the district and national organizations to unnecessary liability. The U.S. Court of Appeals determined that there was no employer/employee relationship with the local, district or national organizations.

- ***What to do if your employer gives you Form 1099 instead of Form W-2?***

1. Have your employer prepare a corrected Form 1099 with -0- income shown. Then prepare a Form W-2 correctly reporting the taxable salary in Box 1. This correction may prevent an audit.
2. When an employed dual-status minister, paid by a church or church controlled organization, receives Form 1099 rather than a Form W-2 **and the employer will not prepare corrected forms,** we recommend the following procedure for preparing Form 1040:
   a. Enter the amount shown as income on the Form 1099 on Schedule C as gross income because IRS computers will scan the tax return and expect it to be there.
   b. Subtract the same amount as "wages taken to Form 1040, line 7" in the expense section of Schedule C to have a net result of zero on Schedule C to the extent of the salary.
   c. Then enter the amount as income on Form 1040, line 7 as though it were wages on a W-2. IRS computers will accept an amount on line 7 that is greater than the total wages reported on W-2's attached to the return. Use Form 2106 and Schedule A to deduct any unreimbursed employee business expenses.

Even though IRS has conducted many audits for taxpayers who enter income on Schedule C from one source (Form 1099), there will be no additional tax assessed for a correctly prepared Form 1040.

Taxable Sources Of Income

Gross income, according to Sec. 61, includes all income (cash, value of property, or value of services) from whatever source, unless it is specifically excluded by a section in the Internal Revenue Code. It is important to understand that regardless of what a payor or payee calls a sum of money, property or value of service; facts and circumstances will determine whether it is taxable or not. **Any income that is received because you performed a service is taxable.** Generally, the employee will be taxed on all remuneration that is not a qualified fringe benefit (Chapter One), housing allowance (Chapter Two), or reimbursement for professional expenses under an accountable plan (Chapter Three).

Professional Income

Fees, offerings, or gifts for speaking, performing weddings, funerals or baptisms are considered professional income. An independent contractor evangelist or missionary receives professional income from the churches to which he ministers as well as from individual supporters. When as a minister you have provided a service and the person receiving the benefit of your ministry gives you money, it should be considered as earned professional income according to Reg 1.61-2(a)(1).

When an independent religious worker personally receives his support from individual contributions, it becomes necessary to show these amounts on Schedule C and to deduct the expenses of doing ministry to arrive at net income. If large amounts of money for work projects are received, it becomes difficult to prove they are legitimate ordinary and necessary ministry expenses to the IRS in an audit. **The ideal solution for this Schedule C problem is for the independent religious worker to establish an employer/employee relationship with a church.** (See complete discussion of this recommendation in Chapter Six.)

Income received from writing, lecturing, radio or television appearances, etc., are additional types of professional income. The income or royalties and expenses of selling religious tapes and books are to be shown on Schedule C as professional income, according to Revenue Ruling 59-50. For ministers not exempt from social security, the net profit will be subject to social security.

Professional income and any expenses incurred in connection with earning the professional income are to be shown on Schedule C. Only when honorariums and fees for weddings, funerals, etc., are paid directly to the employer, are they not taxable to the individual minister.

Gift or Bonus From Employer

When an employer gives a bonus or "love gift" to an employee it is simply additional salary and should be included in the W-2, Box 1. **Cash gifts** that result from special offerings received from the congregation for a minister are to be included in the W-2, Box 1. Cash gifts that are received by the minister from individuals to whom he ministers or from whom he receives support are to be included with honorariums on Schedule C. Two court cases, Banks v. Commissioner, T.C. Memo 1991-641 and Goodwin v. United States Court of Appeals, KTC 1995-479 (8th Cir. 1995), both involved ministers who had received three or four large special occasion offerings each year on a regular basis and had not included them on their tax returns. Both ministers were assessed large sums of income tax and Social Security tax for three years plus many penalties and several years of interest by the time the court decisions were final.

Gifts of other than cash should be considered at their fair market value and, if from the employer, included in the W-2. A common occurrence involves a contributor giving an auto to the church. The church then "pays" or transfers the auto to their pastor. The contributor should be given a statement that the auto was given to the church, then it is a Schedule A contribution at the FMV (donor must determine FMV). The church then must include in the pastor's income the FMV of the auto given as extra compensation.

When an employer sells at a bargain price or transfers without payment any property, such as the parsonage, it results in taxable compensation. The difference between the amount paid and the amount of its fair market value at the time of the transfer is taxable according to Reg. 1.61-2(d)(2). To avoid an excessive tax burden in the year of transfer we suggest the following: The employer should loan the employee the amount of the difference between the FMV and the amount paid by the employee and, over a period of time, forgive a portion of the loan each year. The annual income would be the amount of forgiveness and if the loan is secured by a home, it would be principal payment that can be parsonage allowance. (See discussion of "Loans from employers" in Chapter Two)

Small gifts of merchandise: According to Revenue Ruling 59-58, "The value of a turkey, ham or other item of merchandise purchased by an employer and distributed generally to each of the employees engaged in his business at Christmas, or a comparable holiday, as a means of promoting their good will, does not constitute wages." The ruling also states that this rule "will not apply to distributions of cash, gift certificates, and similar items of readily convertible cash value, regardless of the amount involved."

Benevolence to an employee or a family member: When an employer helps an employee or a member of an employee's family with crisis needs it will result in taxable compensation. **To avoid this, we recommend** that a local non-employer, not-for-profit organization (such as Red Cross) be utilized to solicit help for an employee with crisis needs.

Social Security Paid By the Employer

When an employer agrees to provide extra payment to a dual-status minister to pay all or part of his social security tax, **it must be shown as taxable salary** according to Revenue Ruling 68-507. Dual-status ministers are treated as self-employed taxpayers when computing their social security on Schedule SE. Their combined rate of social security tax and medicare tax is 15.3% less adjustments. It may be convenient to have the employer pay this amount to the minister on a quarterly basis, to coincide with the due dates of his estimated tax payments.

On Schedule SE the gross social security base is adjusted to allow ½ of social security as a deduction. On Form 1040, page 1, an adjustment for ½ of the social security paid by the self-employed taxpayer is allowed.

The wage base for the two parts of the social security tax (social security and medicare) are different. **The 7.65% combined rate** is made up of 6.2% rate for social security and 1.45% rate for medicare.

Here is the schedule of what has happened since 1993:

YEAR	SOC SECURITY WAGE BASE	MEDICARE WAGE BASE	EMPLOYEE RATE FICA	EMPLOYEE RATE Medicare	SELF-EMPLOYED RATE
1993	$57,600	$135,000	6.20%	1.45%	15.30%
1994	$60,600	No limit	6.20%	1.45%	15.30%
1995	$61,200	No limit	6.20%	1.45%	15.30%
1996	$62,700	No limit	6.20%	1.45%	15.30%
1997	$65,400	No limit	6.20%	1.45%	15.30%
1998	$68,400	No limit	6.20%	1.45%	15.30%
1999	$72,600	No limit	6.20%	1.45%	15.30%
2000	$76,200	No limit	6.20%	1.45%	15.30%

Insurance

The cost of regular term and permanent life insurance (whole, universal, etc.), paid by the employer is a taxable fringe benefit if the minister names the beneficiary of his choosing. Any premium paid for group term life insurance **over $50,000** coverage is also taxable. The Table in Reg. 1.79-3(d)(2) is to be used to compute the amount to be included in an employee's income, even though the employer's actual premium may be more or less.

Housing

We recommend that the dual-status minister "over estimate" his parsonage allowance that is required to be designated in advance by his employer. When filing the tax return, any unused parsonage allowance becomes taxable income and is to be entered on Form 1040, line 21, as "excess parsonage allowance."

The lay employee who is provided living quarters that are not on the premises of the employer, nor for the convenience of the employer, nor a requirement of the job, must show as taxable income the value of the living quarters provided. This value is also subject to social security tax. (Sec. 119 qualifications are not met.)

Non-Accountable Allowances

If you are paid a non-accountable expense allowance or reimbursement and you are not required to submit your records and receipts to your employer, the income has to be shown on your Form W-2. For example: when an employee receives $300 a month for his auto expenses and is not required by a written accountable plan to submit a mileage log to his employer as substantiation, the auto allowance must be reported on Form W-2, Box 1.

It is very important to establish a written accountable reimbursement plan and "adequately account" to your employer in order not to lose some or all of the deduction for your professional expenses. A complete discussion of how to establish an accountable reimbursement plan is in Chapter Three.

Personal Use of Auto Provided by Employer

Strict regulations require the **value of personal use** of an employer owned auto to be included in the W-2 as a taxable fringe benefit. The amount to be included in income is to be reduced by any amount the employee pays the employer for the taxable fringe benefit. (See complete discussion in Chapter Three.)

Non-Taxable Sources of Income---Exclusions

Fringe Benefits

Gross income, for tax purposes, includes all income from whatever source unless specifically excluded by an Internal Revenue Code Section. It is important to follow the rules in the Internal Revenue Code and establish qualified tax-free fringe benefits. **Any non-qualified benefits provided are simply taxable fringes. Before establishing most employee fringe benefits**, seek the assistance of an attorney and/or benefits consultant. With congressional changes happening often, existing plans must be continually examined and revised to meet new requirements.

Fringe benefits are available for either dual-status or lay employees of not-for-profit employers and employees of for-profit employers. Providing qualified fringe benefits in an employee's "pay package" reduces the base upon which both income tax and social security tax are paid.

To be qualified, most fringe benefit options must meet nondiscrimination tests. There are two fringe benefits that are free from the nondiscrimination tests: (1) accident & health insurance provided to an employee and family and (2) certain church plans providing **group term** life insurance to employees.

Qualified Retirement Plan Contributions

For retirement plans, the Internal Revenue Code considers the salaried minister as an "employee." When the employer makes the contribution on the behalf of an employee for a qualified retirement plan under Sec. 401(a), 403(b), 408(k), 408(p) or 414(e), it is not taxable income to an employee during his working years. At retirement or at the time of any withdrawals from an employer's qualified retirement plan, the benefits are taxable. (For exception see "Retired Ministers & Parsonage Designation")

Plans may be available through your denominational headquarters. Several mutual fund vendors and insurance companies specialize in plans for the not-for-profit organizations and their employees.

● *Sec. 401(a) - Employer Qualified Retirement Plan*

For-profit employers generally establish their qualified retirement plans according to Sec. 401(a) rules. Many technical requirements must be met for a plan to be qualified under Sec. 401(a). These rules prohibit discrimination and plans must be established for the benefit of the employer's employees in general. The cost of administration of a qualified 401(a) retirement plan is great. Not-for-profit organizations generally establish retirement plans according to Sec. 403(b), 408(k), 408(p) or Sec. 414(e) rules because they are less strict and are less expensive to administer. Annual contributions by an employer to a qualified retirement plan on the behalf of an employee cannot exceed the lesser of (1) $30,000 or (2) 25% of the employee's compensation for the year.

● *Sec. 401(k) - Salary Reduction*

Beginning in 1997, tax-exempt organizations are allowed to establish 401(k) or CODA plans. Between July 2, 1986 and December 31,1996, tax-exempt employers generally could not establish 401(k) or CODA plans. 401(k) plans that existed before July 2, 1986 were allowed to continue.

Organizations who employ larger staffs and wish to contribute matching contributions should consider a prototype Sec. 401(k). However, the cost of administration of a Sec. 401(k) plan is greater than a Sec. 403(b) plan.

● *Sec. 403(b) - Tax Sheltered Account (TSA)*

Tax Sheltered Accounts are available to public school employees and employees of tax-exempt organizations. Ministers employed by a tax-exempt organization are eligible for making contributions to a Sec. 403(b) retirement account. Since January 1, 1997, a minister or chaplain, who in connection with the exercise of his ministry is a self-employed individual or is working for an employer that is not a qualified tax-exempt organization, can also contribute to a TSA. TSAs are the most popular retirement plans to be established by tax-exempt employers. This code section provides two different methods of funding.

Forfeitable Contributions (employee loses if not vested) can be made by the **employer** to a Sec. 403(b) account on the behalf of its employees. The maximum limit for a defined contribution plan applies (lesser of $30,000 or 25% of pay). The cost to establish and administer this type of Sec. 403(b) employer plan causes it to not be cost effective for an employer with a small number of employees.

An employer's plan can be established to accept both forfeitable contributions by the employer and non-forfeitable contributions made by the employee through a salary reduction plan or just forfeitable contributions.

Non-Forfeitable Contributions (employee is always 100% vested) can be made for the **employee** to a Sec. 403(b) account established by the employer for voluntary salary reduction contributions. Generally an employee can contribute up to 20% of includible compensation or $10,000. Contributions to a TSA account by a dual-status minister **are not** subject to social security and medicare tax. However, contributions to a TSA account by a lay employee **are** subject to social security and medicare tax withholding.

A Sec. 403(b) retirement plan can be established to accept only **non-forfeitable** voluntary contributions from one or several employees. Many employers establish Sec. 403(b) plans that only allow salary reduction non-forfeitable voluntary contributions because **they are quick to establish and involve very little cost of administration.** Employees of not-for-profit organizations who change employers from time to time like the "portability" of a Sec. 403(b) non-forfeitable type of plan. (See additional discussion of non-forfeitable TSA plans under "Voluntary Tax Shelter Retirement Plans".)

- ***Sec. 408(k) - Simplified Employee Pension (SEP)***

Only an **employer** may establish a SEP. The employer makes contributions directly to a SEP-IRA account or annuity that has been set up for each employee with a broker, bank, or insurance company qualified to sponsor an IRA under Sec. 408(k). Contributions are limited to $30,000 or 15% of an employee's compensation, whichever is less. Employer contributions must be made to a SEP for each employee age 21 or over who has worked for the employer for at least 3 of the last 5 years and received annual compensation of $400 or more. Contributions to SEPs must not discriminate in favor of highly compensated employees. Employer contributions must be determined under a definite written allocation formula and withdrawals must be allowed. Because the SEP-IRA is established in the employee's name it is 100% vested and portable.

Employees of tax-exempt organizations and state or local governments **may not** make additional voluntary salary reduction contributions to a Sec. 408(k) SEP. They are eligible for Sec. 403(b) salary reduction plans instead.

- ***Sec. 408(p) - Simple Retirement Plan***

Savings Incentive Match Plan for Employees (SIMPLE). For years beginning after December 31, 1996, A SIMPLE retirement plan is a written salary reduction arrangement that allows a **small employer** (an employer with 100 or fewer employees) to make elective contributions to a simple retirement account (IRA) on behalf of each eligible employee. The amount that the employee elects to have deferred must not exceed $6,000 for any year and must be expressed as a percentage of the employee's compensation. The employer is required to match the employees' contributions on a dollar for dollar basis, up to 3% of compensation, or elect to make 2% nonelective contributions on behalf of all eligible employees. Eligible employees are those who earned at least $5,000 in compensation from the employer during any two prior years and who is reasonably expected to receive at least $5,000 in compensation during the year. An eligible employer is not allowed to maintain another retirement plan.

If the employer desires to allow the employees to designate their own investment and financial institution, Form 5304-SIMPLE should be used to establish the plan. If the employer desires to designate one financial institution, Form 5305-SIMPLE should be used to establish the plan. Both the employee contributions and the employer contributions are **non-forfeitable** (employee is always 100% vested).

Distributions from a SIMPLE retirement account are subject to IRA rules. However, withdrawals of contributions during the two-year period beginning on the date the employee first participated in the SIMPLE plan are subject to a 25% early withdrawal penalty (rather than 10%).

- ***Sec. 414(e) - Church plans***

A plan established and maintained for its employees by a church or by a convention or association of churches exempt from tax under Sec. 501 is excluded from minimum participation, vesting, and funding rules. These rules may be elected. A church plan may be administered by an independent organization, such as a retirement board or a bank. Amounts contributed are limited according to Sec. 415(c). Contribution allowed is the least of: 25% of includible compensation plus $4,000; the exclusion allowance under Sec. 403(b)(2); or $15,000 according to Sec. 415(c)(4)(B).

- ***Distributions from Employer Qualified Retirement Plans (QRP)***

Upon retiring, resigning, or disability an employee usually has a choice of receiving their employer's qualified retirement all at once as a lump-sum distribution or as an annuitized monthly income distribution. **Tax Planning Is Important.** Information about the rate of return, survivor benefits, etc., are going to enter into the decision you must make at retirement time. Each taxpayer's tax situation will differ. **Ask your tax advisor** which choice of distribution provided by your plan will have the least tax liability.

Periodic income distribution: The choice of monthly income from a qualified plan is more attractive to dual-status ministers because of the ability to designate it as tax-free parsonage allowance.

Lump-Sum Distributions have a special 5 or 10-year averaging available if you were born before 1936, receive the entire balance from all of the qualified plans in one year and do not "roll-over" any portion of the lump-sum distribution. Only 5-year averaging is available if you were born after 1935. It is a computation that often results in a lesser tax liability. (The election to use 5-year averaging is repealed starting in the year 2000.)

If you have the ability to "roll-over" a lump-sum distribution into another tax-sheltered Sec. 403(b) account within a 60 day period, you will avoid tax in the year of distribution and the 10% early withdrawal penalty assessed if you are not age 59½ or disabled. Doing so will retain the proper identity of earnings from the ministry and preserve the opportunity for designated parsonage allowance. If you "roll-over" a lump-sum distribution into an IRA, you will not be able to designate the distributions from the IRA account as tax-free parsonage allowance.

The payor of a lump-sum distribution from an employer's Qualified Retirement Plan is required to withhold 20% of the distribution for income tax **unless** you ask for a transfer from trustee to trustee.

● *Penalties*

Early distributions are generally subject to 10% early withdrawal penalties if received before age 59½ or disability. There are **two ways to avoid the 10% penalty**: (1) Early distributions can be rolled over to another qualified TSA or IRA or (2) can be received as part of a series of substantially equal periodic payments received at least once a year for the life or life expectancy of the taxpayer or for joint lives of taxpayer and beneficiary. (Sec. 72(T)(2)(A)(iv)).

● *Retired Ministers & Parsonage Designation*

A **retired minister** receiving an otherwise taxable distribution from a qualified Sec. 401(a), Sec. 403(b), Sec. 408(k), Sec. 408(p) or Sec. 414(e) plan may have a **"parsonage allowance"** designated by the former employer or denominational pension board. We recommend that a perpetually worded designation state that 100% of the retirement income be designated as parsonage allowance and be tax free to the extent spent for housing. (Revenue Ruling 63-156) Language found in the Department of Labor Regulations under ERISA that seem to consider either type of contribution to Sec. 403(b) **(forfeitable and non-forfeitable) to be considered as an employer's plan and eligible for parsonage allowance designation.** (Labor Regs. 2520.3-2(f)(3))

However, distributions from an IRA or a Keogh retirement plan cannot be designated as non-taxable housing.

Third party payors of retirement plan distributions should include the gross distribution on Form 1099-R, Box 1. Not being able to determine the taxable amount, Box 2a should be left blank and Box 2b should be checked. As a retired minister receiving distributions from a retirement plan that has been designated as "parsonage allowance" you are to enter the gross amount on Form 1040, line 16a. It is the responsibility of the retired minister to show as taxable, on Form 1040, line 16b, any designated distributions not spent for parsonage expenses. If all of the distribution has been spent for parsonage expenses enter -0- on line 16b.

Group Term Life Insurance

Premiums paid by an employer for group term life insurance on the first $50,000 coverage are not to be included in income according to Sec. 79. New lower rates are available for 1999. **An exemption from the nondiscrimination rules** of Sec. 79 applies to certain church plans providing group term life insurance to

Cost Per $1,000 of group term life insurance protection for 1-Month Period [Reg. 1.79-3(d)(2)]

Age	Cost
Under 25	5¢
25 through 29	6¢
30 through 34	8¢
35 through 39	9¢
40 through 44	10¢
45 through 49	15¢
50 through 54	23¢
55 through 59	43¢
60 through 64	66¢
65 through 69	$1.27
70 and above	$2.06

employees. Any coverage for group term life insurance **over $50,000** is taxable. Use the Table from Reg. 1.79-3(d)(2) to compute the amount to be included in an employee's income, even though the employer's actual premium may be more or less.

The only time premiums paid by the employer for regular term or permanent life insurance are not taxable is when the employer is named as beneficiary.

Accident And Health Insurance

Premiums paid for group accident and health insurance by an employer are not taxable income according to Sec. 106. Premiums for group accident and health plans are able to be a "tax free" fringe benefit. **There are no discrimination rules that apply to insured accident and health plans.** A plan underwritten by an insurance policy or a prepaid health care plan must involve the shifting of risk to an unrelated third party to be considered an insured plan.

Tax qualified long-term care insurance contracts issued after 1996 will be treated the same for income tax purposes as accident and health insurance contracts. For those not able to use the cost as a deduction, non-tax qualified long-term care contracts are available.

The Health Insurance Portability and Accountability Act of 1996 (HIPAA) provides for improved access, portability and renewability of health insurance coverage. **An unfortunate byproduct of HIPAA's very complex requirements affects the tax-free fringe benefit treatment of some individual policies.** Effective after June 30, 1997, HIPAA requires health insurance companies to offer group coverage to all employers with two or more employees. (State governments must adopt guidelines and have the option to require group policies to be offered to employers with one employee.) Employers with an existing health plan must review it with their insurer or administrator and make sure it meets all of the new requirements.

Some **individual** health policies have been amended to prohibit tax-free fringe benefit treatment for their premiums. Some insurers are requiring participants to sign statements indicating that their individual premiums are not being paid by their employer or reimbursed by their employer as a fringe benefit. Employers who were unable to obtain a group policy before HIPAA's changes **should seek group coverage** for their employees and replace such individual policies. Pre-existing condition exclusions are reduced by the employee's period of creditable coverage as of the enrollment date, so long as the person does not have more than a 63-day break in coverage. **To continue paying for an individual health policy, that requires the insured to sign a statement as described above, will cause the employee to be taxed on the premiums as a "taxable fringe benefit."**

For years beginning in 1997, Medical Savings Accounts (MSAs) may be offered by employers who on average had no more than 50 employees in either of the two preceding years and who provide high-deductible health plans. Employers contributions to MSAs are not taxable to their employees and can accumulate tax-free if used to pay medical expenses not covered by the high deductible policy.

Fraternal form of insurance carriers, such as Brotherhood Newsletter, Good Samaritan, etc, are not normally incorporated under state insurance laws as are insurance companies. Fraternities were popular at the close of the Civil War. Lutheran Brotherhood, Woodmen of the World and others have existed for a long time. The monthly payments to a fraternal form of medical non-insurance **still qualifies** for "tax free" fringe benefit treatment. These co-op providers have group characteristics and will not require participants to sign any statement as described above.

If an employee were to receive taxable salary and pay their own medical insurance premiums, two costly things happen:

1. *Because of the 7.5% limitation on Schedule A or not having enough to itemize, the premium may not be deductible, and*
2. *Social security tax will be paid on that portion of the salary.*

NOTE: Employed ministers who pay their own health insurance premiums cannot deduct 60% of the cost on Form 1040, line 28.

Self-Insured Medical Reimbursement Plans

A qualified medical expense reimbursement plan is a plan or arrangement under which an employer pays the medical expenses incurred by its eligible employees, their spouses and dependents and is non-taxable according to Sec 105(b). Strict discrimination rules in Sec. 105(h) do apply to self-insured plans and **it is wise to seek the assistance of an attorney and/or benefits consultant to draft a qualified self-insured plan.** The employer may make direct payments to the provider of the service (the physician, hospital, or insurer) or it may reimburse the employees.

Often a self-insured medical reimbursement plan is established as a supplement to an insured accident and health insurance plan. The upper limit or cap, for example, $500 or $1,000, must be uniform for all employees eligible for the plan. As a fringe benefit, available amounts not used for medical expenses cannot be paid as additional compensation. It is a **"use it or lose it"** fringe benefit.

A self-insured medical reimbursement plan can be included in a qualified Sec. 125 Cafeteria Plan also. As a non-taxable option in a Sec. 125 Cafeteria Plan, each employee would be allowed to choose the "cap" that would best fit their family.

Disability Insurance

Premiums for disability insurance paid by the employer are not taxable income according to Sec. 105(e). The income from a disability plan provided by the employer is taxable as sick pay. Either the employer or the third party payor must report benefits as salary on Form W-2, subject to the appropriate withholding requirements. As salary, it will be subject to social security for dual-status ministers who are not exempt.

However, if the **employee** pays the premium for a private disability insurance policy, the cost of the premium is not deductible, and the income from the plan is **not taxable.**

Cafeteria Plans

A cafeteria plan is a separate, written benefit plan maintained by an employer under which all participants are employees and each participant has the opportunity to select the particular benefits that he desires according to Sec. 125. A plan must offer both a cash benefit and at least one statutory nontaxable benefit. Nontaxable benefits include group term life insurance up to $50,000 coverage, dependent care assistance, disability benefits, accident and health benefits, self-insured medical reimbursement benefits, and group legal services.

Salary reduction agreements under which participants elect to reduce their compensation or to forgo increases in compensation can be utilized to begin a cafeteria plan. Benefits are of the **"use it or lose it"** nature and therefore should be set conservatively.

Qualified Moving Reimbursement

Unreimbursed qualified moving expenses to move the family when there is a change of job location is an adjustment on Form 1040, page 1. They are an above-the-line deduction subtracted from gross income in arriving at adjusted gross income under Sec. 62(a). Reimbursed qualified moving expenses from an employer are excludable from an employee's gross income as a qualified fringe benefit under Sec. 132(a)(6).

Qualified moving expenses are limited to the reasonable cost of:

1. moving household goods and personal effects from the former residence to the new residence; and
2. traveling, including lodging during the period of travel, from the former residence to the new place of residence. Auto travel can be the actual gas and oil expenses for the trip or the IRS mileage allowance for moving of 10¢ a mile.

The following costs of moving are unqualified and nondeductible: meals, temporary living expenses, pre-move house hunting trips, expenses of sale or lease of a home, and expenses of purchase or lease of a home. An employer reimbursement to an employee for costs of moving that are not allowable is taxable salary and must be reported on Form W-2.

Two requirements of **Sec. 217** must be met for moving expenses to be allowable. The new place of work must be at least **50 miles** farther from the former home than was the former place of work. Employment in the new area must be full-time for **39 weeks** during the 12 month period immediately following the move. Self-employed persons must be working 78 weeks during a 24-month period immediately following the move. **Employed ministers** are subject to the 39 week work requirement.

If the employer expects the employee to satisfy the 50 mile and 39 weeks of work requirements for deduction, the allowable moving reimbursement is not subject to income tax withholding or social security. Dual-status ministers and lay employees do not pay social security on allowable moving reimbursements.

If the employer knows that the requirements of Sec. 217 **will not be met**, the nonqualifying moving reimbursement is subject to both income tax and social security tax withholding for the lay employee. Nonqualifying moving expense reimbursement paid to a dual-status minister is subject to income tax and social security tax and the additional tax liability should be included in his estimate or optional withholding.

Educational Assistance Programs

The tax-free status of employer provided educational assistance programs according to Sec. 127 has been slated to terminate from time to time, only to be restored as a tax-free fringe for a brief time. This benefit has been extended to June 1, 2000. The exclusion does not apply to graduate level courses after June 30, 1996. (H.R. 3448)

The annual excludable educational assistance is $5,250. An educational assistance program is a plan established and maintained by an employer under which the employer provides educational assistance to employees. Education expenses that improve or develop the capabilities of an individual, not limited to courses that are job related or part of a degree program, qualify under Sec. 127.

Notice in **Chapter Three that educational expenses that are job related** can be reimbursed by an employer as business expenses or deductible on Schedule A if unreimbursed.

Qualified Tuition Reduction

Effective for education furnished after 6-30-85, employees of qualified educational organizations described in **Sec. 170(b)(1)(A)(ii)** can exclude from gross income qualified tuition reduction, including cash grants.

An educational organization is described in Sec. 170(b)(1)(A)(ii) if it has as its primary function the presentation of formal instruction, and it normally maintains a regular faculty and curriculum and normally has a regularly enrolled body of pupils or students in attendance at the place where its educational activities are regularly carried on.

This fringe benefit is **not available** for any other type of not-for-profit organizations according to Revenue Ruling 78-184. A church that provides tuition payments for employee's children must treat the payments as a **taxable fringe benefit**, as payment for services. (Private Letter Ruling 9226008)

According to Sec. 117(d)(2), the exclusion applies to tuition for education provided at the employer's school as well as at any educational institution. The exclusion is limited to education below graduate level. A special rule applies to graduate students at eligible educational institutions who are engaged in teaching or research activities for the institution.

Qualified tuition reduction applies to: (1) an individual currently employed by the educational institution; (2) a person separated from service with the institution due to retirement or disability; (3) a widow or widower of an employee who died while employed by the institution, (4) spouses and dependent children of the above.

Effective 1-1-88, the nondiscrimination rules under Sec. 414(q) apply to a qualified tuition reduction plan.

Qualified Scholarships

While scholarships are typically provided to non-employees, we felt it important to include the following "non-fringe benefit" discussion, following the educational topics we have just discussed.

Sec. 117(a) provides for qualified scholarships given to degree candidates to be excluded from income to the extent amounts are used for "qualified tuition and related expenses." Related expenses include fees, books, supplies, and equipment required for courses of instruction. Additional amounts for room, board, or incidental expenses are not excludable. So that recipients understand their tax liabilities, they should be formally advised in writing that amounts granted for expenses incurred are taxable income if the total amount exceeds tuition and fees required for enrollment and related expenses according to IRS Notice 87-31. Form 1040 instructions say, add the taxable amount to any other amounts on Form 1040, line 7. Then write "SCH" and the taxable ount in the space to the left of line 7.

To establish a private foundation that can grant qualified scholarships requires legal assistance. Revenue Procedure 76-47 (clarified by 85-51, amplified by 94-78) establishes seven conditions and a percentage test or a facts and circumstances test for a qualified scholarship program. The program must impose minimum eligibility requirements that limit the independent selection committee's consideration to those children of employees who meet the minimum standards for admission to an educational institution. No more than 10% of the program's recipients can be employee's children.

Voluntary Tax Shelter Retirement Plans

The following "sheltered" retirement plans are those to which a taxpayer can contribute on a voluntary basis and reduce their taxable earnings by the amount of the contribution. When a taxpayer has an income tax liability, it is good tax planning to consider making contributions to a "sheltered" retirement plan. **Even when a minister has no income tax liability, he may wish to contribute to a Sec. 403(b) Tax Sheltered Account and reduce his social security base.**

Employees of not-for-profit organizations contributing to a Sec. 403(b) voluntary salary reduction plan can also make contributions to an individual IRA account or annuity. Between July 2, 1986, and January 1, 1997, a not-for-profit organization could not establish a Sec. 401(k). Beginning in 1997, tax exempt organizations can setup 401(k) plans. Contributions to self-employed Keogh Plans can only be made to the extent of Schedule C honorariums and professional income.

- ***Effect of Sec. 911 Foreign Earned Income Exclusion***

According to Reg. 1.403(b)-1(e)(2), foreign earned income counts as includible compensation if an employee wishes to make contributions to a TSA.

According to Reg. 1.219-1(c)(1), for IRA purposes compensation does not include foreign earned income and/or housing that is excluded from income and contributions to an IRA are not allowed.

- ***Distributions and Penalties***

Early distributions of voluntary plans before age 59½ or disability are subject to the 10% early withdrawal penalty. To transfer or "roll-over" distributions within 60 days to another qualified tax shelter plan will prevent tax in the year of distribution and the 10% penalty. However, early distributions which are part of a series of substantially equal periodic payments received at least once a year for the life or life expectancy of the taxpayer or for joint lives of taxpayer and beneficiary will not be subject to the 10% penalty regardless of taxpayer's age, according to Sec. 72(T)(2)(A)(iv).

Mandatory distributions from a qualified plan must begin by April 1 of the calendar year following the later of: (1) the calendar year in which you reach 70½, or (2) the calendar year in which you retire.

Tax Sheltered Accounts - (TSA)

TSA's are available for employees of tax exempt organizations or public schools according to Sec. 403(b). IRS Publication 571 contains additional information on TSA's. An employee of a qualified organization can make an election to reduce their taxable salary and request that the employer make **non-forfeitable** (employee is always 100% vested) contributions to a Sec. 403(b) plan.

Salary reduction contributions to a TSA are not to be shown on the W-2 as income in Box 1. The amount of the contribution is required to be shown as a memo in Box 13, Form W-2.

Contributions **are subject** to social security tax and medicare tax for the lay employee, according to **Revenue Ruling 65-208**, and must be shown on the W-2, Box 3 and Box 5.

Contributions to a TSA by a dual-status minister **are not subject** to social security according to **Revenue Ruling 68-395**. If you have paid social security on contributions to a TSA as a dual-status minister you should file amended returns for the open years and request a refund.

For years beginning after 1995, you can enter into more than one salary reduction agreement during a year.

Beginning in years after December 31, 1996, a self-employed minister will be treated as his own employer that is presumed to be an exempt organization eligible to participate on his behalf in a Sec. 403(b) plan. Ministers employed by non-exempt organizations can participate in Sec. 403(b) plans so long as their duties consist of the exercise of ministry.

An employee can exclude up to 20% of "includible compensation" multiplied by the number of years of service, less amounts contributed in prior years. For tax years beginning after December 31, 1997, the maximum amount of such deferrals cannot exceed $10,000. If a taxpayer can participate in a Sec. 401(k) plan with another for-profit employer, the combined limit for both plans will be $10,000. There is an exception to the annual limit on contributions to Sec. 403(b) accounts. Any "qualified" employee who has completed 15 years of service with a qualified organization can make additional salary reduction contributions. An additional contribution of up to $3,000 can be made in any one year. An aggregate or total limit of $15,000 applies to additional contributions. Additional contributions are not available if a taxpayer's lifetime elective deferrals top his lifetime limit ($5,000 X years of service performed by the individual with the employer). The above limit of $10,000 and this additional $3,000 can be combined for a total limit of $13,000.

Other complex elections are available and IRS Publication 571 contains the rules and worksheets.

According to IRS Publication 571, page 6, "Includible compensation—self-employed minister: Beginning in 1997, compensation of a self-employed minister who is treated as employed by a tax-exempt organization is the ministers net earnings from self-employment reduced by contributions to retirement plans and the deduction for one-half of the self-employment tax." This new definition for "includible compensation" clearly takes the combination of salary and housing from Schedule SE. **Yes!** Parsonage allowance or value of parsonage provided is a part of **"includible compensation."**

Beginning in 1998, Sec. 403(b)'s definition of "includible compensation" has been expanded to include (1) elective deferrals (your employer's contributions made on your behalf under a salary reduction agreement), (2) amounts contributed or deferred by your employer under a Sec. 125 cafeteria plan, and (3) amounts contributed or deferred by your employer under a Sec. 457 plan.

Individual Retirement Accounts - (IRA)

You may also contribute, and possibly deduct, up to $2,000 annually to an IRA. IRS Publication 590 contains additional information on IRA's. Since January 1, 1997 the maximum IRA deduction for a married couple filing jointly is $4,000, up to $2,000 each, as long as their combined compensation is at least that much. Contributions for 1999 must be made by April 15th, 2000. You can set up and make contributions to an IRA if you received taxable compensation during the year and have not reached age 70½ by the end of the year.

Total individual contributions to all IRAs (regular & Roth) for a tax year cannot exceed $2,000.

● *Sec. 408(a) - Regular Individual Retirement Accounts*

Payments to a regular Individual Retirement Account (IRA) are to remain shown as salary, are subject to social security, and subtracted as an adjustment on Form 1040, line 23, if allowed as deductible contributions.

You will receive a Form 5498 by May 31, from the trustee of your account, each year stating the amount you have contributed for the current year and the value of your account. The earnings of an IRA accrue tax-free as long as you do not withdraw them.

For those who are active participants in an employer retirement plan, SEP, TSA, or a Keogh; contributions to an IRA can still be made but may not be deductible contributions. Beginning in 1998, active participation in an employer-sponsored plan by one spouse will not prevent the non-participating spouse from making a deductible contribution to an IRA unless their combined AGI reaches the phaseout level between $150,000 and $160,000. For active participants in 1999, the AGI phaseout range for making deductible IRA contributions for single persons is $31,000 to $41,000. For married persons filing jointly the range is $51,000 to $61,000. For married persons filing separately, if they lived together for any part of the year, the phaseout range is $0 to $10,000. From 1999 through 2002, these ranges expand each year by an additional $1,000 at each end. Starting in 2003, bigger jumps will apply until the phase-out range reaches $50,000 to $60,000 in 2005 for single persons and $80,000-$100,000 in 2007 for married persons filing jointly.

There is a provision that allows you to designate contributions as non-deductible, even if they qualify as deductible. **This prevents "wasted" deductions when there is no tax liability.** It allows the combination of "sheltered" and "non-sheltered" contributions to the same plan. Contributions that you choose to designate as non-deductible can be changed to deductible on an amended return for three open years.

Recordkeeping for non-deductible contributions to an IRA is the **responsibility of the taxpayer!!** Form 8606 is necessary to be completed and attached to your Form 1040. The non-deductible basis or contributions will be returned to you in retirement as non-taxable. If a taxpayer fails to keep record of the basis of his IRA account, the IRS can treat it as fully taxable upon withdrawal. Keeping copies of your tax returns in a safe place for your total working lifetime is your responsibility. The earnings of non-deductible or designated contributions are sheltered from tax until withdrawal.

Beginning in 1998, **penalty free** withdrawals from IRAs can be used for qualified higher education expenses and up to $10,000 (lifetime cap) of qualifying "first time" home-buyer expenses. You are a "first time" home buyer if you did not have a present ownership interest in a principal residence in the two year period before the acquisition of a new home. Such distributions would be subject to regular tax.

● ***Sec. 408A - Roth Individual Retirement Accounts***

Beginning in 1998, the Roth IRA, a new form of IRA, is available. Contributions to a Roth IRA will be non-deductible in the year of the contribution. As with other IRAs, **earnings accumulate** within a Roth IRA **tax free**. Qualified **distributions** from a Roth IRA **are also tax free** and not subject to a 10% penalty. Qualified distributions are those made after a 5 year period, and in addition, made after age 59½, after death to a beneficiary, after becoming disabled or distributed to pay for "qualified first time home buyer expenses." Nonqualified distributions are includible in income to the extent they exceed total contributions and are subject to a 10% penalty unless an exception applies. You can contribute up to $2,000 annually to a Roth IRA. For single persons the phaseout range is $95,000 to $110,000. For married taxpayers filing a joint return the phaseout range is $150,000 to $160,000. We feel this will be a wonderful choice for the non-tax paying minister's retirement planning. A Roth IRA invested in a mutual fund will capture the long term growth of the capital market.

Existing IRAs may be rolled over to Roth IRAs if your modified adjusted gross income is $100,000 or less. The rollover or conversion of a regular IRA to a Roth IRA is treated as a taxable distribution. During 1998 a special provision allowed you to spread the tax over a four year period. After 1998 a rollover or conversion from a regular IRA to a Roth IRA is taxable in the year it is made.

If you have contributed to or converted to a Roth IRA during the year and later become ineligible because your income is too high or because you are filing a married separate return, there are provisions for recharacterizing or unconverting back to a regular IRA. Timely recharacterizing can be chosen because you or your tax advisor discover that it was unwise to convert to a Roth IRA and pay tax. IRS Announcement 99-57 provides the latest deadlines and information.

Self-Employed Keogh Plans (H.R. 10)

Salaries received as "employees" are not eligible for making contributions to self-employed Keogh plans. Only income from honorariums or true independent contractor status qualify as income from which Keogh contributions can be made under Sec. 401(c). Annual contributions cannot exceed the lesser of (1) $30,000 or (2) 25% of the Schedule C income.

Housing Exclusion

Two separate types of housing are provided in the tax law. Dual-status employees **must use** Sec. 107 housing. Lay employees that meet the requirements must use Sec. 119 housing.

Lay Employees - Sec. 119

For the lay employee (janitor, dorm parents, managers, caretakers, etc.), the value of employer-furnished lodging and utilities is not taxable if:

1. Furnished on your employer's business premises;
2. For your employer's convenience;
3. And as a condition of your employment. Regular and emergency duties must be continuous, on constant 24-hour call.

All three conditions must be met or the value of housing provided is taxable. The exclusion does not apply if an employee can take cash instead of the housing.

Employees furnished lodging in a camp located in a foreign country by or on behalf of his employer, such camp shall be considered to be the business premises of the employer according to Sec. 119(c).

Employees of colleges, universities, and other educational institutions described in Sec. 170(b)(1)(A)(ii), can exclude the value of qualified campus lodging, provided they satisfy a rent-payment requirement. The rent must be at least equal to:

1. *5% of the appraised value of the lodging, determined at close of year or*
2. *the average of rentals paid to the educational institution for comparable housing during such calendar year, whichever is the lesser figure.*

If the rent paid equals the lesser of (1) or (2), the employee gets to exclude the entire lodging's value according to Sec. 119(d) and IRS Pub 525.

In the past, Sec. 119 housing was subject to social security. A Supreme Court Decision (Rowan Companies, Inc. v. United States) and Revenue Ruling 81-222 states that the IRS cannot have a different definition for wages for the lay employee for income and social security purposes. Therefore, the value of the meals and lodging that had been subject to social security in the past became exempt retroactively.

Dual-Status Minister - Sec. 107

Dual-status ministers are not taxed on the parsonage provided them and/or the parsonage allowance paid to them as a part of their compensation. Chapter Two gives full detailed discussion on how to designate in advance and compute tax-free parsonage allowance.

Unfortunately, the Rowan court case has no effect on the Sec. 107 for the dual-status minister. According to Flowers v. Commissioner, TC Memo 1991-542, parsonage provided and/or parsonage allowance paid **are still subject to social security** unless Form 4361 has been timely filed. Some tax advisors have applied the Rowan case to Sec. 107, **out of context**, and the IRS has assessed the preparer the $1,000 negligence penalty for each return filed in error. If you have failed to pay social security on your housing under Sec. 107, we would advise you to amend your returns and pay the correct amount of social security.

Gifts

When you **have not performed a service** and someone gives you a gift **and it does not come from an employer**, the gift can be considered non-taxable according to Sec. 102. Gifts received directly from relatives and personal friends for personal reasons are not taxable.

Often a church is asked to "funnel" a designated contribution to a specific individual. If that individual is involved in a ministry or missionary endeavor and the church finance committee chooses to honor the request, it should be treated as compensation to the individual receiving it, and included in the church's payroll reports. When the gift can be forwarded to a mission organization with which the individual is employed, that organization can include the amount in their payroll reports. If the individual to whom the gift is designated is not involved in a ministry, extreme caution must be exercised by the church. **Deductible contribution receipts should not be issued when the church does not have the right to control the monies.** When a designated recipient is not involved in a ministry, deductible contribution receipts should not be issued when the donor and the designated recipient are related.

When an employer helps an employee or a member of an employee's family with crisis needs it will result in taxable compensation. **We recommend** that a local non-employer, not-for-profit organization (such as Red Cross) be utilized to solicit help for an employee with crisis needs.

Deacon's Fund or Benevolence Fund: Churches should never hesitate to help people in the community who are unemployed, have a catastrophic illness, been an accident victim, or aged. Benevolent gifts to non-employees that are based on their needs are **non-taxable and are never** to be reported on an information return (Form 1099). Churches should be actively meeting the benevolent needs of their community.

Accountable Reimbursement Plan for Professional Expenses

Auto, travel, and professional expenses are able to be deducted from gross income if they are reimbursed by the employer according to Sec. 62(2)(A). You must "adequately account" to your employer. Several beneficial reasons will be given in Chapter Three for establishing an accountable reimbursement plan with your employer.

Sec. 457 Deferred Compensation Plans

Employees who have fully funded qualified tax shelter retirement plans may be able to defer additional taxable income through a Sec. 457 "non-qualified deferred compensation plan." These plans, which frequently use a trust arrangement known as a "rabbi trust," may be adopted with a model rabbi trust published by the IRS in Rev. Proc. 92-64.

To successfully defer taxes under a "non-qualified plan," the compensation deferred must, until actual payment, continue to be owned by the employer and be available to the employer's creditors if the employer becomes bankrupt or insolvent. The annual limitation for Sec. 457 deferrals is $8,000.

Before establishing a non-qualified deferred compensation plan, an employer should seek the assistance of an attorney and/or benefits consultant.

Prizes and Awards

Prizes and awards received in recognition of past accomplishments, even if you are selected without action on your part and you are not expected to render any future services, are taxable according to Sec. 102(c). They can be non-taxable if you "designate" the prize to charity according to Sec. 74.

Gratuity Payments to a Retired Minister

Payments made by a congregation to a retired minister (because of age or disability), if he is not expected to perform any further services, are non-taxable. Such non-taxable gifts based on gratitude and appreciation can be given after a minister retires in addition to his receiving taxable pension from an established plan. It is also necessary that the payments not be required by an established plan or agreement entered into before retirement and that they are based on his needs and the ability of the congregation to pay.

A statement in Osborne v Commissioner, T.C. Memo 1995-71: "In Revenue Ruling 55-422, the Service indicated that a payment by a congregation to a retiring clergyman would qualify as an excludable gift where, among other circumstances, there was a closer personal relationship between the recipient and the congregation than is found in secular employment situations."

This is a unique special provision for retired clergy. In all other careers all payments after retirement are taxable to the retiree because of past services. (Sec. 102(c)(1)) In Goodwin v. United States, KTC 1995-479, the judge said, "...the legislative history suggests that section 102(c)(1) was enacted to address other fact situations..."

CHAPTER TWO

Parsonage Allowance

The understanding of this chapter will result in tremendous income tax savings. Some dual-status ministers have spent many years in the ministry and have not been aware of how to "designate" their expenses of providing a home as non-taxable parsonage allowance. Internal Revenue Code Sec. 107 says:

"In the case of a minister of the Gospel, gross income does not include---

1. **The rental value of a home furnished to him as part of his compensation; or**
2. **The rental allowance paid to him as part of his compensation, to the extent used by him to rent or provide a home."**

Are You Entitled to the Parsonage Allowance Exclusion?

The answer to the question, "Are you entitled to parsonage allowance?" is also going to answer another question, "Are you considered self-employed for social security purposes?" **Sec. 107's** regulations refers us to **Sec. 1402(c)'s** regulations for the definition of some important terms. When we determine that you are entitled to tax-free parsonage allowance, we will have also determined that you are to be considered self-employed for social security purposes. **Dual-status means** that you are an **employee** for income reporting, fringe benefit, and expense deducting purposes and **self-employed** for social security purposes.

When we determine that you are not entitled to tax-free parsonage allowance, we will have also determined that you are to be considered as a lay employee for income tax and social security withholding purposes.

Generally, there are three circumstances to be considered. (1) Are you employed by a church or an integral agency of a church? (2) Are you performing ministerial services? and (3) Are you ordained by a church or "the equivalent thereof?" While all three tests must be satisfied for you to be treated as a dual-status minister for tax purposes, recent court cases and letter rulings reflect a very liberal and friendly definition of circumstance #3.

Are You Employed by a Church or An Integral Agency of a Church?

To qualify for minister's tax treatment and tax-free parsonage allowance your employer must be a church or an integral agency of a church. (See "Two Exceptions")

Churches (or a convention or association of churches) are exempt from federal income tax under Sec. 501(a) as a religious organization described in Sec. 501(c)(3) and further described in Sec. 170(b)(1)(A)**(i)**. A church **is not required to file Form 1023** to be exempt from federal income tax or to receive tax deductible contributions. In many states a church is not required to become incorporated. We feel it is wise for a church to protect themselves legally by incorporating at the state level. A church has a membership, separate accounting, and holds regular worship services. **Many churches do not have and do not need a determination letter from the IRS**. When a church voluntarily files Form 1023 to obtain formal recognition of their exemption they will receive a determination letter. Form 8718 must accompany the Form 1023 and requires a $500 fee to the IRS.

Religious organizations that are not churches can be under the control of a church or group of churches by drafting their bylaws to meet most of the requirements of **Revenue Ruling 72-606** and be an integral agency of a church. Such an organization, after filing Form 1023, would receive a determination letter stating that they are an organization described in Sec. 501(c)(3) and further described in Sec. 170(b)(1)(A)**(vi)**.

- ***Two Exceptions***

An exception to the requirement that your employer must be a church or an integral agency is provided if you are assigned or appointed to perform services at an organization that is not a church by your denomination or church. When you are considering employment by an organization that is not a church or an integral agency, have your church or denomination assign you to the position during the hiring process **before** you accept the position. (See "Qualifying Service Includes" from Reg. 1.1402(c)-5(b), item #7)

Another exception is provided when the services you are performing is that of conducting religious worship or ministering sacerdotal functions.

Since only a church or an integral agency can give authority to a minister to perform the duties of the ministry, we feel it is important for him/her to have been formally ordained, licensed or commissioned for either of these exceptions to be available.

Definition of Church

The following definitions will help you determine your correct status. Regulations for Sec. 107 state:

> *"The term, religious organization, has the same meaning and application as is given to the term for income tax purposes."*

The scope of what organizations are included in the definition of "churches" is found in the instructions of **IRS Pub. 557, page 20.** Because beliefs and practices vary so widely, there is no single definition of the term "church" for tax purposes. The Internal Revenue Service considers the facts and circumstances of each organization applying for church status. A separate organization affiliated with a church will be considered an integrated auxiliary if the principal activity of the organization is exclusively religious. Examples of organizations considered to be integrated auxiliaries of a church are a men's or women's organization, a religious school (such as a seminary), a mission society, or a youth group.

A church or organization may be liable for tax on its unrelated business income. Unrelated business income is income from a trade or business, regularly carried on, that is not substantially related to the charitable, educational or other purpose constituting the basis for the organization's exemption. An organization must file Form 990T if it has $1,000 or more gross income from an unrelated business. No part of an organization's net income may inure to the benefit of any individual.

The following list of organizations that are not required to file an annual information return (Form 990) gives us an **"expanded definition"** of what the IRS deems to be a church to satisfy Sec. 107 and Sec. 1402(c). *(Summary from Pub. 557, page 7 & 8:)*

1. A church, an interchurch organization of local units of a church, a convention or association of churches, an integrated auxiliary of a church, or an internally supported, church-affiliated organization.
2. An exclusively religious activity of any religious order. Specifically a religious order that is not opposed to insurance. (See complete discussion of "Religious Orders" in Chapter Five.)
3. A mission society sponsored by or affiliated with one or more churches or church denominations, more than one-half of the activities of which society are conducted in, or directed at persons in, foreign countries.
4. A school below college level affiliated with a church or operated by a religious order, even though it is not an integrated auxiliary of a church.

Integral Agency of a Church

A not-for-profit organization with a determination letter showing it is not a church but is described as an organization for charitable, educational, or other purposes in Sec. 170(b)(1)(A)**(vi)**, would be able to treat an employee performing ministerial duties as a dual-status minister for tax purposes and designate parsonage allowance if it meets **most of the requirements** of Revenue Ruling 72-606 to be an integral agency of a church.

Revenue Ruling 70-549 and Revenue Ruling 72-606 clearly state what is required for a school, mission, or other religious organization to be under the control of a church and qualify as an integral agency of a church. The eight criteria listed in **Revenue Ruling 72-606** are:

1. whether the religious organization incorporated the institution;

2. whether the corporate name of the institution indicates a church relationship;
3. whether the religious organization continuously controls, manages, and maintains the institution;
4. whether the trustees or directors of the institution are approved by or must be approved by the religious organization or church;
5. whether trustees or directors may be removed by the religious organization or church;
6. whether annual reports of finances and general operations are required to be made to the religious organization or church;
7. whether the religious organization or church contributes to the support of the institution; and
8. whether, in the event of dissolution of the institution, its assets would be turned over to the religious organization or church.

The only time a not-for-profit organization that is neither a church nor an integral agency of a church can treat an employee as a dual-status minister is when he has been assigned or appointed by a church or when his duties are conducting worship or ministering sacerdotal functions. All other employees will be lay employees regardless of their duties.

In the court case, Flowers v. U.S. CA 4-79-376-E, 11/25/81, it was found that Texas Christian University only met two of the possible eight tests of Revenue Ruling 72-606. Therefore, an ordained employee could not have a parsonage allowance as allowed by Sec. 107. Though Texas Christian University has a close relationship with the Disciples of Christ they did not evidence direct or indirect control by the church.

In Private Letter Ruling, 9144047, the teaching staff of a college was allowed to be dual-status, because their employing college was deemed to be an integral agency of a church.

We advise any organization that is unsure of their standing to examine their determination letter from the IRS and their bylaws. We recommend that you consider obtaining legal assistance to amend your bylaws to comply with those areas of control and to become an integral agency of a church.

Are You Performing Ministerial Services?

The salary or honorarium you receive for services which are ordinarily the duties of a minister of the gospel is eligible for minister's tax treatment and tax-free parsonage allowance. There is no parsonage allowance exclusion for a minister who volunteers and receives no ministerial income.

As a minister you are not required to be performing all of the duties or even able to perform all of the duties to be a dual-status minister for tax purposes. Since 1978, according to Revenue Ruling 78-301, it is only necessary that a minister be able to perform **"substantially all"** of the duties of the ministry to be a minister for tax purposes.

Regulations describe the types of services that a minister in the exercise of his ministry performs. These services include:

1. the ministration of sacerdotal functions,
2. the conduct of religious worship,
3. service in the administration, control, conduct, and maintenance of religious organizations, including integral agencies, under the authority of a church or church denomination, and
4. the performance of teaching and administrative duties at theological seminaries.

- **Qualifying Services Include *(Summary from Reg. 1.1402(c)-5(b).)***

1. A minister employed as pastor of a church is eligible for parsonage allowance. If more than one minister is on the staff, they may all exclude their parsonage allowance as long as their duties are those of ministers of the gospel.
2. Conducting religious worship services or ministering sacerdotal functions are ministerial services whether or not performed for a church or integral agency of a church. This provision makes it possible for a **chaplain** to qualify for dual-status treatment, even though he may be employed by a secular organization.
3. Service performed by a chaplain at either a church-related hospital or health and welfare institution, or a private non-profit hospital is considered to be in the exercise of his ministry according to Revenue Ruling 71-258.
4. A minister engaged in the control, conduct and maintenance of an integral agency of a religious organization or church. Members of the executive staff and those serving as

departmental managers are performing qualifying ministerial services according to Revenue Ruling 57-129.

5. A minister serving on the faculty as a teacher or administrator of a college or seminary which is operated as an integral agency of a church according to Revenue Ruling 71-7.
6. A minister serving on the faculty as a teacher or administrator of an undergraduate school that is affiliated with a church. (Included in the "expanded definition" of a church)
7. A minister **assigned or designated by a church to perform services for an organization that is not a church,** even though such service may not involve the conduct of religious worship or the ministration of sacerdotal functions, is in the exercise of his ministry. **Example:** A minister assigned to perform advisory service to a printing company in connection with the publication of a book dealing with the history of his church denomination. (Reg. 1.1402(c)-5(b)(v)) Your services are ordinarily not considered to have been assigned or designated by your church if any of the following is true:
   A. The organization for which you perform the services did not arrange with your church for your services.
   B. You perform the same services for the organization as those performed by its other employees who were not designated as you were.
   C. You perform the same services before and after the designation.
8. A rabbi is a minister of the gospel and qualifies for the parsonage allowance. Cantors also qualify according to Revenue Ruling 78-301.
9. A minister who performs evangelistic services at churches away from his permanent home may exclude parsonage allowance paid to him by the churches according to Revenue Ruling 64-326.
10. Writing or producing religious books, articles, audio or video tapes is considered to be in the exercise of your ministry. Royalty income from their sale is self-employment income.

- **Non-Qualifying Duties Include** ***(Summary from Reg. 1.1402(c)-5(c).)***

1. Ministers who were administrators of non-profit nursing homes. The nursing homes were not a religious organization nor an integral agency of a church. The services performed by the ministers were not the type of services that qualified. (Jesse A. Toavs et al., 67 TC 897)
2. If a minister is performing service for an organization which is neither a religious organization nor operated as an integral agency of a religious organization and the service is not performed following an assignment or designation by his ecclesiastical superiors, then the service performed is not in the exercise of his ministry. **Example**: Minister is employed by a university to teach mathematics and history. The university is not a church nor an integral agency of a church. He receives honorariums from time to time performing wedding and funerals for friends. The honorariums are his only ministerial income.
3. Routine services performed by secretaries, stenographers, mail clerks, file clerks, janitors, etc., are not in the exercise of ministry according to Revenue Ruling 57-129. Usually the services performed by doctors, nurses, auto mechanics, pilots, carpenters, cooks, etc., are not in the exercise of ministry.
4. A chaplain in the armed forces is specifically denied this exclusion since he is considered to be a commissioned officer, and as such is not a minister in the exercise of his ministry. Military officers are given tax-free housing, therefore, Sec. 107 is not needed.
5. Similarly, service performed by an employee of a State as a chaplain in a State prison or a government hospital is considered to be performed by a civil servant of the State and not by a minister in the exercise of his ministry. Though not able to be treated as self-employed when an employee of a government entity, Sec 107 parsonage designation was allowed in C.T. Boyd, Jr., 42T.C.M. 1136, T.C. Memo 1982-377 by the Church Federation of Greater Indianapolis, Inc., even though Boyd was employed by the Indianapolis Police Department as Senior Chaplain. This is **an exception** to Sec 107 and Sec 1402(e) qualification being simultaneous.

Are You Ordained By A Church Or "The Equivalent Thereof?"

If you are employed by a church or an integral agency of a church and are performing ministerial services, you are considered to be "the equivalent of" ordained at the time you begin your employment. When a church calls or hires you to be their minister, they have informally given you the authority to conduct religious worship and to administer ordinances at the time of employment. You satisfy the "ability to perform services in control, conduct and maintenance of the church" merely by being employed by a church as their minister. In Salkov v. Commissioner, supra, 46 TC at 190 (1966) it was concluded that the congregation's formal selection of the taxpayer as their cantor constituted commissioning him as their minister.

Here is a very important court definition of a "duly ordained, commissioned, or licensed" minister. In J.M. Ballinger, U.S. Court of Appeals, 10th Circuit, No. 82-1928, 3/7/84, it was stated, *"Not all churches or religions have a formally ordained ministry, whether because of the nature of their beliefs, the lack of a denominational structure or a variety of other reasons. Courts are not in a position to determine the merits of various churches... We interpret Congress' language providing an exemption for any individual who is 'a duly ordained, commissioned, or licensed minister of a church' to mean that **the triggering event is the assumption of the duties and functions of a minister**."*

It is very important for a minister who wishes to become exempt from social security to be aware of the date his/her ministry begins. The deadline for a timely filed "Application for Exemption from Self-Employment Tax for Ministers," Form 4361, is the due date of the tax return (including extensions) for the second year in which he/she earns more than $400 from the ministry. The minister who is formally ordained, licensed, or commissioned by his church or denomination experiences a very important and meaningful event. However, **when he receives formal credentials after the date of his hiring, it is not an important event for tax purposes**. On the date he was hired, he was entitled to ministerial tax status.

Only a church or an integral agency can give authority to a minister to perform the duties of the ministry. **When a minister is not employed by a church or an integral agency,** it is important for him to have been formally ordained, licensed or commissioned as a minister by a church before being "assigned or designated" to a position with a non-church. When a minister, as **an independent evangelist or a chaplain,** performs worship and/or ministers sacerdotal functions at locations outside of a church, it is also important for him to have been formally ordained, licensed or commissioned as a minister by a church.

Prior to 1978, Revenue Ruling 65-124 was very strict in stating that a minister had to be able to perform **"all"** the religious functions of the church to be defined as "ordained" for tax purposes.

Since 1978, Revenue Ruling 78-301 added the word **"substantially"** to the definition in order to allow Jewish cantors to qualify for parsonage allowance. Exactly what was meant by "substantially all" was a mystery until 1989. Two tax court cases involving ministers with limited authority who waited until formal ordination to file Form 4361 to become exempt from social security were decided. IRS denied both applications as being untimely filed. In Private Letter Ruling 9221025 the teaching staff of school below college level were deemed to be ministers for tax purposes even though they were unable to conduct public adult worship or any of the sacerdotal functions. In Private Letter Ruling 199910055 it was determined that the Minister of Education, Minister of Music and Minister of Stewardship, all ordained deacons, were ministers for tax purposes. Performing ministerial duties and being recognized as a religious leader by his church qualifies a minister for ministerial tax status.

James S. Wingo, 89 TC No. 64, Docket No. 8613-85: Taxpayer was an ordained "deacon" and licensed as a probationary pastor of the United Methodist Church beginning in 1980. He became an ordained "elder" in 1984 and wished to become exempt from social security. The United Methodist Church considers both "deacons" and "elders" as ordained ministers of the Church, and as an appointed full-time pastor Rev. Wingo was permitted to administer the sacraments, provide for the organizational concerns of the local church, conduct divine worship, preach the Word, perform marriage ceremonies, and bury the dead. IRS determined that for purposes of applying for the exemption from self-employment tax **under Sec. 1402** or for obtaining the parsonage exclusion **under Sec. 107**, Rev. Wingo was a minister.

John G. Knight, 92 TC No. 12, Docket Nos. 45505-86, 27182-87: Taxpayer was a licentiate of the Cumberland Presbyterian Church and served as a supply pastor. He preached, conducted the worship service, visited the sick, performed funerals, and ministered to the needy. Because he was not ordained, he could not moderate the session, administer sacraments, or solemnize marriages. Duties and functions were considered by the court to be appropriate for a "duly ordained, commissioned or licensed minister."

Private Letter Ruling 9221025: Because some churches allow both genders to be given full authority in the ministry and others extended full authority only to the men, an unequal tax advantage resulted for some women in the ministry. On February 20, 1992, Private Letter Ruling 9221025, gave a positive answer to a major denomination concerning their "commissioned" female teachers being eligible for dual-status treatment. The female staff performed full-time public ministry functions including: classroom teaching; evangelizing; counseling individuals; leading Bible study groups, devotions, worship services for youth and a congregation's music ministry; giving the children's sermon at the regular Sunday worship service, coordinating lay church workers; caring spiritually for the sick and imprisoned and their families; etc., It is important to understand that Sec. 6110(j)(3) of the Code provides that a letter ruling may not be used or cited as precedent.

The impact of a church or an integral agency of a church making the switch to dual-status tax treatment for their staff should be carefully administered with good communication and instruction. **An additional salary factor** equal to the matching portion of social security should be paid to each staff member affected. Otherwise, an employee with little or no parsonage expense would experience an economic loss. Whether or not an employee has an opportunity to elect to become exempt from Social Security will depend on the date they were hired or began performing ministerial duties.

Private Letter Ruling 199910055: A local church requested rulings for three "ordained deacons" whose duties were to assist the senior pastor. The Minister of Education's duties included planning and supervising youth, adult, and family activities. He selected the curriculum, scheduled activities and coordinated lay volunteers. The Minister of Music coordinated all choir and music activities. The Minister of Stewardship performed financial and managerial functions. He encouraged members of the congregation to give their time, talent and money to the church. They met with the elder to plan the worship services, assist with the sacraments and officiate at weddings and funerals. All three positions were deemed to be eligible for ministerial tax treatment.

Haimowitz v. Commissioner, T.C. Memo 1997-40: Mr. Haimowitz served for 30 years as an executive director of a temple. He never claimed ministerial tax status or housing allowance during his working years. He eventually performed more religious duties, such as helping students with memorization of blessings, Torah readings, and elocution. He frequently helped plan weddings and participated in the wedding ceremony as a witness to the contract, but he never officiated. After he retired, never having **shown himself to have been recognized as a religious leader** by the temple, he claimed that his pension should be tax-free parsonage allowance. He provided no evidence that a housing allowance had been designated in advance, so it was not allowed and was not appealable.

Parsonage Allowance Exclusion Rules

What Does the Parsonage Allowance Exclusion Include?

It includes anything spent to provide a home for the dual-status minister and his family. Regulations for Sec. 107 state that the parsonage allowance does not include food or a maid. Parsonage allowance is the tax-free treatment of a ministers **personal** home expenses on a **cash basis.** Do not use business capital asset rules. Do not depreciate home capital expenses. Parsonage allowance expenses include those for the house, its contents, the garage and the yard. The following list shows typical expenses that are to be considered in computing the amount of parsonage allowance:

1. Rent or principal payments, cost of buying a home and down payments. (See limitations below)
2. Real estate taxes and mortgage interest for the home. These expenses are deductible again as itemized deductions. **A DOUBLE DEDUCTION**, but allowable by IRS!! (Revenue Ruling 62-212 and Sec. 265(a)(6)) **An amazing "tax shelter"!**
3. Insurance on the home and/or contents.
4. Improvements, repairs and upkeep of the home and/or contents. Such as a new roof, room addition, garage, patio, fence, pool, appliance repair, etc.

5. Furnishings and appliances: dish washer, vacuum sweeper, TV, VCR, stereo, piano, computer (personal use), washer, dryer, beds, small kitchen appliances, cookware, dishes, sewing machine, garage door opener, lawnmower, hedge trimmer, etc.
6. Decorator items: drapes, throw rugs, pictures, knick knacks, painting, wallpapering, bedspreads, sheets, towels, etc.
7. Utilities - heat, electric, non-business telephone, water, cable TV, sewer charge, garbage removal, etc. (Show long distance business telephone calls and the business % of cellular phone usage as a professional expense. Both income tax and self-employment tax will be reduced.)
8. Miscellaneous - any thing that maintains the home and its contents that you have not included in repairs or decorator items: cleaning supplies for the home, brooms, light bulbs, dry cleaning of drapes, shampooing carpet, expense to run lawnmower, tools for landscaping, garden hose to water lawn, etc. (Rasmussen v. Commissioner, July 6, 1994, T.C. Memo 1994-311.)

The expenses in item No. 8 are often purchased at the grocery or variety store. It is a good practice to buy a supply of household cleaning supplies separately and save the receipt. An easy way to keep record of them is to use the "Housing Expense" section of our **"Professional Tax Record Book."**

Do Not Include the following: Maid (or hired lawn care), groceries, personal toiletries such as toothpaste, shampoo, deodorant, laundry and dish soap, paper products; personal clothing, coats, shoes, jewelry; toys, bicycles, hobby items, cassette tapes, CD's, computer games, computer application software, VCR movies, etc. Because a cellular phone is used outside of the home, do not use the personal portion as parsonage allowance.

Parsonage allowance is free from income tax, **but subject to social security and medicare tax**. Parsonage expense details, receipts, and records are **not to be submitted to the employer.** They are handled differently than the professional business expenses we will discuss in Chapter Three. The personal home expenses can remain confidential. If the designated amount is greater than the amount substantiated, it is the responsibility of the individual minister to show the "excess parsonage allowance" as income on Form 1040, line 21.

Double Deduction of Interest & Taxes

Sec. 265(a)(6) provides for the deduction of home mortgage interest and property taxes on Schedule A even though all or part of the mortgage is paid with funds you get through a nontaxable parsonage allowance. In 1983 Congress attempted to end the "double deduction," but Revenue Ruling 83-3 was revoked by Sec. 265(a)(6). This "double deduction" has been available since 1962. Revenue Ruling 62-212 provided for this amazing "tax shelter" and it has been strengthened with an addition to Sec. 265.

Interest Rules

Interest for the purchase of a home and furnishings can be used for parsonage allowance exclusion. However non-mortgage interest for home purchases will not be allowable on Schedule A as "personal interest." Mortgage and home equity loan interest will qualify as Schedule A "mortgage interest" deduction because the home is used as collateral. Mortgage and home equity loan interest for the purchase of and improvement of the parsonage can also be used for parsonage allowance exclusion. Mortgage and home equity loan interest for any other purpose will not be allowable as parsonage allowance exclusion. If a home equity loan is used for home improvements and the purchase of an auto, only the home improvement portion of the interest can be used as parsonage allowance exclusion. (Rasmussen v. Commissioner, July 6, 1994, T.C. Memo 1994-311.)

Cash Basis

Since capital expenditures for home principal, improvements, furniture, and appliances are on a cash basis, it is important to understand when to deduct them if the purchase involves borrowed funds. Any purchases with bank charge cards are treated the same as if you paid cash for the item. Any purchases for the home that involves a loan from a bank, store, or individual are treated as not paid for in full. Non-credit card loan payments for home, improvements, and furniture are to be deducted as they are paid.

● ***Transition Periods***

Generally, a minister can use the expenses of one home for his parsonage allowance exclusion. When he owns a vacation or second home on a permanent basis, he can only use the expenses for the "main" home as parsonage allowance exclusion.

During a temporary period of changing employers, changing parsonages, or building a parsonage; expenses for two parsonages is allowable according to a tax court case, Fred B. Marine, 47 TC 609 (1967). The temporary period would continue as long as both homes remained personal use. If before a sale, the previous home is rented, the rental income and expenses will generally be reportable on Schedule E.

● ***Sale of Personal Residence***

There is no requirement that the cost of purchasing and improving a residence be adjusted or reduced by the tax-free principal portion of parsonage allowance. Therefore, in reporting the sale of a personal residence, the whole cost basis is used to determine gain or loss. If the sale of a personal residence results in a loss, it is not deductible from other taxable income.

The Taxpayer Relief Act of 1997 provides for an exclusion of $250,000 of gains on the sale of a personal residence ($500,000 for couples.) There are two tests:

1. "Once-in-two-years." You must not have used this rule for at least two years prior to the current sale.
2. "Used-as-your-home." In the 5 year period before the current sale, you must have used the property as your home for a total of at least two years.

If you can meet the tests, you can exclude the gain. This new exclusion eliminates the need to buy a larger and more expensive replacement home to defer tax. Ministers who have owned their home and relocate to a church that provides them a parsonage can now sell without incurring tax on the gain if the two tests are met. If the two tests are not met, the gain is taxable even if a more expensive replacement home is purchased. However, you can claim a reduced exclusion if you sold the home due to a change in health or job transfer by employer.

The above rules for the sale of a personal residence never apply to the sale of business or rental property. Business property sales will result in taxable gains or deductible losses.

How Much of a Minister's Salary Can Be Designated?

Nothing in the Internal Revenue code or regulations establish a "flat" dollar limitation or a percentage of income limitation for the parsonage allowance exclusion. **The amount designated as parsonage allowance must be a specific dollar amount or a specific percentage of salary.** Employers can designate a blanket percentage of their staff's salaries as parsonage allowance. Individuals on their staff who anticipate incurring a greater amount for parsonage expenses should be allowed to ask for a higher amount to be designated.

Publication 517, page 7, gives a very clear explanation of how much the parsonage allowance can be:

> *"If you own your home and you receive as part of your pay a housing or rental allowance, you may exclude from gross income the* ***smallest*** *of the following:*
>
> *1. The amount actually used to provide a home,*
> *2. The amount officially designated as a rental allowance, or*
> *3. The fair rental value of the home, including furnishings, utilities, garage, etc.*
>
> *You must include in gross income any rental allowance that is more than the smallest of your reasonable pay, the fair rental value of the home plus utilities, or the amount actually used to provide a home."*

The **"top limit"** that can be claimed by a minister as parsonage allowance exclusion is based on his furnished home's fair rental value, cost of utilities, etc. Actual expenses incurred up to this "top limit" can be used as parsonage allowance exclusion. In the year of purchase, or a year in which a major payment of principal or a large outlay is made for improvements or furniture is made, it is important to carefully compute the "top limit" as follows:

FRV of house + FRV of furniture + decorator items + utilities + miscellaneous

To support the computation of your housing allowance in a year of major expenditures we recommend you obtain a professional appraisal of your home's fair rental value. Fair rental value is what it would cost to rent a comparable home in your neighborhood. A "rule of thumb" among realtors nationwide is that the fair rental value of a home (without furnishings) amounts to **1% of the appraised fair market value** per month. This formula is fairly accurate. However, **the condition, location, local market demand, and local economic conditions** of your home will need to be considered.

Example: If your home is appraised at $115,000, the monthly FRV could be $1,150. Annual FRV could be $13,800 ($1,150 X 12).

The fair rental value of furniture is more difficult to compute. Based on the amount, age, and condition, we recommend that you estimate your furniture FRV conservatively.

We have included space on the "Worksheet for Form 2106" to compute the limitation in a year of major expense. FRV of the home would take the place of principal, interest, taxes, insurance and major repairs (line 2 through line 6). FRV of the furniture would take the place of actual furniture purchases (line 7). Actual costs of decorator items (line 8), utilities (line 9), and miscellaneous items (line 10) are to be used. We have included an example of the computation of the "top limit" in Rev. Snodrass's return in Chapter 7.

When actual expenses exceed the fair rental value limitation they are lost. There are no provisions for carryover of unused portions. Rather than lose the ability to exclude your down payment or major home expenses, consider obtaining a second mortgage and spreading the cost over a few years and keep within the "top limit" each year.

Loans from employers can be used to accomplish the above suggestion to avoid "wasting" parsonage allowance expenses. It is important that interest be charged if the loan exceeds $3,000 and that the loan be secured by the home and recorded at the courthouse. Sec. 483 rules concerning "below market" interest loans require that the Applicable Federal Rate (published monthly by the IRS) be charged for loans over $3,000. Based on the date of the loan, apply that month's rate for the duration of the loan.

Often the minister's employer would rather not charge him interest for a loan. But Sec. 483 says it is required. This requirement has a **positive tax benefit** for the minister employee. If the loan is secured by the home, the interest will qualify for deductible "home interest" on Schedule A and also as a part of tax-free parsonage allowance. Therefore, we recommend the following procedure: (1) pay an additional salary factor to equal the correct interest (annually or monthly); (2) increase the designated parsonage allowance as needed; (3) accept the interest payment from the minister (annually or monthly).

Loan forgiveness: In the event the employing church who loans their minister money for a down payment or major improvement desires or decides to forgive a loan we recommend the following procedure: (1) secure the loan with the home and record at the courthouse; (2) forgive a portion of the loan each year so that the "top limit" is not exceeded; (3) increase the designated parsonage allowance as needed; (4) treat the amount of principle and/or interest forgiven as income; (5) deduct interest forgiven on Sch A.

In Sec. 7872, loans with "below-market interest rates," not involved with real or personal property, require that the Applicable Federal Rate be charged for loans over $10,000.

Reasonable compensation means that a minister should not be over-compensated for the amount of time spent and amount of work accomplished. Usually the opposite is true, a minister is under-compensated. In Revenue Ruling 78-448, a tax protest minister was considered to have been over-compensated and was not allowed to have 100% of his compensation be tax-free housing allowance **because he did not perform any services to earn it**. The Revenue Ruling deals with a tax protest situation, and has no application to a legitimate church/minister employment relationship. Some IRS auditors have misapplied Revenue Ruling 78-448 and claim it prevents a minister from using 100% housing designation. They are wrong as the only limits to the amount of parsonage allowance a minister can claim are those we quoted from IRS Pub 517 earlier in the chapter.

● *Tax Plan*

Good tax planning for a minister is to **"over designate"** his parsonage allowance and allow for unexpected expenses and increases in utility costs to be covered. The "unused parsonage allowance" will be shown as income on Form 1040, line 21.

● *Part-Time Ministers*

For a minister who is serving part-time and is not fully supported by the employer, it is possible to designate all or 100% of his salary as parsonage allowance. Since parsonage allowance is not required to be shown on Form W-2, a Form W-2 generally does not need to be prepared.

When a minister is employed outside the church and a new or small congregation cannot fully support him, it is good tax-planning for the minister to make substantial Schedule A contributions to the church. The church will then have the funds to pay an adequate salary, designate it as parsonage allowance, and allow him to take full advantage of Sec. 107. The minister who is not exempt from social security will have to pay social security taxes on the parsonage allowance.

● *What If Your Home Is Debt Free?*

For the minister whose home is paid for or nearly so, the amount of actual expenses for taxes, insurance, upkeep, utilities, etc., does not allow as much tax-free parsonage allowance. In Swaggart v. Commissioner, TC Memo 1984-409, the taxpayer argued that rental allowance was fully excludable from gross income regardless of how the funds were spent.... In rejecting such argument, the court concluded that Congress intended to exclude from the minister's gross income only that portion of his compensation paid by the church which was **actually used** by the minister for providing a home for himself. In a previous case, Reed et al, 82 TC 208, the court had also restricted tax-free parsonage to out-of-pocket expenses.

In Private Letter Ruling 9115051, the IRS tells us their position in regards to "refinancing the debt-free parsonage." It is important to understand that Sec. 6110(j)(3) of the Code provides that a letter ruling may not be used or cited as precedent.

The IRS was asked to respond to these questions: "Are payments made on a home equity line of credit (secured by the debt-free home) expenses for which a parsonage allowance may be granted by the church? Would taking out a loan secured by a mortgage on the home result in expenses for which a parsonage allowance may be granted by the church?"

The response of IRS was: "Neither payments made on the home equity line of credit nor on the mortgage secured by the house are being used to rent or provide a home as required by Sec. 107 and the regulations. Therefore, amounts designated by the church to pay for these expenditures are not excludable from the minister's gross income as a parsonage allowance under Sec. 107."

What is Meant By "Official Designation"?

"Official designation" means that the employer designates, by official action, **IN ADVANCE**, the amount the dual-status minister expects to spend for all the expenses of his home. The designation can be done by the official board or the congregation, and should be recorded in their minutes. **The amount designated as parsonage allowance must be a specific dollar amount or a specific percentage of salary.** Reg. 1.107-1(b) says:

> *"The term 'rental allowance' means an amount paid to a minister to rent or otherwise provide a home..... if such amount is designated as rental allowance pursuant to official action taken* ***in advance*** *of such payment by the employing church or other qualified organization.*
>
> *The designation of an amount as rental allowance may be evidenced in an employment contract, in minutes of or in a resolution by a church or other qualified organization or in its budget, or in any other appropriate instrument evidencing such official action. The designation referred to in this paragraph is a sufficient designation if it permits a payment or a part thereof to be identified as a payment of rental allowance as distinguished from salary or other remuneration."*

Because the IRS will accept **a perpetually worded designation**, we recommend using a perpetual clause as a **safety net.** Example: "As long as .....the above amount....shall apply to all future years until modified." We recommend that a minister "tax plan" annually and consider if the amount designated needs to be modified for the coming year.

If you were not aware of how to designate your parsonage allowance or you have had an inadequate amount designated, there is no way to fix the problem for the past. **Now** is the time to designate an adequate parsonage allowance for the rest of the year. In advance of a major unexpected expense or a change from a parsonage provided to buying your own home, do not hesitate to **amend and increase** your designation for the balance of the year.

- ***Qualified Organization***

This regulation requires that an independent party make the designation and prevents "self-designation." A qualified organization does not have to be a religiously affiliated entity to be able to designate parsonage allowance. Nor is it necessary that the designation come from the payor of a minister's compensation. In C.T. Boyd, Jr., 42T.C.M. 1136, T.C. Memo 1982-377, the advance designation requirement was considered to be met by designation of the Church Federation of Greater Indianapolis, Inc., a non-profit corporation, even though Boyd was employed by the Indianapolis Police Department as Senior Chaplain. IRS Letter Ruling 8519004 supports this inclusive scope of a "qualified organization."

- ***Ministers Who Own***

Ministers who own their homes will want to designate an amount to cover the total cost of owning, cost of their furnishings, cost of decorating, utilities, and etc.

When the title to the home and the real estate mortgage is in the minister's name, the employer should not make the payments for him. Pay the minister enough salary to pay all the home expenses, and designate an adequate amount as parsonage allowance. The minister who owns his own home should pay his payment and all of the home expenses himself. **Keep it simple**. Hybrid arrangements where the employer pays some of the expenses and the minister pays others, causes confusion and may result in an inadequate designation of parsonage allowance.

Do not do this: Often, to avoid paying real estate taxes, creative arrangements of "we'll put the house in the churches name" create huge income tax problems. Any transfer of title to the minister can result in a taxable event for the entire value of the home.

- ***Ministers Who Rent***

Ministers who rent their homes will want to designate an amount to cover the actual rent paid, cost of their furnishings, cost of decorating, insurance, utilities, and etc.

- ***Church Owns The Parsonage***

If the employer provides the home and/or pays the utilities, its value is income tax-free automatically. The minister then needs to estimate how much he expects to spend in all of the other categories of home expenses and have that amount of his cash salary designated. It is important to understand that the minister living in a church-owned parsonage has **"two pieces"** to his parsonage allowance:

1. a value provided and
2. a designated portion of his cash salary for the additional home expenses.

- ***Evangelists***

According to Revenue Ruling 64-326, a traveling evangelist may exclude amounts he receives from various churches or meetings as tax-free parsonage allowance. There are two ways to handle the designation in advance: (1) A supporting or home church could designate an annual amount even though they do not pay or handle the honorariums, or (2) individual host churches can designate a portion of his honorarium as parsonage allowance. This involves communicating with the various churches in advance and sending them a statement requesting that they take action to "designate" a portion of your honorarium as parsonage allowance. We recommend that you get duplicate non-carbon copies of the "Statement of Parsonage for An Evangelist" printed. Each church on your itinerary can keep a copy and easily provide you a copy.

A traveling evangelist or conference speaker with a permanent home will incur deductible travel expenses for lodging and meals while on the road and use parsonage allowance exclusion for his permanent home. If he lives in a motor home or travel trailer and does not have a permanent home, his lodging and meal expenses will not be deductible as business expenses. His tax home for tax purposes is wherever he "hangs his hat." He may treat the motor home as his parsonage, but his meals would not be deductible.

An evangelist who forms his own not-for-profit corporation, will be an employee of the corporation. An evangelist, as long as the services he performs is that of conducting worship and the ministration of sacerdotal functions, is a dual-status minister for tax purposes. The organization's board can easily designate his parsonage allowance.

- ***Missionaries***

Sec. 911 foreign earned income exclusion allows most missionaries serving outside of the United States to be able to earn as much as $74,000 ($76,000 in 2000) and pay no income tax.

If they do not qualify to use the $74,000 exclusion, the mission should definitely designate the parsonage allowance for the dual-status missionary. Missionaries who are dual-status ministers should always designate a parsonage allowance so that their home expenses will be excluded while on furlough or sick leave. Chapter Five contains a detailed discussion of the special tax situation for missionaries serving outside of the United States.

● ***Retired Ministers & Parsonage Designation***

A retired minister receiving an otherwise taxable distribution from a qualified Sec. 401(a), Sec. 403(b), Sec. 408(k), 408(p) or Sec. 414(e) plan may have a **"parsonage allowance"** designated by the former employer or denominational pension board. It is possible for 100% of the retirement income to be non-taxable to the extent it is used for parsonage expenses. (Revenue Ruling 63-156). We have found language in the Department of Labor Regulations under ERISA that seem to consider either type of contribution to Sec. 403(b) **(forfeitable and non-forfeitable)** to be considered as an employer's plan and eligible for parsonage allowance designation. (Labor Regs. 2520.3-2(f)(3))

However, distributions from an IRA or a Keogh retirement plan are fully taxable and cannot be designated as non-taxable housing.

Third party payors of retirement plan distributions should include the gross distribution on Form 1099-R, Box 1. Not being able to determine the taxable amount Box 2a should be left blank and Box 2b should be checked. As a retired minister receiving distributions from a retirement plan that has been designated as "parsonage allowance" you are to enter the gross amount on Form 1040, line 16a. It is the responsibility of the retired minister to show as taxable on Form 1040, line 16b, any designated distributions not spent for parsonage expenses. If all of the distribution has been spent for parsonage expenses enter -0- on line 16b.

Steps in Designating & Deducting Parsonage Allowance

1. The dual-status minister is to estimate the amount he expects to spend for the coming year and present this to his employer. It is good to over estimate and allow for unexpected expenses and utility cost increases. In advance of a major unexpected expense, or a change from a parsonage provided to buying your own home, do not hesitate to "amend" and increase your designation for the balance of the year.
2. The employer then makes an official written designation based on the dual-status minister's estimate. You may use the suggested wordings we provide.
3. At the close of the tax year, the dual-status minister then compares his actual expenses with the amount designated. If he has incurred any major expenses he will compute the FRV limit. The smallest amount is allowed as his parsonage allowance exclusion.

Parsonage expense details, receipts, and records are **not to be submitted to the employer.** They are handled differently than the professional business expenses we will discuss in Chapter Three. The personal home expenses can **remain confidential**. If the designated amount is greater than the amount substantiated, it is the responsibility of the individual minister to show the "excess parsonage allowance" as income on Form 1040, line 21. Use the "Worksheet for Form 2106" provided in this publication to compute taxable unused parsonage allowance, if any.

A minister who moves and/or changes amounts of parsonage allowance during the year should allocate the annual designations by the week. For example: You were at ABC Church for 17 weeks and your annual parsonage allowance was $5,200. You were at XYZ Church for 35 weeks and your annual parsonage allowance was $13,000. Compute as follows:

$ 5,200 ÷ 52 = $100 X 17 weeks = $1,700
$13,000 ÷ 52 = $250 X 35 weeks = $8,750

Total parsonage allowance for the two positions would be:

$1,700 + $8,750 = $10,450.

Once the parsonage allowance has been timely designated, there is no need to attach a copy of the official designation to the tax return itself. Merely show the amount properly designated on the "Worksheet for Form 2106." In the event you are chosen for an audit, the IRS will ask for a verification of the timely official designation from the church records.

We recommend that the "Worksheet for Form 2106" be attached to Form 1040 to explain how you arrived at amount of "excess parsonage allowance" entered on Form 1040, line 21.

Suggested Wording of the Official Designation

When The Church Owns The Parsonage

The chairman informed the meeting that under the tax law, a minister of the Gospel is not subject to federal income tax on "the parsonage allowance paid to him as a part of his compensation to the extent used by him to rent or provide a home."

The parsonage is owned by the church and the actual utility expenses will be paid by the church.

After considering the estimate of Rev. ________ of his additional home expenses, a motion was made by __________, seconded by _________ and passed to adopt the following resolution:

Resolved that of the total cash salary for the year 19___, $_________ is hereby designated as parsonage allowance.

Resolved that as long as Rev. ________ is our employee the above amount of designated parsonage allowance shall apply to all future years until modified.

When A Minister Owns Or Rents His/Her Own Home

The chairman informed the meeting that under the tax law, a minister of the Gospel is not subject to federal income tax on "the parsonage allowance paid to him as part of his compensation to the extent used by him to rent or provide a home."

After considering the estimate of Rev.________ of his home expenses, a motion was made by _________, seconded by _________ and passed to adopt the following resolution:

Resolved that of the total cash salary for the year 19____, $_________ is hereby designated as parsonage allowance.

Resolved that as long as Rev. ________ is our employee the above amount of designated parsonage allowance shall apply to all future years until modified.

When A Minister Is Employed By A School, College, Or Mission

Most teachers and administrators working for a church or integral agency of a church have an annual contract of employment with that organization. It is convenient to include the necessary written designation within the contract itself. An annual "Agreement for the Designation of the Parsonage Allowance" could be worded as follows:

According to the provisions in income tax law, a minister of the Gospel is not subject to federal income tax on the "parsonage allowance paid to him as part of his compensation to the extent used by him to rent or provide a home."

Based on Rev.________'s estimate of his home expenses, it is agreed to officially designate $_________ of his total cash salary as parsonage allowance.

Resolved that as long as Rev. ________ is our employee the above amount of designated parsonage allowance shall apply to all future years until modified.

Statement Of Parsonage For An Evangelist

Evangelists can have a supporting or home church designate an annual amount of the honorariums they will receive as parsonage allowance or they can send a statement to churches on their itinerary and have a portion or all of the honorarium designated as parsonage allowance, in advance of the engagement. **Get duplicate non-carbon sets printed of the following statement:**

According to the provisions in income tax law, a minister of the Gospel is not subject to federal income tax on the "parsonage allowance paid to him as a part of his compensation to the extent used by him to rent or provide a home."

After considering the request of Rev._________, our evangelist, to designate $_________ or ________% of his honorarium as parsonage, a motion was made by __________, seconded by __________ and passed to adopt the following resolution:

Resolved that of the total cash honorarium paid to our evangelist, we hereby designate $_________ or _______% as parsonage allowance.

Name of Church ____

Signature ____

Title ____

Date ____

Computation of Parsonage Allowance -"Worksheet For Form 2106"

- ***Column A***

Enter the value of a home and utilities provided by the employer in this column. It is subject to social security tax. Though it seems to be contradictory, we do not have to use the same formula we used earlier in the chapter for computing the "top limit" for the minister who owns his own home. The fair rental value of the parsonage provided should be reasonable, but has historically been allowed to be a conservative amount in audits. **Do not be guilty of understating your rental value** below a reasonable amount and thereby understating your social security liability.

A conservative, but realistic rental value estimate of a $115,000 home including utilities, considering all the facts and circumstances stated above, might be **$10,000 to $12,000** a year.

You may wish to consult a local realtor for an appraisal, or make inquiries of local landlords. **The condition, location, local market demand, and local economic conditions will help you to determine a reasonable value.** The fact that you must live in a particular home as a part of your employment, gives reason for a more conservative estimate of the value of a parsonage provided.

We would like to refer you to the guidelines in Sec. 119 for qualified campus lodging. (See discussion in Chapter One, Lay Employees - Sec. 119.) The guidelines for Sec. 119 are not necessarily applicable to Sec. 107, but they do represent guidelines for housing in another setting. A "bare minimum" rental value should be at least 5% x the appraised value of the home provided. Example: 5% x $115,000 = $5,750 annual FRV of home including utilities. The guidelines for Sec. 119 further require that the appraised value be determined at the end of each year by an independent appraiser, not the employer. However, it is intended that the appraisal be reviewed annually without undue cost to the employer.

- ***Column B***

Enter amounts for all parsonage allowance expenses the minister pays or provides for himself on a cash basis in this column. The actual expenses of the home, furniture, utilities, decorating, and miscellaneous expenses, are to be shown in Column B. Enter their total on line 11 of the worksheet.

In a year of incurring major expenses, show the computation of fair rental value of furnished home, utilities, etc., on line 12. Examine the sample computation we have shown on Rev. Snodgrass's return in Chapter Seven. Enter the lesser of line 11 or line 12 on line 13.

Show the amount that has been officially designated as parsonage allowance by the employer on line 14. If line 14 is greater than line 13, enter the "excess parsonage allowance" on line 15 and as income on Form 1040, line 21.

Parsonage allowance, as an exclusion, **is not to be included on Form W-2, Box 1 according to Publication 15-A, page 8.** When the parsonage allowance is included in error on Form W-2, Box 1, we recommend that a corrected Form W-2c be prepared. When it becomes necessary to deduct a large negative parsonage allowance amount on Form 1040, line 21, exposure to an IRS audit is greatly increased. Though not required, we recommend using Form W-2, Box 14, to show a memo of the amount designated as parsonage allowance.

Computation of Social Security -"Worksheet For Form 2106"

Parsonage allowance is free from income tax, but subject to social security and medicare tax. Enter Column A, line 11 and/or Column B, line 14 amounts on the lines provided. A minister who has elected to be exempt from social security and has an approved Form 4361 does not have to compute this value for Schedule SE.

A minister who qualifies for earned income credit must include the value of a parsonage provided and/or a parsonage allowance on Schedule EIC.

CHAPTER THREE

Professional Expenses

In any profession, the ordinary and necessary expenses incurred in order to be able to earn income are deductible according to Sec. 162. In this Chapter we will explain how to have an accountable reimbursement plan. The IRS provides very detailed regulations on how to handle reimbursed employee business expenses. It is good stewardship to take the time to learn the rules and legally reduce income tax by adopting a written accountable plan for professional expenses.

- ***Contributions ARE NOT allowable as Professional Expenses***

Contributions, tithes, or offerings paid to a not-for-profit organization are **always Schedule A itemized deductions**. Some tax advisors suggest that you reduce your salary by the amount you would tithe and thereby save tax if you are unable to itemize. According to Sec. 61, the assignment of income rule, "Income received for personal services is taxable to the person who earns it, even though he assigns it to another."

Other tax avoidance suggestions include renaming tithes as "dues" and treating them as a professional expense. The MSSP for Ministers, an IRS training manual, contains this comment, *"Ministers often pay a small annual renewal fee to maintain their credentials, which constitutes a deductible expense. However, ministers' contributions to the church are not deductible as business expenses."* Even if a contract or other arrangement states that excessive dues must be paid by the employee to retain their position, facts and circumstances will determine whether it is taxable compensation.

The business expense code Sec. 162(b) specifically states that contributions are Schedule A deductions:

> *"No deductions shall be allowed under subsection 162(a) for any contribution or gift which would be allowable as a deduction under section 170 (Schedule A) were it not for the percentage limitations, the dollar limitations or the requirements as to the time of payment, set forth in such section."*

- ***Babysitting expense not allowable as Professional Expenses***

The cost of babysitting for your children is never a business expense. Child care incurred while both parents are working results in a potential credit to be computed on Form 2441.

- ***Difference Between Parsonage Expense and Professional Expense***

It is important to separate in our thinking the parsonage expense from professional expense since their tax treatment is so different. **Parsonage expense** details, receipts, and records **are not to be submitted to the employer.** The personal home expenses can remain confidential. If the designated amount is greater than the amount substantiated, it is the responsibility of the individual minister to show the "excess parsonage allowance" as income on Form 1040, line 21.

For the best tax advantage, professional expenses must be adequately accounted to the employer and be reimbursed. An IRS regulation requires a written reimbursement plan between an employer and an employee. Professional expense details, receipts and records **must be submitted** to the employer for reimbursement.

- ***Professional Expense Rules are not Unique to Ministers***

The professional expenses discussed in this chapter are available to all religious workers – both the dual-status minister and lay employee. All of the information in this chapter about auto, travel, and professional expenses is also applicable to for-profit employers and their employees. Independent contractors or evangelists can adequately account their expenses to a payor.

- ***Volunteer Workers***

When a religious worker receives no income as a volunteer for a qualified organization, but incurs out-of-pocket expenses, they are deductible as contributions on Schedule A. Any miles driven for charitable work are deductible at the rate of 14¢ per mile or actual cost of gas and oil. Do not deduct the miles driven for personal worship to regular church services. Do not deduct any value for your time given, it is not allowable. Travel away from home expenses are limited to actual cost of lodging and meals.

Volunteer workers who are reimbursed for travel and ministry expenses must adequately account to the organization making the reimbursement. According to IRS Publication 526, charitable travel expenses are not business related. Reimbursement must be the actual travel expenses incurred and 14¢ a mile for auto mileage or the actual gas and oil expense. If a volunteer does not submit diaries and receipts to the organization, the organization will be required to treat the payments as compensation, prepare Form W-2, and withhold taxes.

Recordkeeping a Must!!

We recommend a careful reading of **IRS Publication 463**, "Travel, Entertainment, Gift and Car Expenses." Recordkeeping rules have always existed, adequate records or sufficient evidence must be available to support deductions for auto and professional expenses. A record of the elements of an expense made at or near the time of the expense, supported by sufficient documentary evidence, has more value than a statement prepared later when generally there is a lack of accurate recall. A log maintained on a **weekly basis** is considered a record made at or near the time of the expense. If you charge business expense items on your employer's credit card or charge account, you must make a record of the details for the amounts you spend. It cannot be stressed enough – **adequate records and receipts must be kept to substantiate all expenses.** Good stewardship means keeping good records!

IRS regulations require that careful and adequate records be kept for submitting to the employer for reimbursement. "Adequate accounting" means you will give your employer the same type of records and supporting information that you would be required to show to the IRS if they questioned a deduction on your return. There is **no relief** from keeping adequate records!

We have available a **"Professional Tax Record Book"** for ministers, religious workers, and professional individuals. It is designed to provide a convenient and efficient way to keep the auto, travel, and professional expense record details required by the IRS. Monthly summary pages are provided. You can easily photocopy the pages and receipts and submit them to your employer for reimbursement. For those who only need to keep records for auto business miles and auto expenses, we have available an **"Auto Log."** Information for ordering these books is given in the back of this publication.

Unreimbursed Professional Expenses

There is no dispute that in order to adopt a written accountable reimbursement plan both the employer and the employee must learn the rules. Therefore, the following results of not establishing such a plan will hopefully provide the motivation to do so and save tax dollars legally. **It is good stewardship to** reduce income tax by **adopting a written accountable plan** for professional expenses!

Unreimbursed professional expenses, other than auto and travel, carry the extra burden of being "required by your employer" and as "a condition of your employment". Establishing an accountable plan and becoming reimbursed for them by your employer is a good way to show they meet these requirements.

If an employer chooses to provide an expense allowance arrangement that **does not meet** the accountable plan requirements the employer **must report all amounts paid** under the non-accountable plan **as wages** on the employee's Form W-2, Box 1, even though an employee might voluntarily substantiate expenses to the employer and return any excess amounts to the employer. Such allowances paid to lay employees are subject to withholding of income tax and social security withholding and matching. The dual-status minister will incur the additional income tax for estimated tax purposes.

Tax Savings Illustrated: Our sample return for Rev. Snodgrass in Chapter Seven is computed "without reimbursement" and "with accountable reimbursement." The difference in tax liability illustrates the value of establishing an accountable reimbursement plan.

If You Do Not Adequately Account To Your Employer

Reg. 1.274-5(e)(3) says, **"Reporting of expenses for which the employee is not required to make an adequate accounting to his employer. If the employee is not required to make an adequate accounting to his employer for his business expenses or,**

though required, fails to make an adequate accounting for such expenses, he must submit, as a part of his tax return, a statement showing. . ."

all amounts received as advances or reimbursements from his employer. He must complete Form 2106 based on his records and supporting evidence. His employer must show amounts not adequately accounted for on Form W-2, Box 1. **The following consequences will happen:**

1. The expenses become "below the line" deductions on Form 2106 and Schedule A. Meals and entertainment are first reduced by 50%, then combined with other miscellaneous expenses, and further reduced by 2% of the employee's Adjusted Gross Income. With higher standard deductions, many taxpayers do not have enough deductions to itemize. **UNLESS** – they adopt a written reimbursement plan and adequately account to their employer and become reimbursed for all their professional expenses they may lose the income tax deduction entirely. The standard deduction for 1999 is $7,200 for a joint return and $4,300 for a single return. Reimbursed auto, travel, and professional expenses are not reduced by 2% of AGI. Employees can be 100% reimbursed for meals. Employers deduct only 50% of reimbursed meals & entertainment as a business expense. Not-for-profit employers are not affected since they have no tax liability.
2. A large amount of unreimbursed professional expenses deducted on Schedule A causes many employees to be audited. It is a high "dif" score area of a tax return. Establishing an accountable reimbursement plan with your employer could prevent the time consuming trauma of proving your expenses to an IRS auditor.
3. Many states do not allow itemized deductions. Therefore, unreimbursed professional expenses cause additional state income tax.
4. Items such as earned income credit, deductible IRA's, percentage of medical deduction limitation, percentage of child care credit allowable, educational credits, taxable social security benefits, etc., are all affected by the amount of the Adjusted Gross Income figure. Establishing a written accountable reimbursement plan with your employer may qualify you for other deductions and credits. **Parents of college students may qualify for more financial aid.**
5. For lay employees the social security base for both the employer and the employee is greater when there are unreimbursed professional expenses. Establishing an accountable reimbursement plan with your employer will allow the employer to compute social security withholding and matching on just the salary. Dual-status ministers have always been able to reduce their social security base by unreimbursed business expenses.
6. When a dual-status minister's income is a combination of taxable salary and Sec. 107 non-taxable parsonage allowance only the percentage of **unreimbursed** professional expenses that were spent in earning the taxable salary are allowable. The percentage of expenses spent in earning the non-taxable housing are not allowed. Read the following explanation.

Sec. 265 - Proration of Unreimbursed Expenses

If you establish a written accountable expense reimbursement plan and are adequately accounting to your employer for your auto, travel, and professional expenses, **the following facts WILL NOT affect you.**

A 1988 court case, Melvin H. Dalan & Lillian J. Dalan, Docket No. 8278-87, T.C. Memo 1988-106, filed March 9, 1988, resurrected an old IRS application of Sec. 265. Unreimbursed ministerial trade or business expenses are not deductible to the extent they are spent to earn non-taxable housing.

Example: A minister receives $20,000, including $8,000 housing allowance. His unreimbursed professional expenses amount to $4,000. ($8,000 divided by $20,000 = 40% X $4,000 = $1,600) $1,600 is the amount of the unreimbursed expenses spent to earn the non-taxable housing that he would not be able to deduct. The proration of unreimbursed expenses is to be computed on Schedule A for the employed minister and on Schedule C for the self-employed evangelist.

History of the issue goes back to the David E. Deason case, Docket No. 3993-62, January 10, 1964. During the 60's and early 70's we prorated and did not deduct a minister's expenses spent to earn his non-taxable housing allowance. In 1977, the Internal Revenue Manual – Audit, 45(11)3 said that the interpretation of the Service was that Sec. 265 should not be applied to a minister's unreimbursed employee business expenses. The promise of a revenue ruling in the 1977 Memo never happened. Instead, the memo seems to have vanished. Therefore several decisions, such as the Dalan case, are being made in certain regions of the country that are contrary to the IRS's 1977 position. A 1992 court case, Robert H. McFarland and Georgia W. McFarland, Docket No. 28246-90, T.C. Memo 1992-440, filed August 4, 1992, upholds Deason and Dalan cases. The IRS drafted a Revenue Ruling on this allocation issue in December 1990. It stated the IRS position to be parallel to the three court cases. It was never finalized, the IRS chose to state their position in IRS Publication 517.

● ***The Official Position of the IRS***

The official position of the IRS since 1988 has been to follow the Deason and Dalan Court Cases. **IRS Publication 517**, page 8, contains the published position of the IRS: unreimbursed ministerial trade or business expenses are not deductible to the extent they are spent to earn non-taxable housing. If you receive a tax-free rental or parsonage allowance and have ministerial expenses, you must attach a statement to your tax return showing how you computed the percentage of unreimbursed expenses that are not allowed. In Publication 517, pages 10 through 19, a comprehensive example of a completed minister's tax return illustrates the allocation computation.

Our sample return for Rev. Snodgrass, "Without Reimbursement," in Chapter Seven shows the computation for prorating unreimbursed expenses and the worksheet we use.

Reimbursed Professional Expenses

An employee may deduct from gross income, to arrive at adjusted gross income, only those expenses paid or incurred by him in connection with his employment that are reimbursed under a reimbursement or other expense arrangement with his employer.

To be an accountable reimbursement plan, the plan must meet the following three requirements: **(1)** business connection, **(2)** adequate accounting, and **(3)** return of any excess reimbursement. Each requirement is fully discussed in this chapter.

Reg. 1.62-2(d)(1) requires evidence of an obligation by the employee to make an adequate accounting to the employer for the employee's business expense. **Therefore a written reimbursement plan is required.** The regulation also requires that the payment for an "adequately accounted reimbursement" be identified either by making a separate payment or by specifically indicating the separate amount if both wages and the reimbursement are combined in a single payment. If you pay salary, housing, and professional expense reimbursement to your employees with one check, identify the different amounts on their checks and in your accounting. **We recommend separate checks** to be written for reimbursement of employee business expenses.

We recommend that an employee submit his substantiation of employee business expenses for reimbursement no less often than **monthly**. If an employee has a cash flow problem and needs to be reimbursed more often, allow him to submit his records on a **weekly** basis.

CAUTION: When an employer and employee have established an accountable reimbursement plan, it is important to be careful to submit all allowable expenses. An employee cannot deduct expenses on his tax return that he failed to submit to the employer for reimbursement. (Drury v. Commissioner, T.C. Memo 1977-199)

CAUTION: Showing reimbursements for non-business meals, overseas travel that does not qualify as business, and personal family members travel expenses as **income** on the employee's Form W-2 is an acceptable practice.

Tax Law & Regulations

Sec. 62(a)(2)(A) says, "**General Rule.—....the term 'adjusted gross income' means, in the case of an individual, gross income minus the following deductions:....**
(A) Reimbursed expenses of employees.—The deductions allowed by part VI (section 161 and following) which consist of expenses paid or incurred by the taxpayer, in connection with the performance by him of services as an employee, under a reimbursement or other expense allowance arrangement with his employer...."

Sec. 62(c) says, "**Certain Arrangements Not Treated as Reimbursement Arrangements:—For purposes of subsection (a)(2)(A), an arrangement shall in no event be treated as a reimbursement or other expense allowance arrangement if:**
(1) such arrangement does not require the employee to substantiate the expenses covered by the arrangement to the person providing the reimbursement, or

(2) such arrangement provides the employee the right to retain any amount in excess of the substantiated expenses covered under the arrangement. The substantiation requirements of the preceding sentence shall not apply to any expense to the extent that substantiation is not required under section 274(d) for such expense by reason of the regulations prescribed under the 2nd sentence thereof."

Regulation 1.62-2(d)(3) says: **"Reimbursement requirement— (i) In general. If a payor arranges to pay an amount to an employee regardless of whether the employee incurs (or is reasonably expected to incur) business expenses of a type described in paragraph (d)(1) or (d)(2) of this section, the arrangement does not satisfy this paragraph (d) and all amounts paid under the arrangement are treated as paid under a nonaccountable plan."**

Business Connection

This requirement means that no part of an employee's salary may be **recharacterized** as being paid under a reimbursement arrangement or other expense allowance arrangement.

The Past: Employees of not-for-profit organizations have historically had to absorb the "cost of doing ministry business." Especially small to medium size congregations have said, "Pastor we understand you will incur auto and professional expenses and we will include enough in your salary to cover them. Just do not bother us with the details." Under the temporary regulations it was permissible for the employee to adequately account to the employer for expenses incurred, and subtract that amount from the gross salary and report the remaining portion as taxable salary. It was not necessary to change the cash flow. **This was recharacterization.**

The Present (Since January 1, 1991): Regulation 1.62-2(d)(3)'s narrow definition of "business connection" was not included in the temporary regulations in effect before 1-1-91. To establish an accountable plan under this new definition means that there will be a change in the "cash flow." Salary and reimbursements must be two separate budget items. The reimbursement for auto and professional expenses will be in addition to the salary. The tax benefits and reduced audit exposure gained by having an accountable reimbursement plan should convince employers and their employees to carefully meet the requirements of an accountable plan. There are two choices for the employer: (Sample policy wording is provided later in this chapter.)

1. If the employer is willing to bear the burden of the "cost of doing ministry business" they can adopt a policy to fully reimburse the employee for all adequately accounted business expenses incurred.
2. If the employer feels that they can not assume the unknown amount of the "cost of doing ministry business" they can adopt a policy to reimburse the employee for adequately accounted business expenses up to a fixed limit.

We want to teach you how to start a reimbursement policy when no policy exists or only partial reimbursement has been available. It is important to understand that it can be accomplished without any additional cost to the employer. From the employee's past business expense records determine what the average annual amount he has been incurring. From the salary or compensation being paid subtract this **conservative** expense average. The adjusted salary and the money available for the reimbursement of accounted professional expenses will become two completely separate budget amounts for the year.

Employers who initially adjust the employee's salary and adopt an "unlimited" policy will simply reimburse the employee each year for the actual expenses adequately accounted.

Employers who initially adjust the employee's salary and adopt a "fixed limit", according to two Private Letter Rulings (9822044 and 199916011), can prior to the start of a calendar year determine the amount the "fixed limit" will be in the succeeding year. Computing the "fixed limit" annually is a welcome relief. In past editions of this book, we asked you to visualize your hands fully extended and that your right hand represented the "salary" and your left hand represented the "accountable reimbursement plan." We further stated that the two budget categories could independently be given increases, but that they were to always remain separate budget items. **Put your hands down!** It is acceptable to readjust the "fixed limit" amount and the salary amount for the following calendar year. So whether an increase in the accountable reimbursement plan be funded by a salary adjustment or a salary increase from the employer, what is important is that it is set apart and the employee will not receive any unused portion and that it is not carried over to another year.

When a "fixed limit" policy is adopted this is what happens:

1. If the employee's expenses end up being greater than the fixed limit amount, he can deduct what was not able to be reimbursed as "below the line" Schedule A itemized deductions subject to limitations.
2. If the employee's expenses are less than the fixed limit amount, the difference between the expenses and the fixed limit will not be received by the employee and will not be carried over from one calendar year to the next. This **"use it or lose it"** nature of an accountable reimbursement plan is similar to the tax treatment that applies to self-insured medical reimbursement and cafeteria fringe benefit plans. For this reason we recommend that an accountable reimbursement plan be carefully planned and not overstated.

- ***Examples***

Example (1). Community Church pays its pastor $500 per week or $26,000 annually. $10,400 has been designated as parsonage allowance. At the end of the month he adequately accounts his employee business expenses of $265 for the month. Community Church designates $265 of the $500 as paid to reimburse the pastor's employee business expenses. Because Community Church would pay the pastor $500 a week regardless of whether the pastor incurred employee business expenses, the arrangement **does not satisfy** the reimbursement requirement of Reg. 1.62-2(d)(3)(i). Community Church must report ($26,000 - $10,400) $15,600 as wages on Form W-2. (This plan would have been an accountable plan for years ending before 1-1-1991.)

Example (2). Community Church pays its pastor $500 per week or $26,000 annually. Community Church initially adjusts its pastor's salary to $23,000, designates parsonage allowance of $10,400 and adopts a fixed limit reimbursement plan of $3,000. Each month the pastor received an expense reimbursement check for the amount of employee business expenses he adequately accounted to his employer. At the end of the year, Community Church had paid their pastor expense reimbursements of only $2,400. They decided that they would give him a bonus of $600. The entire $3,000 must be included on Form W-2. Community Church must report ($26,000 - $10,400) $15,600 as wages on Form W-2. The plan **does not satisfy** the reimbursement requirement of Reg. 1.62-2(d)(3)(i)

Example (3). Community Church pays its pastor $500 per week or $26,000 annually. Community Church initially adjusts its pastor's salary to $23,000, designates parsonage allowance of $10,400 and adopts a fixed limit reimbursement plan of $3,000. Each month the pastor received an expense reimbursement check for the amount of employee business expenses he adequately accounted to his employer. At the end of the year, Community Church had paid their pastor expense reimbursements of $2,400. Community Church correctly included ($23,000 - $10,400) $12,600 on Form W-2 for their pastor. Their reimbursement plan **does satisfy** all the conditions of an "accountable plan."

Example (4). Community Church pays its pastor $500 per week or $26,000 annually. Community Church initially adjusts its pastor's salary to $23,000, designates parsonage allowance of $10,400 and adopts an unlimited reimbursement plan for employee business expenses. Each month the pastor received an expense reimbursement check for the amount of employee business expenses he adequately accounted to his employer. At the end of the year, Community Church had paid their pastor expense reimbursements of $3,600. Community Church correctly included ($23,000 - $10,400) $12,600 on Form W-2 for their pastor. Their reimbursement plan **does satisfy** all the conditions of an "accountable plan."

Adequate Accounting

- ***Definition Of Adequate Accounting***

Reg. 1.274-5A(e)(4) says, **"Definition of an 'adequate accounting' to the employer.... means the submission to the employer of an account book, diary, statement of expense, or similar record maintained by the employee in which the information as to each element of an expenditure is recorded at or near the time of the expenditure, together with supporting documentary evidence, in a manner which conforms to all the 'adequate records' requirements of paragraph (c)(2) of this section."**

Regulations further instruct us that a responsible person other than the employee must verify and approve the records and amounts of expense. Such a person should be careful not to allow personal expenses to be submitted. Employers are to maintain or keep records of reimbursed business expenses for at least three years after the due date of the employee's tax return. Even though it is not required, we would recommend that the records and receipts be photocopied and that both the employee and the employer keep the records. Our **"Professional Tax Record Book"** contains monthly summary pages, is easily photocopied, and has been designed to make it easy to adequately account to your employer. **The instructions for each section of the record book outline the requirements of Sec. 274 and the necessary details to record for each category of expense.**

The details of time, place, destination, business purpose, business discussion, etc., are very important details to record at or near the time of the business expense or trip. Each type of business expense and Sec. 274 requirements that apply to it are discussed in more detail later in this chapter. A record of the elements of an expense made at or near the time of the expense, supported by sufficient documentary evidence, has more value than a statement prepared later when generally there is a lack of accurate recall. A log maintained on a **weekly basis** is considered a record made at or near the time of the expense. If you charge business expense items on your employer's credit card you must make a record of the required details for the amounts you spend.

You must have **actual receipts** for **lodging** and any other **professional expense of $75.00** or more. Ask for and get receipts and pay by check when possible. Both forms of proof will be strong substantiation. Canceled checks alone may not provide adequate record. You may maintain an **account book or diary** for any **expense under $75.00** according to IRS Notice 95-50.

It is **not sufficient** if an employee merely groups expenses into broad categories such as "travel" or reports individual expenses through the use of vague, nondescriptive terms such as "miscellaneous business expenses," according to Reg. 1.162-2(e)(3).

● *If You Do Adequately Account To Your Employer*

Reg. 1.274-5A(e)(2) says, **"Reporting of expenses for which the employee is required to make an adequate accounting to his employer—(i) Reimbursements equal to expenses. For purposes of computing tax liability, an employee need not report on his tax return business expenses for travel, transportation, entertainment, gifts, and similar purposes, paid or incurred by him solely for the benefit of his employer for which he is required to, and does make an adequate accounting to his employer and which are charged directly or indirectly to the employer or for which the employee is paid through advances, reimbursements, or otherwise, provided that the total amount of such advances, reimbursements and charges is equal to such expenses."**

If you do adequately account to your employer the following will occur:

1. You do not report on your tax return the reimbursement for professional business expenses when you establish an accountable reimbursement plan with your employer.
2. You do not have to keep records for possible IRS audit. You do not have to substantiate your expense account for the IRS auditor as you have already done so with your employer. The employer must retain the records and receipts submitted by you. If your return is audited, show the IRS auditor a copy of the written accountable reimbursement plan you established with your employer.
3. The employer does not include the reimbursements on the W-2, Box 1.

Other references to support the above discussion of reimbursement policies are Reg. 1.62-2 and Reg. 1.162-17.

If you are reimbursed more than your allowable expenses, you must return the excess reimbursement to your employer. If your employer has an "accountable plan" and you fail to either adequately account or return excess reimbursement, it will be deemed to be a "non-accountable" plan for you and your employer is required to report all of your reimbursements as salary on Form W-2. You will then be required to treat such non-accountable expenses as "below the line" deductions on Form 2106 and Schedule A, subject to the limitations.

● *Adequate Accounting Requirement Is Satisfied by Mileage Allowance & Per Diem*

Adequate accounting requirement is satisfied when the amount of reimbursement is based on the auto mileage allowance of **31¢** (**32½¢** from 1-1-99 to 3-31-99) per mile and the employee's log of business miles, date, place, and purpose. Likewise, when the amount of reimbursement for travel away from home is based on the per diem allowance of **$185 or $115** (see IRS list of eligible high cost cities later in the chapter) per day and the employee's record of number of days, place, and purpose of travel. Likewise, when the amount of reimbursement for meals away from home (incurred without cost of lodging) is based on the city by city M&IE rate from the IRS tables per day and the employee's record of number of days, place, and purpose. (Rev. Proc. 98-64)

Per diem rates are adjusted for inflation and cover a convenient calendar year time period now. Employee mileage allowances and per diem travel subsistence allowances that are not in excess of IRS-set maximums may relieve difficulty of substantiation and generate a deduction that is greater than actual travel expenses. You must use the same method of accounting for the whole year. We will give more detailed discussion under "travel" later in this chapter. Compare the options shown in our discussion of "travel," and use the method that allows the greater deduction.

On December 28, 1998, Rev. Proc. 98-63 announced the **31¢ mileage allowance rate** for **1999.** Historically, this is the first time ever for the mileage rate to be less than it was in the previous year. Then IRS Announcement 99-7 postponed the effective date until April 1, 1999 to give employers time to implement the new lower rate.

IRS has already announced in Rev. Proc. 99-38 that the mileage allowance rate for **2000** is **32½¢.** ☺

Since 1990, the mileage allowance rate is available for all business miles. With or without a reimbursement plan taxpayers are allowed **31¢** (**32½¢** from 1-1-99 to 3-31-99) per mile for all of their business miles.

● ***When Actual Auto Expenses Exceed The Cents Per Mile Computation***

If you are incurring more than **31¢** (**32½¢** from 1-1-99 to 3-31-99) per mile to operate your auto, it may be beneficial to submit your business percentage of actual expenses to your employer. Otherwise, any unreimbursed excess expense becomes a Schedule A deduction subject to the 2% of AGI limitation and the Sec. 265 limitation. **Annually** choose to become reimbursed for actual expenses **or** mileage allowance. Rev. Proc. 98-63, Sec. 8, describes a fixed and variable rate (FAVR) allowance that is acceptable to the IRS. However, we recommend the following procedure of computing actual:

1. Compute auto depreciation for year and divide by 12.
2. Total actual monthly expenses for gas, oil, repairs, etc., (omit auto payment).
3. Estimate what your annual percentage of business use will be or use the business percentage that you recorded for previous year.
4. Multiply business percentage by the total of depreciation and expenses for the month and submit to your employer for reimbursement.
5. At the end of the year: Divide business miles by total miles for the year to know what your ACTUAL business percentage is.
6. Multiply actual business percentage by the total of depreciation and expenses for the full year.
7. Submit the difference between the annual auto expense computed and what has been reimbursed during the other 11 months of the year to your employer for December's reimbursement.

Return of Amounts Exceeding Expenses

If you are advanced more than your allowable expenses, you must return the excess reimbursement to your employer within a reasonable time. Committee reports for Sec. 62(c)(2) state: In cases where an employee is reimbursed by the employer on **the basis of a per diem or auto mileage allowance up to the IRS-specified rates,** there is deemed to be **no excess retained** by the employee. An "above the line" deduction is allowed up to the IRS-specified rate. Any reimbursement to an employee in excess of the IRS-specified rates can be treated by the employer as "above the line" deductions when the employee submits proof of actual expenses that equal the amount of reimbursement.

An accountable plan must generally require the employee to return any amount paid under the arrangement over and above substantiated expenses within a reasonable period of time. Advances for expenses must be reasonably calculated to not exceed anticipated expenses and any excess must be returned to the employer within a reasonable period of time after receipt. Under the "fixed date method," the following are treated as having occurred within a reasonable period of time:

1. an advance made within 30 days of when an expense is paid or incurred,
2. an expense substantiated to the payor within 60 days after it is paid or incurred, or
3. an amount returned to the employer within 120 days after an expense is paid or incurred.

We recommend that not-for-profit employers **avoid adopting a plan that allows for payment of "advances."** If an "advance" is not paid to an employee this more complex bookkeeping procedure is automatically satisfied. Employers who have volunteer treasurers should chose the **simplicity** of periodically reimbursing their employees for actual expenses and/or IRS-specified rates as they are submitted.

Although the "reasonable time" periods do not specifically apply to plans without "advances," we do recommend that an employee account for his expenses within the guidelines. We also recommend that an employee submit his substantiation of employee business expenses for reimbursement no less often than **monthly**. If the employee has a cash flow problem and needs to be reimbursed more often, allow him to submit his records on a **weekly** basis.

Adopt One of the Following Reimbursement Plans

One of the following plans should be adopted for each employee. An employer does not have to have the same plan for all employees. An accountable reimbursement plan is very important to your employees' economic health! Reg. 1.62-2(d)(1) **requires evidence of an obligation** by the employee to make an adequate accounting to the employer for the employee's business expense.

If you and your employer have not adopted a written reimbursement plan, you must report your expenses as "unreimbursed" on Form 2106 and Schedule A. A plan is not able to be retroactive, it becomes effective for the future at the time it is adopted. Adopting a reimbursement plan on a calendar year basis causes less confusion than a fiscal year plan.

You may customize one of the following policies to clearly state the agreement between the employer and the employee. For example, if you wish to state that the amount of reimbursement will be at the IRS-specified mileage allowance and/or per-diem allowances for travel, add a sentence that clearly states that agreement.

Salary Plus Unlimited Reimbursement

The chairman informed the meeting that according to Sec. 62(a)(2)(A), an employee that adequately accounts to the employer the details of their professional expenses, is allowed a deduction from gross income. Sec. 62(c) further requires an employee to return any excess reimbursement or advance to the employer within a reasonable time. Reg. 1.62-2(d)(3) further requires that no part of our employee's salary be recharacterized as being paid under this reimbursement arrangement.

A motion was made by________, seconded by_________and passed to adopt the following resolution:

Resolved that in addition to the salary provided our employee, we will reimburse him/her for auto, travel and professional expenses considered ordinary and necessary for him/her to carry out his/her duties. ***(Add special modifications here.)***

It is further understood that a person other than the employee will examine the adequately accounted records and that the records will be kept for at least four years by the employer.

Salary Plus Fixed Limit Reimbursement

The chairman informed the meeting that according to Sec. 62(a)(2)(A), an employee that adequately accounts to the employer the details of their professional expenses, is allowed a deduction from gross income. Sec. 62(c) further requires an employee to return any excess reimbursement or advance to the employer within a reasonable time. Reg. 1.62-2(d)(3) further requires that no part of our employee's salary be recharacterized as being paid under this reimbursement arrangement.

A motion was made by________, seconded by_________and passed to adopt the following resolution:

Resolved that in addition to the salary provided our employee, we will reimburse him/her for auto, travel and professional expenses considered ordinary and necessary for him/her to carry out his/her duties up to a fixed limit of $_________. ***(Add special modifications here.)*** *If his/her actual expenses are less than this fixed limit, he/she cannot be given the difference as bonus or salary, nor can it be carried over to the next year. If his/her actual expenses are greater than this fixed limit, he/she will be required to deduct the extra expenses on Form 2106 and Schedule A.*

It is further understood that a person other than the employee will examine the adequately accounted records and that the records will be kept for at least four years by the employer.

Typical Professional Expenses for a Minister

Auto Expense

The cost of business travel is the largest employee business expense that a minister typically incurs. Therefore, it is very important to understand how to arrive at the "largest" deduction or reimbursement that is allowable. We encourage you to read **IRS Publication 463**, "Travel, Entertainment, Gift and Car Expenses."

- ***Effect of Employer Reimbursement Plans***

When you **lease an auto and you adequately account to your employer** for your business mileage, you do have the **choice** of being reimbursed at the mileage allowance rate. If the business percentage of the cost of your lease (reduced by inclusion factor discussed later), combined with other operating expenses, is greater than the mileage allowance rate, you will want to adequately account to your employer the business percentage of your actual expenses.

When you **own an auto and you adequately account to your employer** for your business mileage, you have the **choice** of being reimbursed at the mileage allowance rate or the business percentage of your actual expenses.

Log Your Business Miles

Dedicate one auto for business use when possible: Because of depreciation limits placed on less than 50% business use autos, it is advisable to concentrate business use to one auto at a time to keep the percentage of business use high. Because the sale or trade of your auto used for business is a reportable transaction, a separate mileage log for each auto used in business must be kept to prove the business percentage of each auto's basis. It is not easy to **keep a log of miles traveled** for business, **but you must.** When you experience the amount of tax savings generated by being able to fully deduct your business mileage expense, you will agree that keeping a business mileage log is very worthwhile.

Revenue Ruling 94-47 clarifies the circumstances under which daily trips between a residence and a work location will be deductible as business mileage. In general, daily trips incurred in going between your residence and a work location is **nondeductible commuting expense**. However, the following circumstances permit deductible business miles:

1. Daily trips between your residence and a temporary work location outside the metropolitan area where you live and normally work qualify as business miles. Daily trips between your residence and a temporary work location within that metropolitan area are not deductible as business miles unless (2) or (3) below applies.
2. If you have one or more regular work locations away from your residence, you may log as business miles the distance between your residence and a temporary work location in the same trade or business, regardless of the distance.
3. If your residence is your principal place of business according to Sec. 280A(c)(1)(A), you may log as business miles the distance between your residence and another work location in the same trade or business, regardless of whether the other location is regular or temporary and regardless of the distance.

Multiple trips between your residence and work location during the day are all non-deductible commuting miles. The distance between your residence and the **first business stop** of the day and/or between the **last business stop** of the day and your residence are non-deductible as commuting miles. Careful planning of your itinerary and daily entries in your mileage log may legally lessen your non-deductible commuting for some days according to Shea v Commissioner, T.C. Memo 1979-303.

How to Log Business Miles: One entry in your mileage log is sufficient to record a daily business trip consisting of several stops without interruption. One entry in your mileage log is sufficient to record a business trip consisting of several days away from home. De minimis personal use, such as a lunch stop between two business stops, is not an interruption in business use. Our **"Professional Tax Record Book"** or **"Auto Log"** have been designed to make it easy to record all the details necessary for your mileage log and actual auto expenses. Your mileage log should contain the following information:

1. Date
2. Odometer reading at beginning of trip
3. Odometer reading at end of trip

4. Business miles driven for the day
5. Place and purpose of the trip

Sale Or Trade Of Business Auto

It is very important that you keep a record of your auto's basis because, upon sale or trade, you must properly compute the gain or loss. The only way to accurately compute each auto's basis is to keep **separate** mileage records for each auto used.

Regardless of whether you have used optional mileage allowance or actual expense method, the sale or trade of an auto with business use results in a reportable transaction on Form 4797 or Form 8824. Form 8824, Like Kind Exchanges, is required to be attached to your tax return to report a trade transaction. **A trade** will affect the basis of the new auto, according to Sec. 1031. **A sale** will result in **a gain that is taxable** or **a loss that is deductible** on Form 4797. We have included an example of an auto trade and Form 8824 in Chapter Seven for Rev. Snodgrass.

Knowing the basis of your auto makes it possible to tax plan. If the potential value of your auto would cause a **gain upon sale**, generally it would be **best to trade autos.** If the potential value of your auto would cause a **loss upon sale**, generally it would be **best to sell the auto outright,** deduct the loss and buy the replacement auto outright. (IRS Publication 463, page 21)

● ***Depreciation Adjustment to Basis***

If the actual cost method and MACRS method of depreciation is chosen in the first year, you must use the MACRS depreciation for the life of the auto. Even if your employer reimburses you under an accountable plan at the optional rate, you still must use your choice of MACRS to determine your basis.

If the optional mileage allowance method to deduct the business use of your auto is chosen for the first year your auto is placed in service, an optional depreciation factor reduces the basis of your auto in determining the adjusted basis when you dispose of it. From 1994 through 1999, all business miles should be multiplied by **12¢** to determine the optional depreciation factor. (Rev. Proc. 98-63)

Exception: If the actual cost method is used to deduct the business use of your auto for **any year other than the first year**, you must use 5 year straight line as the depreciation method. You will combine the optional factor for years of mileage allowance method with the actual depreciation for years of actual expense method to determine your basis.

We have designed a **"Worksheet to Compute Auto Basis."** The backside of the worksheet contains the technical rules that we are detailing in this chapter. We advise you to enter your auto information on our worksheet each year, unstaple it each year and bring it forward to the current return. In a year of sale or trade you will have the necessary information to make the required basis calculations. Information for ordering this form is given in the back of this publication. We feel the best way to illustrate the basis computation on the worksheet is to include an auto trade situation in our sample problem for Rev. Snodgrass in Chapter Seven.

If you are sending your information to us for preparation of your return, please give us the type of information you see on the form and **copies of prior year tax returns** showing how your auto basis has been handled. Our **"Checklist"** in the back of the book allows for your auto information to be separated for each auto.

Auto Interest & Personal Property Tax

Auto interest and personal property tax are not available as an employee business expense. Do not become reimbursed for the business percentage of auto interest and personal property tax. Interest on an auto for an employee is considered "personal interest" and is not deductible on Schedule A. Personal property or excise tax is deductible on Schedule A by employees. Sales tax for the purchase of an auto used in business is to be added to the cost basis as a capital expense.

Self-employed business use or farm use have the advantage of being able to deduct the business percentage of interest and personal property tax on Schedule C or F. Based on Revenue Ruling 80-110, Sec. 1402(a) and Sec. 62(1), it is correct to **use the business percentage of auto interest and personal property tax as a subtraction from a minister's social security base**

The portion of tax preparation fee that is attributable to the reporting of ministry transactions can also be a subtraction from a minister's social security base according to Revenue Ruling 92-29.

Lease or Own

Although leasing an auto is subject to luxury limitations, it could be advantageous to lease rather than to own. Lease payments may generate more deduction since auto interest is considered to be nondeductible personal interest for the employee. **The question of whether to lease or own is a difficult question to answer.** Our advice is to shop and negotiate for the best deal that provides you with dependable and comfortable travel. Be sure to read the "fine print" conditions of the lease. There is usually a limit as to how many miles you can drive the leased auto before an extra charge per mile is assessed.

Spending additional dollars for transportation because it is tax deductible is not sensible. To spend an additional $500 and be in the 15% tax bracket would only reduce your tax by $75. The difference of $425 is a real cost out of your pocket.

Choose the Best Method of Deducting Auto Expenses

There are two methods of computing the deduction for the cost of operating your auto for business. It is important to keep records of your actual expenses so that you can compare optional with actual and use the method that results in the largest deduction. Due to the luxury auto limitations on depreciation and better gas economy, fewer taxpayers benefit from the actual expense computation.

Mileage Allowance Method

IRS allows you to be reimbursed or deduct **31¢** (**32½¢** from 1-1-99 to 3-31-99) a mile for all business miles driven in 1999. In addition, you may be reimbursed or deduct your actual tolls and parking fees. A daily log book of miles driven must be kept in order to use this method. **The mileage allowance is now available for leased autos, since 1-1-1998, according to Rev. Proc. 97-58.**

To use the mileage allowance rate for **unreimbursed** business use you must:

1. Own or lease the auto,
2. Not use the auto for hire, such as for a taxi,
3. Not operate a fleet of autos using two or more at the same time.
4. Not have claimed depreciation using any method other than the straight-line method.
5. Not have claimed the Sec. 179 deduction on the auto.
6. Not have claimed actual expenses during entire lease period of leased auto.

Actual Method

This is an itemized list of your actual auto expenses such as: gas, oil, lubrication, repairs, parts, tires, batteries, tune-ups, auto washes, insurance, auto club dues, licenses, parking fees, tolls, and auto depreciation or auto lease.

If the actual cost method and MACRS method of depreciation is chosen in the first year, you must use the MACRS depreciation for the life of the auto. Even if your employer reimburses you under an accountable plan at the optional rate, you still must use your choice of MACRS to determine your basis.

If the actual cost method is used to deduct the business use of your auto for **any year other than the first year**, you must use 5 year straight line as the depreciation method. You will combine the optional factor for years of mileage allowance method with the actual depreciation for years of actual expense method to determine your basis.

● ***Listed Property - Deductions Limited For Less Than 50% Business Use***

Tax Reform Act of 1984 began to limit depreciation deductions for autos, computers, cellular phones, etc. placed in service after June 18, 1984 that are not **predominantly used in business**. When less than 50% use of the property is business, Sec. 179 expensing is not available and the auto's basis must be recovered over five years using the straight-line method and the half-year convention.

Depreciation recapture is to be computed when an accelerated depreciation method is used in the year of purchase and business use drops below 50% in any future year during the 5 year life. Recapture means "pay back." If you used your auto more than 50% in your business in the year you placed it in service, but 50% or less for business in a later year, you must include in gross income the difference between depreciation and Sec. 179 expensing claimed and the amount of depreciation recomputed at the 5 year straight-line method. You must continue using 5 year straight-line even if business use rises back above 50%.

The recapture amount is shown as a memo on Form 4797. Employees enter the income on Form 1040, line 21 and dual-status ministers also include the income on Schedule SE.

● ***Deductions Limited For Luxury Automobiles***

Yes, if you purchased an auto in 1999 and it **cost $15,500** or more, **you drive a luxury auto!** Even though an automobile is used more than 50% for business purposes, the law placed further limits on the amounts of annual depreciation deductions that could be taken on automobiles. The amount of annual limits are based on 100% business use. If the business use is less than 100%, the maximum annual limits must be reduced to reflect the actual business use percentage. The depreciation limit amounts apply to regular depreciation and Sec. 179 expensing. The limits are indexed for inflation.

● ***Luxury Limits for autos purchased after 12-31-86 and before 1-1-2000*** —

Date Auto Placed in Service

		1-1-87 thru 12-31-88	1-1-89 thru 12-31-90	1-1-91 thru 12-31-91	1-1-92 thru 12-31-92	1-1-93 thru 12-31-93	1-1-94 thru 12-31-94	1-1-95 thru 12-31-96	1-1-97 thru 12-31-97	1-1-98 thru 12-31-98	1-1-99 thru 12-31-99
Number of years owned	1st Year	$2,560	$2,660	$2,660	$2,760	$2,860	$2,960	$3,060	$3,160	$3,160	$3,060
	2nd Year	$4,100	$4,200	$4,300	$4,400	$4,600	$4,700	$4,900	$5,000	$5,000	$5,000
	3rd Year	$2,450	$2,550	$2,550	$2,650	$2,750	$2,850	$2,950	$3,050	$2,950	$2,950
	4th - 6th	$1,475	$1,475	$1,575	$1,575	$1,675	$1,675	$1,775	$1,775	$1,775	$1,775

How To Compute Auto Depreciation

Methods and limits of depreciation apply to autos according to the date of purchase. Follow the same column of the table **applicable in the year of purchase** until you change autos.

● ***Autos Purchased After 12-31-86 and before 1-1-2000*** —

Under Modified Accelerated Cost Recovery System (MACRS) autos are 5-year Class property. The percentage method is based on 200% declining balance method. The alternative recovery method is 5 year straight-line. **Sec. 179 expensing** of up to $17,500 (1993 to 1996), $18,000 (1997), $18,500 (1998), **$19,000 (1999)** or $20,000 (2000) can very rarely be used within the luxury auto limits. If business use is 50% or less in year of purchase, then the auto's basis must be recovered over five years using the straight-line method and the half-year convention. The most depreciation allowed per year, regardless of your auto's basis, is the business percentage of the luxury auto limits shown above. MACRS allows depreciation deduction in the year of sale. The IRS tables below have computed the mid-year and mid-quarter factors for the year of purchase automatically.

Mid-year convention allows ½ of the annual percentage available in the year of purchase and in the year of sale.

Mid-quarter convention allows the mid-quarter computation percentage depending on which quarter the purchase or sale occurs. If more than **40% of the year's** depreciable assets are placed in service in the **final quarter**, then all non-realty assets for that year **must** be depreciated using "mid-quarter" convention instead of the normal mid-year convention.

Here are the percentages for both mid-year and mid-quarter for autos and other 5-year class equipment.

Depreciation Table - MACRS 5-year Class Property

		Mid-quarter			
Year	Mid-year	(1st)	(2nd)	(3rd)	(4th)
1	20.00%	35.00%	25.00%	15.00%	5.00%
2	32.00%	26.00%	30.00%	34.00%	38.00%
3	19.20%	15.60%	18.00%	20.40%	22.80%
4	11.52%	11.01%	11.37%	12.24%	13.68%
5	11.52%	11.01%	11.37%	11.30%	10.94%
6	5.76%	1.38%	4.26%	7.06%	9.58%

Leased Automobiles

The mileage allowance is now available for leased autos, **since 1-1-1998**, according to Rev. Proc. 97-58. If you drove a leased auto for business use and you were not reimbursed by your employer, before December 31, 1997, you had to use actual expenses for your deduction on Form 2106. You can now choose to deduct the greater of **31¢** (**32½¢** from 1-1-99 to 3-31-99) a mile or the business percentage of the actual cost of the lease, gas, oil, and any other expense you incur. You cannot deduct any part of a lease payment that is for commuting or other personal use of the auto. When you lease an auto for business use, the **luxury auto limitations** are applied by the computation of an **income inclusion factor**. **IRS Publication 463** contains special tables to compute the income inclusion factor. The inclusion amount is prorated for the number of days of the lease term included in the tax year. The amount computed would be shown on line 24b, Part II, of Form 2106. The net amount of vehicle rental expenses will be shown on line 24c. In determining the inclusion amount, different rules apply depending on when the auto is leased.

- ***Autos Leased After 12-31-86 And Before 1-1-2000*** —

For each taxable year that a taxpayer leases an auto with a FMV of more than the amounts listed below, you must include in gross income an inclusion amount. There is **no** additional inclusion amount if you have 50% or less business use for this period. Easy to use tables are in **IRS Publication 463**.

Year	FMV	Table
1987 to 1992	$12,800	Use Appendix B-6 for autos leased after 12-31-86.
1993	$14,300	Use Appendix B-6 for autos leased after 12-31-92.
1994	$14,600	Use Appendix B-5 for autos leased after 12-31-93.
1995	$15,500	Use Appendix B-4 for autos leased after 12-31-94.
1996	$15,500	Use Appendix B-3 for autos leased after 12-31-95.
1997	$15,800	Use Appendix B-2 for autos leased after 12-31-96.
1998	$15,800	Use Appendix B-1 for autos leased after 12-31-97
1999	$15,500	Use Rev. Proc. 99-14 Table 3 for autos leased after 12-31-98

Employer Provided Autos

The value of an employee's personal use of an employer provided vehicle must be included in his income minus any reimbursement he made to his employer. **Publication 535**, "Business Expenses," contains instructions for the employer providing this "working condition" fringe benefit. **Reg. 1.61-21(c),(d),(e), and (f)** is a thorough presentation of the "working condition" fringe benefit.

It is best for the employer providing the auto to pay for all costs or all costs except gasoline. Hybrid arrangements cause confusion and cause the employee to pay tax on a value he did not receive. Regulations only allow for a gasoline factor of 5½¢ a mile to be added if the employer pays for the gasoline or omitted if the employee pays for the gasoline.

In order for an employer to exclude from the employee's gross income the value of an employer-provided vehicle, the **employee must keep** a log of business miles and submit the log to the employer. If the employer does not receive such a log of business miles, the whole value of the vehicle is income to be reported on Form W-2. (Please do not let this happen.)

- ***General Valuation Rule*** —

Whenever an employer does not choose one of the special valuation rules by a timely notification to the employee, **the value of the fringe benefit must be determined** under the general valuation rule. Under the general valuation rule, FMV is the amount your employee would have to pay a third party to lease the vehicle in the geographic area where he uses the vehicle.

If you want to adopt one of the three Special Valuation Rules to calculate the value of personal use to report as income for your employee, you must adopt in writing what rule you have chosen by the first day you make the vehicle available to the employee.

Three special valuation rules are available

- ***The Vehicle Lease Rule***

The value of availability of an auto to the employee must first be determined. This value of availability is then reduced by the percentage of business use to determine the value of the employee's personal use of the auto to be treated as compensation.

ANNUAL LEASE VALUE TABLE / Vehicle Lease Rule

IRS Publication 535

Automobile Fair Market Value	Annual Lease Value	Automobile Fair Market Value	Annual Lease Value
$ 0 - 999	$ 600	$ 22,000 - 22,999	$ 6,100
1,000 - 1,999	850	23,000 - 23,999	6,350
2,000 - 2,999	1,100	24,000 - 24,999	6,600
3,000 - 3,999	1,350	25,000 - 25,999	6,850
4,000 - 4,999	1,600	26,000 - 27,999	7,250
5,000 - 5,999	1,850	28,000 - 29,999	7,750
6,000 - 6,999	2,100	30,000 - 31,999	8,250
7,000 - 7,999	2,350	32,000 - 33,999	8,750
8,000 - 8,999	2,600	34,000 - 35,999	9,250
9,000 - 9,999	2,850	36,000 - 37,999	9,750
10,000 - 10,999	3,100	38,000 - 39,999	10,250
11,000 - 11,999	3,350	40,000 - 41,999	10,750
12,000 - 12,999	3,600	42,000 - 43,999	11,250
13,000 - 13,999	3,850	44,000 - 45,999	11,750
14,000 - 14,999	4,100	46,000 - 47,999	12,250
15,000 - 15,999	4,350	48,000 - 49,999	12,750
16,000 - 16,999	4,600	50,000 - 51,999	13,250
17,000 - 17,999	4,850	52,000 - 53,999	13,750
18,000 - 18,999	5,100	54,000 - 55,999	14,250
19,000 - 19,999	5,350	56,000 - 57,999	14,750
20,000 - 20,999	5,600	58,000 - 59,999	15,250
21,000 - 21,999	5,850	over $59,999	Auto's FMV X 0.25 + $500

EXAMPLE: *An employer makes an auto available for all of 1999. Its fair market value is $16,000; its annual lease value from the table is $4,600. Employee uses the auto 20% for personal use. Thus, the employer must include in the employee's income 20% of $4,600 or* ***$920****. If fuel is provided by the employer and personal use of 20% was 4,000 miles, (4,000 X 5½¢) an additional* ***$220*** *must be included in income.*

1. Employer must request from the employee a statement as to the business mileage and the total mileage driven by the employee. Where the employee supplies such statement or record within a reasonable period of time, the employer must compute the personal use percentage and the amount of payroll taxes to withhold on the basis of such information.
2. Determine the FMV of the automobile on the first date the automobile is available to any employee for personal use. Use the Annual Lease Value Table to determine an annual value. When an automobile is provided for only part of a year, the value is determined by multiplying the annual lease value by a fraction (days automobile is available to the employee divided by 365).
3. The figures in the annual lease value table are applicable for a four-year period starting on the date on which the special rule is applied and ending on December 31st of the fourth full year following that date. After that period, the annual lease value for each calendar year is based on the fair market value of the auto on January 1st of the applicable year.
4. If an employer provides fuel; its fair market value or 5½¢ per mile must be an additional computation.

● ***The Vehicle Cents-per-Mile Rule***

Under this cents-per-mile rule, an employer values the benefit using the standard mileage rate multiplied by the total miles the employee drives the automobile for personal purposes. For 1999, this rate is **31¢** (**32½¢** from 1-1-99 to 3-31-99). All of the following conditions must be met:

1. Employer must request from the employee a statement as to the business mileage and the total mileage driven by the employee.
2. This rule cannot be used if the FMV of the auto, as of the first date the auto is made available to any employee for personal use, exceeds $15,500 (Rev. Proc. 99-14).
3. It must be reasonably expected that the auto will be regularly used in employer's business, or actually driven primarily by employees at least 10,000 (personal and business) miles during a calendar year.
4. The cents-per mile rule includes all costs of operating the auto. Neither the employer or the employee may adjust the rate for services not provided, such as repairs. The only

adjustment allowed is that if fuel is not provided by the employer, the cents-per mile value may be reduced by no more than 5½ cents.

- ***Commuting Rule***

Under this rule, the value of the commuting use of an automobile an employer provides is $1.50 per one-way commute ($3.00 for each round-trip) for each employee who commutes in the vehicle. An employer can use this special rule if all of the following requirements are met.

1. Employer owns or leases the automobile and provides it to one or more employees for use in his trade or business.
2. For bona fide noncompensatory business reasons, an employer requires the employee to commute in the automobile.
3. Employer establishes a written policy under which they do not allow employees to use the vehicle for personal purposes, other than for commuting or *de minimis* personal use (such as a stop for a personal errand on the way between a business delivery and the employee's home.)
4. The employee does not use the automobile for personal purposes, other than commuting and de minimus personal use.
5. If this vehicle is an automobile, the employee required to use it for commuting is not a control employee.

A **control employee** of a nongovernmental employer is any employee who (1) is a board-appointed, shareholder-appointed, confirmed, or elected officer of the employer whose compensation equals or exceeds $70,000, (2) is the director of the employer, (3) owns a one percent or greater equity, capital or profit interest in the employer, or (4) receives $145,000 or more in compensation. (IRS Publication 535)

- ***100% Business Use Rule (Very Unlikely)***

If an employer **prohibited all personal use** and commuting by the employee, no value would be taxable to the employee. Without personal use, no log of business miles would be required.
All of the following conditions must be met:

1. The vehicle is owned or leased by the employer and is provided to an employee for use in the employer's trade or business.
2. The vehicle is kept on the employer's premises.
3. Only de minimis stop on the way between a business delivery and the employer's place of business.
4. The vehicle is not being used for personal purposes.
5. No employee using the vehicle lives at the employer's place of business.
6. There must be evidence that the vehicle meets all these conditions.

Withholding of Tax: When an auto is either owned or leased by the employer for an employee's use, the personal value of the automobile's use is a taxable fringe benefit subject to withholding of income tax and social security for the lay employee. The dual-status minister will incur the additional income tax and social security tax for estimated tax purposes.

When an employee pays the employer for personal use, the amount to be included in income is reduced by what the employee pays. If the proper amount is computed (general valuation rule or one of the three special valuation rules timely chosen) and paid to the employer, nothing would need to be shown on the W-2, nor any taxes withheld for the lay employee.

Travel

Ordinary and necessary travel expenses incurred in order to be able to earn income include: train, airplane, boat, bus fares, auto rental, taxi, hotel, motel, rooming house, meals, gratuities, telephone, fax, travel insurance, baggage charges, cleaning, and laundry costs. Unreimbursed meals while away from home are subject to a 50% limitation.

To substantiate your travel expenses, you must record the following at or near the time of the travel: the amount spent, the date of the business trip, the place traveled to, and the business reason or purpose of the trip. You must have actual receipts for lodging and any other professional expense of $75.00 or more. You may maintain an **account book or diary** for any **expense under $75.00** according to IRS Notice 95-50.

"**Tax home**" is defined as a taxpayer's place of business or employment where he earns most of his income regardless of where the family residence is maintained. Travel **away from home**

overnight is necessary for the above expenses to be deductible. "Overnight" does not necessarily mean a 24-hour period but there must be enough time allowed for you to be released from activities for 6 hours of sleep, even if it is from noon to 6 p.m.

Temporary work location: A place where your work assignment is realistically expected to last (and does in fact last) one year or less. You can deduct transportation expenses to a temporary location outside your metropolitan area.

Second Job: If you regularly work at two or more places in one day, you can deduct your transportation expenses of getting from one workplace to another.

A minister may incur away-from-home expenses for the following: attendance at a church convention, speaking engagements, lectures, travel to perform a wedding or a funeral, travel for pulpit supply, evangelistic meetings, deputation for missionaries, travel to youth camps, etc.

Do not deduct or adequately account to your employer for **meal expenses when you are not away from home overnight.**

Most overseas travel will not qualify as deductible. The primary purpose of a trip has to be business and your employer has to send or require you to make the trip. Be sure the rules are satisfied before deducting or becoming reimbursed for overseas travel. No deduction is allowed for costs of travel claimed as a **form of education. For example, a trip to the Holy Land is not deductible.** Enrollment in a formal course of study in the Holy Land **may** qualify as an education expense.

If a trip is primarily for business and you extend your stay for a vacation or have other nonbusiness activities, you may deduct the travel expense to and from the business destination. You would not be able to deduct side-trip mileage or the extra cost of the meals and lodging for the personal time.

If a trip is primarily for business and you have weekend or off duty days, all of the meals and lodging will be deductible. Personal side-trip miles would not be deductible. Saturday lodging and meals is considered an allowable business day when required to obtain a cheaper air fare.

If a trip is primarily for vacation or personal reasons, the entire cost of the trip is a nondeductible personal expense. However, you can deduct any expenses while there that are directly related to your business.

Travel expenses for business reasons are only allowable for the person earning an income. Expenses for a non-salaried spouse and children to accompany you on a trip are personal and not allowable as business expenses. The single room rate can be used instead of ½ of double room rate. Except for bona fide entertainment the spouse's meals are not deductible.

Reconciliation Act of 1993 added Sec. 274(m)(3) and states: "No deduction shall be allowed under this chapter for travel expenses paid or incurred with respect to a spouse, dependent, or other individual accompanying the taxpayer (or an officer or employee of the taxpayer) on business travel, unless--

(A) the spouse, dependent, or other individual is an employee of the taxpayer,
(B) the travel of the spouse, dependent, or other individual is for a bona fide business purpose, and
(C) such expenses would otherwise be deductible by the spouse, dependent, or other individual."

However, if a non-salaried spouse was attending a convention as an official representative of a church or organization, the actual travel expenses (14¢ per mile) as a delegate can be adequately accounted for and reimbursed. If no reimbursement is received, such travel expenses as a delegate are allowable as a contribution deduction on Schedule A.

CAUTION: Showing reimbursements for non-business meals, overseas travel that does not qualify as business, and personal family members travel expenses as **income** on the employee's Form W-2 is an acceptable practice.

Lodging, Meal, And Incidental Expense Per Diem Rates

Periodically, the IRS publishes per diem rates that may be used by **employers who reimburse employees** for their traveling expenses. The IRS per diem rates are adjusted for inflation. These per diem rates include an individual's lodging, meals and incidental (M&IE) travel expenses. **Incidental expenses** covered by a per diem arrangement includes laundry, cleaning, and tips for services, but do not include cab fares, business calls, fax, or other communication costs.

The applicable per diem amount depends on the locality of travel. For travel within the continental United States (CONUS) and for foreign and non-foreign travel outside the continental

48 states (OCONUS), separate lodging and M&IE rates are published periodically in the Federal Register, U.S. Government Printing Office. **IRS Publication 1542** contains the CONUS tables.

How to prorate partial travel days: You can use either of the following methods to prorate the full-day rate for M&IE:

1. use ¾ of the M&IE rate for the day of departure and the day of arrival back home, or
2. use any method that you consistently apply and that is in accordance with reasonable business practice. For example, for travel away from home from 9 a.m. of one day to 5 p.m. of the next day can be treated as 2 full days of M&IE, even though federal employees are limited to 1½ days of M&IE.

Unreimbursed employees and self-employed individuals may only use the per diem rate established for meals and incidental expenses found in the IRS CONUS tables. The city by city rates for M&IE range from $30 a day to $46 a day. IRS Publication 463, Appendix A, page 38, list all of cities that are higher than $30. The entire M&IE rate is subject to the 50% limitation on meal expenses. Actual lodging expenses must be used. In addition, the high-low rate available to employers and discussed below may not be used by unreimbursed employees and self-employed individuals.

● ***Alternative Method for Employers —***

A **high-low per diem method** is available to simplify the administrative burden of sifting through some 10 pages of per diem rates in order to determine the correct rate for an employee's particular areas of travel. Under the high-low per diem method, the IRS publishes a list of localities that are classified as high-cost areas. All other localities within the continental United States are classified as low-cost areas. The IRS then establishes a per diem rate for the two types of localities. The 1999 per diem rates are **$185** for high-cost localities and **$115** for low-cost localities. The M&IE portion of the alternative method is **$42** for high-cost localities and **$34** for low-cost localities. The remaining **$143 or $81** is the lodging portion of the per diem allowance.

The high-low method may not be used to reimburse an employee for M&IE expenses only. The employer can use the M&IE rate from the IRS tables if the employer pays for lodging, provides lodging or the employee does not incur lodging. The city by city rates for M&IE range from $30 a day to $46 a day. IRS Publication 463, Appendix A, page 38, lists all of cities that are higher than $30.

The **same method of reimbursement** must be used for the whole year of travel within the continental United States. Annually compare the three options for computing your best travel reimbursement and use the greater of:

1. Individual location rates from the conus or oconus tables
2. High-low per diem alternative method (both lodging & M&IE)
3. Your actual cost of lodging and M&IE from the conus or oconus tables

Become reimbursed throughout the year according to the method you expect to be the greater, then at year end, calculate all three. If another method is greater, become reimbursed for the adjusting differential at the end of the year.

High-low Per Diem Rates

Effective Dates	*Lodging & Meals*	*Lodging Only*	*Meals & Incidentals*
1/1/99 - 12/31/99	$185 high/$115 low	$143 high/$81 low	$42 high/$34 low
1/1/98 - 12/31/98	$180 high/$113 low	$140 high/$81 low	$40 high/$32 low
1/1/97 - 12/31/97	$166 high/$109 low	$126 high/$77 low	$40 high/$32 low
1/1/94 - 12/31/96	$152 high/$95 low	$116 high/$67 low	$36 high/$28 low
3/12/93 - 12/31/93	$150 high/$94 low	$114 high/$66 low	$36 high/$28 low
3/1/92 - 3/11/93	$147 high/$93 low	$113 high/$67 low	$34 high/$26 low
1/1/91 - 2/29/92	$130 high/$88 low	$ 96 high/$62 low	$34 high/$26 low
1/1/90 -12/31/90	$122 high/$85 low	$ 88 high/$59 low	$34 high/$26 low

The locations listed on the next page are eligible for the high cost rates. Some locations are high cost for only a portion of the year. Effective date for the list was January 1, 1999. (Rev. Proc. 98-64)

High Cost Localities *(Rev. Proc 98-64)*

Key City	Specified Dates	County or Other Defined Location
Alabama		
Gulf Shores	5/1 - 9/30	Baldwin
California		
Gualala		City limits of Gualala
Palo Alto		City limits of Palo Alto
San Francisco		San Francisco
Sunnyvale		City limits of Sunnyvale
Yosemite National Park	4/1 - 10/31	Mariposa
Colorado		
Aspen	6/1 - 3/31	Pitkin
Telluride	11/1 - 3/31	San Miguel
Vail		Eagle
District of Columbia		
Washington, D.C.		District of Columbia
Florida		
Delray Beach	11/1 - 3/31	City limits of Delray Beach
Jupiter	1/1 - 4/30	City limits of Jupiter
Key West	12/1 - 4/30	Monroe
Palm Beach	1/1 - 4/30	City limits of Palm Beach
Singer Island	1/1 - 4/30	City limits of Singer Island
Idaho		
Sun Valley	4/1 - 9/30	City limits of Sun Valley
Illinois		
Chicago		Cook
Lake County		Lake County
Maine		
Bar Harbor		Hancock
Maryland		
Baltimore		Baltimore
Montgomery County		Montgomery County
Ocean City	4/1 - 8/31	Worchester
Massachusetts		
Boston		City limits of Cambridge
Martha's Vineyard	6/1 - 9/30	Dukes
Michigan		
Charlevoix	7/1 -9/30	Charlevoix
Mackinac Island		Mackinac
Nevada		
Stateline		Douglas
New Jersey		
Cape May	6/1 - 9/30	Cape May (except Ocean City)
Ocean City	6/1 - 8/31	City limits of Ocean City
Piscataway		City limits of Piscataway
Union County		Union County
New York		
The Bronx		The Bronx
Brooklyn		Brooklyn
Manhattan		Manhattan
Queens Borough		Queens
Saratoga Springs	8/1 - 8/31	Saratoga
Tarrytown/White Plains		Westchester
West Point		Orange
North Carolina		
Kill Devil Hills	5/1 - 8/31	Dare
Pennsylvania		
Hershey	5/1 - 10/31	City limits of Hershey
Philadelphia		Philadelphia; city of Bala Cynwyd in Montgomery County
Rhode Island		
Newport	6/1 - 9/30	Newport
South Carolina		
Hilton Head	3/1 - 8/31	Beaufort
Myrtle Beach	6/1 - 9/30	Horry; Myrtle Beach A.F. Base
Utah		
Park City	12/1 - 3/31	Summit
Virginia		
Alexandria		City limits of Alexandria
Arlington		Arlington
Fairfax County		Fairfax County (includes the cities of Falls Church and Fairfax)
Wintergreen	6/1 -10/31	Nelson
Washington		
Seattle		King

Entertainment

Entertainment expenses and meals for entertainment that are not reimbursed will be subject to the 50% limitation, then combined with other unreimbursed professional expenses and further limited by 2% of AGI and Sec. 265 allocation limitation. An employee can be reimbursed for 100% of meal and entertainment expense. Employers will deduct only 50% of reimbursed meals and entertainment as a business expense. Not-for-profit employers will not be affected since they have no tax liability.

Restrictive tests for meals and entertainment require that the event was directly related to the active conduct of your job and directly preceding or following a substantial and bona fide business discussion on a subject associated with the active conduct of your business or ministry.

The record-keeping rules for entertainment, **Sec. 274**, are very strict. The entertainment diary section in our **"Professional Tax Record Book"** is designed to help you keep all of the necessary facts. **You must have the name of the persons entertained, their title or position, where the entertainment took place, what purpose or discussion took place and the amount.** Receipts are important if expense exceeds $75.00. When the entertainment is in the home and the occasion is over the $75 threshold, keep the receipt from the grocery store.

By adopting an accountable reimbursement plan, you will be submitting your expense records to your employer. **Due to the confidential nature of a minister's entertainment activity,** we suggest that the diary showing who was entertained and what business was transacted should be retained by the minister and a dollar amount be submitted to your employer for reimbursement. An IRS regulation allows this confidential treatment, Reg. 1.274-5T(c)(2)(ii)(C).

Most ministers are required to do substantial entertaining in their home. Since the cost of the home itself is non-taxable as parsonage allowance, the main expense of entertaining is the cost of meals provided. Special speakers, missionaries, board members, prospective faculty, etc., are entertained and a record of the number of meals provided in the home, multiplied by an average cost per meal, will result in a sizable deduction. A reasonable amount per meal, depending on your actual circumstances and service practices, might vary between $6.00 to $8.00 per meal. Those afternoon meetings with refreshments, or after evening service snacks for the youth group, etc., might vary between $1.50 to $2.00 per person.

If the meals are eaten outside the home, then the receipt for the actual cost of the meals is deductible. If you entertain business and non-business individuals at the same event, you must divide your entertainment expenses between business and non-business. For example, if you entertain a group of individuals that **includes yourself**, three business prospects, and seven social guests, 4/11 of the expenses qualifies for the deduction.

If your spouse is present during an occasion of entertainment because the spouse of the person being entertained is present, you may deduct the meal cost for both spouses. Meal expenses for your children are not business deductions.

Educational Expenses

Educational expenses incurred for the purpose of maintaining or improving present job or professional skills or meeting the expressed requirements of an employer to retain the job are deductible. The deduction will not be allowed if the education qualifies you for a new trade or business or satisfies the minimum requirements of your present job.

For education costs to be deductible as a business expense, you are unable to be absent from your profession for more than a year. A minister who has not been gainfully employed as a minister will not be able to deduct his seminary education. Most seminary degrees require three or more years. Seminary students who have the opportunity to serve as a "part-time" minister while obtaining additional education will be more likely to qualify for the education expense deduction. IRS considers you to have changed careers if you work a secular job while obtaining additional education for a period of more than 12 months.

Tuition, fees, books and supplies, any transportation to school away from your hometown, meals and lodging (if necessary to be away from home overnight to attend classes) are typical educational expenses. Unreimbursed meals are only 50% deductible.

No deduction is allowed for costs of travel claimed as a **form of education.** For example, a trip to the Holy Land is not deductible. Enrollment in a formal course of study in the Holy Land **may** qualify as an education expense.

● *Education Incentives for Taxpayer and Family*

Education tax-planning has become very important. Unreimbursed educational expenses deducted on Form 2106 are not eligible for either the HOPE or Lifetime Learning Credits. Calculate your tax liability both ways, claiming the deductions or claiming the educational credits.

Three new tax breaks began in 1998 with a goal of reducing the cost burden of education for you and your family. The three new tax breaks are HOPE Credits, Lifetime Learning Credits, and Education IRAs.

Credits. The HOPE Credit can pay up to $1,500 of the cost of the first two years of a college education. The Lifetime Learning Credit (LL) can pay up to $1,000 of education costs each year. Each student may only use one or the other in a particular year. HOPE pays the first $1,000 you spend, and 50% of the next $1,000. The annual maximum HOPE credit is $1,500 *per qualifying student in the household.* Lifetime Learning pays 20% of the first $5,000 each year to a maximum of $1,000. The LL credit is up to $1,000 *for the entire family.*

Type of Education. The HOPE credit covers the first two years of a post-secondary program leading to a degree or certificate. This includes attendance at a college, university, vocational school, or other post secondary educational institution. A student may use HOPE in only two different tax years, and can not use LL in the same year. LL can be used for any post-secondary classes (even to acquire or improve job skills). It may be used as often as you qualify. Whenever possible, use the two-year HOPE credit first, then switch to the LL credit.

Eligible Expenses. Qualified tuition and related expenses **paid to the institution** as a condition of enrollment or attendance. Related expenses that are eligible include course-related books, supplies and equipment, and student activity fees paid to the institution. Noneligible expenses include room and board, insurance, student health fees and transportation even if paid to the institution. Noneligible expenses also include books, supplies and equipment that are not purchased from the institution. Qualified tuition and related expenses must be reduced by tax-free funds received from scholarships, Pell grants, employer-provided educational assistance, and veterans' educational assistance.

Who is Eligible? You, your spouse, or any child claimed as your dependent. If the child is your dependent, the money is *considered* to be paid by you even it *is* paid by the child.

Phase Out. The credits phase out as your AGI ranges from $80,000 to $100,000 ($40,000 to $50,000 for single filers).

Qualifying Education. Under HOPE, a student must be enrolled at least half-time. The LL Credit has no half-time rule—even a single class qualifies. The starting date for HOPE was 1/1/98, and for LL it was 7/1/98.

Education IRAs. Since January 1, 1998, taxpayers may deposit up to $500 per year into an Education IRA for a child under age 18. It is *not deductible*. The money is *completely tax-free* when taken out if it is used to pay for the qualifying education of a student. Saving and investing $500 a year in a mutual fund could *compound and grow* to a significant amount if began at a young age.

If a student receives a tax-free withdrawal from an educational IRA in a particular tax year, none of that student's expenses can be used as the basis of a higher education credit for that tax year. However, the student can waive the tax-free treatment and pay any tax owed. The student or the student's parents may then be eligible to claim one of the credits.

Student Loan Interest. Since 1998, you may deduct up to $1,000 of interest on a student loan—even if you do not itemize. The deduction is allowed only for interest paid on a qualified education loan during the first 60 months in which interest payments are required. This deduction phases out as your AGI ranges from $60,000 to $75,000 ($40,000 to $55,000 for single filers.)

Library & Equipment Purchases

When the employer makes the decision to purchase equipment needed for ministry use, the items will be owned by the employer. When an employee makes the decision to purchase equipment needed for ministry use from his accountable reimbursement plan, the items will be owned by the employee. This concept is best understood when we think of the use of an automobile for business. If the employer makes the decision to purchase an auto for an employee's use, it is titled in the employer's name. The rules provided for "employer provided autos" are followed for proper tax treatment. If an employee makes the decision to purchase an auto it is titled in the employee's name. The rules for business use deductions or reimbursements are followed.

First we will discuss the kinds of capital purchases that are to be depreciated. Usually when a minister begins his career he already owns a sizable library. Books and equipment that were purchased during college and seminary training were generally not deductible at the time of purchase and were merely for personal use. When a minister begins receiving an income from their use, they become business property and are "placed in service." The **lesser of the cost or fair market value** of items that are converted from personal to business use should be inventoried and placed on the depreciation schedule. Sec. 179 expensing is not available for converted property.

Library, office furniture, typewriters, computers, printers, overhead projectors, VCR or film projectors, cameras, copiers or cellular phones are examples of items to be depreciated or expensed under Sec. 179. **Tax plan according to your tax liability;** choose to "spread out" or depreciate capital assets in years of no tax liability and choose Sec. 179 expensing during years with tax liability.

If you are fully reimbursed for the purchase of a capital item in the year of purchase, it will be the same as choosing Sec. 179 expensing. We recommend that a depreciation worksheet be completed to show each purchase and any election to expense capital assets.

To be reimbursed by your employer for library and equipment depreciation, compute what this year's depreciation will be for previous assets on your depreciation schedule, divide by 12 and use it as a monthly amount. Then in December, include an extra amount that is the depreciation for the current year's purchases.

Computers

Computers of today are so capable and useful that almost everyone has entered into the age of technology. Bible research CD's, web-site promotions, E-mail with missionaries, word processing for sermon preparation, congregation data bases, etc. are examples of current ministry business use of computers.

Congress has made dual-use (part business and part personal) of computers complex by placing them in a category called "listed property." Complex depreciation treatment can be avoided by dedicating a computer to 100% business use. Now that the cost of owning a computer is more reasonable, it is advisable to purchase one for business use and a second one for the family and personal use. The personal use computer in the parsonage can be deducted as a parsonage allowance purchase.

Employers should be willing to own and provide the business use computer for their employees. When the employer owns the computer and it is used exclusively for business use, no log of personal time needs be kept. The time spent learning how to manipulate the peripheral devices is to be counted as business use. (Keyboard exercises and Solitaire)

When employees purchase and own a computer and it is used for both business and personal, a log of time must be kept to know what the percentage of business use is. If less than 50% of computer use is business, you can not choose Sec. 179 expensing and depreciation is required to be at the rate of 5 years straight-line.

Unreimbursed employee business use of computers has to qualify as being a **mandatory requirement** of the employer and a **condition of employment** to be allowable as an itemized deduction. IRS audit history has not been friendly to the employee. In Cadwallader, T.C. Memo 1989-356 the court allowed the deduction for 100% use. In Muline, T.C. Memo 1996-320 a sales manager convinced the court to allow her a deduction with the help of her supervisor as a witness.

Equipment Purchased After 12-31-86 —

Under Modified Accelerated Cost Recovery System (MACRS) the depreciation percentages are based on 200% declining balance method. Items in the 5-year class are computers, typewriters, copiers, and duplicating equipment. Items in the 7-year class are library, office furniture and fixtures. **Sec. 179 expensing** allows you to "expense" up to $17,500 (1993 to 1996), $18,000 (1997), $18,500 (1998), **$19,000 (1999)** or $20,000 (2000) of the purchase price. The IRS tables below have computed the mid-year and mid-quarter factors for the year of purchase automatically.

Mid-year convention allows ½ of the annual percentage available in the year of purchase and in the year of sale.

Mid-quarter convention allows the mid-quarter computation percentage depending on which quarter the purchase or sale occurs. If more than **40% of the year's** depreciable assets are placed in service in the **final quarter**, then all non-realty assets for that year **must** be depreciated using "mid-quarter" convention instead of the normal mid-year convention.

In our discussion of auto depreciation earlier in this chapter we included the MACRS percentages for 5-year class property. Here are the MACRS percentages for both mid-year and mid-quarter for 7-year class property.

Depreciation Table - MACRS 7-year Class Property

		Mid-quarter			
Year	Mid-year	(1st)	(2nd)	(3rd)	(4th)
1	14.29%	25.00%	17.86%	10.71%	3.57%
2	24.49%	21.43%	23.47%	25.51%	27.55%
3	17.49%	15.31%	16.76%	18.22%	19.68%
4	12.49%	10.93%	11.97%	13.02%	14.06%
5	8.93%	8.75%	8.87%	9.30%	10.04%
6	8.92%	8.74%	8.87%	8.85%	8.73%
7	8.93%	8.75%	8.87%	8.86%	8.73%
8	4.46%	1.09%	3.33%	5.53%	7.64%

Office Expense and Supplies

Typical expenses an employee might have in their ministry are stationery, carbon paper, erasers, ink, stapler, paper clips, record books, secretarial or typing expenses, postage, copier supplies, computer supplies, etc. Any office equipment or machines that have a useful life of more than one year should be depreciated or Sec. 179 expensed. (See depreciation discussion)

If you are required to provide an office outside of your home, any cost to you would be a deductible expense. Rent, furniture, utilities, etc., would be allowable expenses.

Office-in-the-home deduction is not available if your employer provides an office on their premises. It is generally not available when you have 100% of your home expenses tax-free under Sec. 107 parsonage allowance.

To deduct a portion of your home as an office-in-the-home, it must be used regularly and exclusively as the principal place of business. Qualifying office-in-the-home use results in favorable absence of personal commuting miles for business use of the automobile.

Prior to 1999: The Supreme Court in *Soliman* said, "the amount of time spent in the home-office location must be compared to the time spent in each of the other places where business is conducted." Very few office-in-the-home situations passed the strict definition of "principal place of business" in *Soliman*.

Effective 1-1-1999, Congress, as a part of The Tax Relief Act of 1997, has provided the following amendment: a home office that is used regularly and exclusively qualifies if (1) the office is used by the taxpayer to conduct administrative or management activities of a trade or business and (2) there is no other fixed location of the trade or business where the taxpayer conducts substantial administrative or management activities of the trade or business.

In a year of no or inadequate parsonage allowance designation, and you have a qualifying office-in-the-home situation, deduct it. To compute the amount allowable, divide the square footage used as an office by the square footage in your entire home. Use this percentage of the allowable home expenses and depreciation.

Generally, it is best for you to have 100% of your home expenses be tax-free under Sec. 107 parsonage allowance. However, a qualified "office-in-the-home" deduction would reduce your social security base and if "adequately accounted" to your employer would not increase income tax.

Religious Materials

Many trips to the religious bookstore add up to much expense for most employees in the ministry. Tracts and booklets purchased for distribution in the calling ministry, music and musical supplies for the choir; gifts for presentation at marriages, baptisms, or holidays; teaching aids, including video and cassette programs, are but a few of the usual expenses a dual-status or lay employee incurs.

Clothing for the minister is usually not deductible. Tax law states that if something is required as a condition of employment and is not adaptable for general wear, it is deductible. Pulpit robes or special shirt collars and their cleaning expense would qualify as a deduction. Suits and shirts that are adaptable for general wear are not deductible for a salesman, businessman, or a minister.

Seminars And Dues

Fees charged to attend seminars or conference meetings and dues to professional organizations that are directly related to your profession are deductible.

Subscriptions, Paperbacks, Tapes And CDs

A number of periodicals and journals find their way into your mail box. The cost of the subscriptions that are directly related to your ministry is deductible. Magazines and local newspapers give the current events so necessary for sermon illustrations and provide news of the local community. Except for one subscription to a local newspaper (which IRS claims must be personal), deduct the subscriptions you use directly in your ministry.

Small booklets, paperback books, tapes and CDs should be separate from regular library books and the whole cost deducted in full in the year of purchase. **DO NOT deduct** magazine subscriptions, tapes, and books that are purchased for **personal reasons and interests.**

Business Telephone

Long distance business calls need to be separated from the personal portion used in the parsonage allowance computation because as a business expense they will reduce income tax as well as social security and medicare tax. The base rate portion of your home telephone cannot be used as a business expense. However, it is a utility that is a parsonage allowance expense.

The business portion of your cellular phone bill is a legitimate professional expense. (Personal part of your cellular phone should not be included in parsonage allowance, it is not a content of the home.)

Earned Income Credit

Earned income credit is available for the low-income taxpayer who maintains a household in the U.S. for more than one-half of the taxable year and has taxable and nontaxable earned income of less than **$10,200** without a qualifying child; **$26,928** with one qualifying child; **$30,580** if you have more than one qualifying child. It is a refundable credit and, if there is no tax liability, the government "gives" it to the taxpayer.

The amount of the credit was increased and became available for low income individuals without a qualifying child for the first time in 1994. The maximum basic credit for 1999 is **$347** without a qualifying child; **$2,312** with one qualifying child; **$3,816** with two or more qualifying children.

Earned income credit will be denied for taxpayers who have "disqualified income" of over $2,350 for the taxable year. "Disqualified income" consists of (a) interest (taxable and tax-exempt); (b) taxable dividends; (c) gross income from Schedule E less expenses; (d) capital gain net income; (e) net passive income that is not self-employment income. (Welfare Act, P.L. 104-193)

A modified definition of AGI is used for phasing out the earned income credit by disregarding certain losses.

● *Definition of Earned Income for Ministers*

Certain earned income is not taxable but it must be included to see if you can take the earned income credit. Contributions to voluntary salary reduction 401(k) or 403(b) retirement plans and salary reductions for cafeteria plans must be included. Revenue Ruling 79-78 defines "earned income" for the dual-status minister to include parsonage allowance and to include the income of a minister who elected to be exempt from social security if he is **an employee.** Use the following outline to guide you in determining if you are entitled to earned income credit.

1. Ministers who are subject to social security and medicare tax:
    a. An employee of an organization - Earned income includes wages, value of parsonage and/or parsonage allowance, 401(k) or 403(b) contributions and Schedule C net honorariums.
    b. An independent evangelist - Earned income includes Schedule C net honorariums, parsonage allowance and 403(b) contributions.
2. Ministers who have become exempt from social security and medicare tax:
    a. An employee of an organization - Earned income includes wages, value of parsonage and/or parsonage allowance, 401(k) or 403(b) contributions **but not Schedule C net honorariums**.
    b. An independent evangelist - Ministry earnings **do not** qualify for earned income credit.

Follow the "special rules" for clergy for the worksheet provided in your Form 1040 Instruction Booklet. Instructions ask you to determine how much of the income reported on Form 1040, line 7, was also reported on Schedule SE, line 2. Next, subtract that income from the amount on Form 1040, line 7. Then, enter only the result on line 1 of the worksheet provided in your 1040 instruction booklet.

If you are entitled to earned income credit, enter the correct amount on Form 1040, line 59A, and write **"CLERGY"** next to the amount. If you are not entitled to receive earned income credit and your AGI is less then the thresholds of $10,200, $26,928, or $30,580, write **"NO"** next to Form 1040, line 59A.

If you receive an unexpected refund check or a larger refund check than you have had computed, do not cash the check. **You have probably received it in error and you will be charged interest for the time you have had the money if you cash the check.** If such a problem arises, call the IRS's Problems Resolution Department. They will give you specific instructions as to the best way to solve the problem.

CHAPTER FOUR

Social Security and Retirement Planning

Dual-status ministers are treated as self-employed individuals in the performance of ministerial services for social security purposes as a result of written law. Sec. 1402(a)(8) is an exception to the "common law" rules for determining whether a person is an employee or self-employed. **Dual-status means** that the minister is an **employee** for income reporting, fringe benefit, and expense deducting purposes and **self-employed** for social security purposes.

Social Security for Religious Workers

Dual-Status Minister

We presented detailed information in Chapter Two to help you determine your correct treatment for social security purposes. **Summary:** The same regulations for determining if a minister qualifies for self-employed status for social security purposes are used to determine if a minister is entitled to parsonage allowance. Generally, you must be employed by a church or an integral agency of a church, perform the duties of a minister, and be ordained or "the equivalent thereof" to be treated as if you were self-employed for social security purposes. When, according to the regulations, you are to be treated as self-employed for social security purposes, **it is mandatory**. For your employer to withhold and match social security would be in error.

In the absence of a formal ordination, licensing, or commissioning, it is the date a church called or hired you as their pastor and gave you the authority to perform substantially all of the religious duties that your self-employed status begins. It is necessary for your church to have formally ordained, licensed, or commissioned you as a minister before they can "assign or designate" you to a position at a "non-integral agency" and qualify you for dual-status treatment. It is also necessary for your church to have formally ordained, licensed, or commissioned you as a minister if you conduct worship and administer ordinances or sacraments, but are not employed by a church or an integral agency of a church.

Before 1968, services performed by ministers were exempt from social security unless they filed a certificate (Form 2031) stating that they wished to be covered by social security.

Since 1968, ministers are automatically covered under social security unless they file an application for exemption on the grounds of conscientious or religious opposition to social security and the government's involvement in public insurance. **If you choose to be covered, YOU DO NOTHING**. You are automatically liable for paying social security on Schedule SE.

An individual who had elected to be covered by social security by filing Form 2031 (before 1968) made an irrevocable decision and could not file Form 4361 and elect to be exempt. Anyone engaged in the ministry at the time of the law change in 1968 had until April 15, 1970, to file Form 4361 and continue not being covered by social security. A minister is often unaware of his **opportunity to choose** between paying social security or becoming exempt from paying Social Security. Once a minister begins to pay social security and the time expires for filing Form 4361, **and he does not change faiths**, there is no way for him to become exempt. (See discussion "When to File Form 4361")

Computation Of Social Security Base - "Worksheet to be Used with Form 2106"

In Chapter Six we have a chart showing the types of income common to a minister and indicate what is required to be entered as salary on Form 941, line 2, and Form W-2, Box 1. **Parsonage provided and/or parsonage allowance designated is to be omitted from Form W-2, Box 1.** However, both the parsonage provided and/or the parsonage allowance must be added to the taxable amount of salary for social security and medicare tax purposes. From the "Computation of Parsonage Allowance" section of the "Worksheet to be Used with Form 2106," enter the value of the parsonage provided from Column A, line 11, on line 2, and enter the parsonage allowance designated from Column B, line 14, on line 3.

Because a dual-status minister is treated as "self-employed" for social security purposes, you can subtract **all unreimbursed professional expenses** from your income to arrive at the amount of income upon which to compute social security. Revenue Ruling 80-110 clearly states that unreimbursed auto, travel, and professional expenses can be used to reduce the social security base for the dual-status minister. Based on Revenue Ruling 80-110, Sec. 1402(a) and Sec. 62(1), **it is correct to use the business percentage of auto interest and personal property tax as a subtraction** from a minister's social security base. The portion of tax preparation fee that is attributable to the reporting of ministry transactions can be a subtraction from a minister's social security base according to Revenue Ruling 92-29.

Qualifying fringe benefits are not subject to social security and are correct to be omitted from employee's Form W-2, Box 1. Nonqualifying and taxable fringe benefits receive the same treatment as taxable salary. They are to be included in the employee's Form W-2, Box 1, and they are subject to social security.

Contributions to a Sec. 403(b) tax sheltered account by a dual-status minister are not subject to social security according to Revenue Ruling 68-395.

If you have filed Form 4361, and are exempt from social security, write "Exempt - Form 4361" on the self-employment line, Form 1040, page 2. If you are exempt from social security on your earnings from the ministry, but have secular self-employment income, use Schedule. SE, page 2. Check the box on Line A to report that you have filed Form 4361 and compute social security on your secular earnings.

- ***Social Security Deductions For Self-Employed***

On Schedule SE the gross social security base is adjusted to allow ½ of social security as a deduction. On Form 1040, page 1, an adjustment for ½ of the social security paid by the self-employed taxpayer is allowed.

Social Security Exemption

Form 4361 includes a statement that, because of your religious principles, you are conscientiously opposed to accepting, for services performed as a member of the clergy, any public insurance (governmental insurance that makes payments in the event of death, disability, old age, or retirement). This includes public insurance established by the Social Security Act. Your conscientious opposition must be based on the institutional principles and discipline of your particular religious denomination **OR** it must be based on **your individual religious biblical principles**. Opposition based on the general conscience will not satisfy this requirement.

A dual-status minister must prayerfully make his/her own decision as to whether he/she wants to be covered by social security. After a personal study of the scriptures for biblical principals that would show opposition to public or government insurance, a minister choosing to be exempt from social security should informally make sufficient notes of his study and conclusions.

As tax professionals, our job is to inform and teach you that, as a dual-status minister, you have an important decision to make regarding social security. No tax professional can make the choice for you nor should they advise you either way. **You must prayerfully make your own decision.** If you choose to remain subject to social security, you will compute it on Schedule SE and timely prepay your estimate of income tax and social security and medicare tax liability. If you choose to become exempt from social security you must timely file Form 4361. If you choose to become exempt **it must be for the religious and conscientious grounds** stated above. You may not become exempt for solely economic reasons. If you file an application for exemption only for economic reasons, you have not made a valid election.

Ministers who have filed Form 4361 are opposed to **only public** insurance and must provide their own alternative to social security. They most certainly **can** and **should have a private investment plan for retirement needs.**

- ***What Happens To What I Have Already Paid In?***

Form 4361 does not cause you to waive the right to receive social security benefits. Any secular employment or work that is **NOT** in the exercise of your ministry will be subject to either social security or self-employment tax. Any social security you pay on secular earnings will be credited to your account.

Filled Out Example of Form 4361

Form **4361** (Rev. February 1997) Department of the Treasury Internal Revenue Service

Application for Exemption From Self-Employment Tax for Use by Ministers, Members of Religious Orders and Christian Science Practitioners

OMB No. 1545-0168

File Original and Two Copies

File original and two copies and attach supporting documents. This exemption is granted only if the IRS returns a copy to you marked "approved."

Please type or print

1 Name of taxpayer applying for exemption (as shown on Form 1040): HARRY C HIGGENBOTTOM

Social security number: 327-19-9999

Number and street (including apt. no.): 1295 SHADY LANE

Telephone number (optional):

City or town, state, and ZIP code: WHEATON IL 60287

2 Check ONE box: ☐ Christian Science practitioner ☐ Ordained minister, priest, rabbi ☐ Member of religious order not under a vow of poverty ☒ Commissioned or licensed minister (see line 6)

3 Date ordained, licensed, etc. (Attach supporting document. See instructions.): 5/24/98

4 Legal name of ordaining, licensing, or commissioning body or religious order: Calvary Independent Chapel

Number, street, and room or suite no.: 1290 Shady Lane

Employer identification number: 25-1024444

City or town, state, and ZIP code: Wheaton, IL 60287

5 Enter the first 2 years, after the date shown on line 3, that you had net self-employment earnings of $400 or more, any of which came from services as a minister, priest, rabbi, etc.; member of a religious order; or Christian Science practitioner ▶ 1998 1999

6 If you apply for the exemption as a licensed or commissioned minister, and your denomination also ordains ministers, please indicate how your ecclesiastical powers differ from those of an ordained minister of your denomination. Attach a copy of your denomination's bylaws relating to the powers of ordained, commissioned, or licensed ministers.

See Attached

7 I certify that I am conscientiously opposed to, or because of my religious principles I am opposed to, the acceptance (for services I perform as a minister, member of a religious order not under a vow of poverty, or a Christian Science practitioner) of any public insurance that makes payments in the event of death, disability, old age, or retirement; or that makes payments toward the cost of, or provides services for, medical care. (Public insurance includes insurance systems established by the Social Security Act.)

I certify that as a duly ordained, commissioned, or licensed minister of a church or a member of a religious order not under a vow of poverty, I have informed the ordaining, commissioning, or licensing body of my church or order that I am conscientiously opposed to, or because of religious principles, I am opposed to the acceptance (for services I perform as a minister or as a member of a religious order) of any public insurance that makes payments in the event of death, disability, old age, or retirement; or that makes payments toward the cost of, or provides services for, medical care, including the benefits of any insurance system established by the Social Security Act.

I certify that I did not file an effective waiver certificate (Form 2031) electing social security coverage on earnings as a minister, member of a religious order not under a vow of poverty, or a Christian Science practitioner.

I request to be exempted from paying self-employment tax on my earnings from services as a minister, member of a religious order not under a vow of poverty, or a Christian Science practitioner, under section 1402(e) of the Internal Revenue Code. I understand that the exemption, if granted, will apply only to these earnings. Under penalties of perjury, I declare that I have examined this application and to the best of my knowledge and belief, it is true and correct.

Signature ▶ **Date ▶** March 3, 2000

Caution: *Form 4361 is **not proof** of the right to an exemption from Federal income tax withholding or social security tax, the right to a parsonage allowance exclusion (section 107 of the Internal Revenue Code), assignment by your religious superiors to a particular job, or the exemption or church status of the ordaining, licensing, or commissioning body, or religious order.*

For Internal Revenue Service Use

☐ Approved for exemption from self-employment tax on ministerial earnings
☐ Disapproved for exempton from self-employment tax on ministerial earnings

By ______________________ (Director's signature) ______________ (Date)

General Instructions

Section references are to the Internal Revenue Code.

Paperwork Reduction Act Notice. — We ask for the information on this form to carry out the Internal Revenue laws of the United States. You are required to give us the information. We need it to ensure that you are complying with these laws and to allow us to figure and collect the right amount of tax.

You are not required to provide the information requested on a form that is subject to the Paperwork Reduction Act unless the form displays a valid OMB control number. Books or records relating to a form or its instructions must be retained as long as their contents may become material in the administration of any Internal Revenue law. Generally, tax returns and return information are confidential, as required by section 6103.

The time needed to complete and file this form will vary depending on individual circumstances. The estimated average time is:

Recordkeeping, 7 min.; **Learning about the law or the form,** 20 min.; **Preparing the form,** 16 min.; **Copying, assembling, and sending the form to the IRS,** 17 min.

If you have comments concerning the accuracy of these time estimates or suggestions for making this form simpler, we would be happy to hear from you. You can write to the Tax Forms Committee, Western Area Distribution Center, Rancho Cordova, CA 95743-0001. **DO NOT** send the form to this address. Instead, see **Where To File** on page 2.

Purpose of Form. — File Form 4361 to apply for an exemption from self-employment tax if you are:

- An ordained, commissioned, or licensed minister of a church;
- A member of a religious order who has not taken a vow of poverty;
- A Christian Science practitioner; or
- A commissioned or licensed minister of a church or church denomination that ordains ministers, if you have authority to perform substantially all religious duties of your church or denomination.

This application must be based on your religious or conscientious opposition to the acceptance (for services performed as a minister, member of a religious order not under a vow of poverty, or Christian Science practitioner) of any public insurance that makes payments for death, disability, old age, or retirement; or that makes payments for the cost of, or provides services for medical

(continued on page 2)

If vested, you will be entitled to receive social security benefits from all mandatory contributions on secular earnings. **Ten years or forty quarters** of social security contributions result in your being vested and eligible for benefits based on your lifetime average. You can find out the number of quarters you have been credited for by contacting the Social Security Administration. Since secular work is always subject to social security, it would be possible to earn additional quarters by performing secular work after filing Form 4361. Earnings required for a quarter of credit in 1999 is $740 and in 2000 is $780. When you retire, you can choose the **greater source** of benefits, either from **your account** or **your spouse's** account.

- ***Disability Coverage***

Disability coverage under social security will discontinue after you become exempt. When it will discontinue for you, depends upon your age and the number of quarters of credit you have. Knowing this, you may wish to be bi-vocational and earn enough secular earnings to retain disability coverage or obtain private disability coverage. Foreign missionaries have difficulty obtaining comparable life and disability insurance coverages and may wish to remain covered by social security.

- ***Irrevocable***

The exemption, once obtained, is basically irrevocable. However, there have been two periods of time that provisions have been made for revocation. Ministers who revoke their election can never become exempt again. For a short period of time, and if filed by the due date of the 1978 return, Form 4361-A did give opportunity for ministers who were exempt to revoke their election.

The Tax Reform Act of 1986 provided another "window." Application for revocation, Form 2031, had to be filed no later than April 15, 1988 due date (including extensions), but before the applicant became entitled to benefits.

Both the House and the Senate have introduced bills to provide another window for exempt ministers to opt back into social security during 1997, 1998 and again in 1999. Nothing has yet been enacted but it is a revenue raiser and has strong backing in both the House and the Senate.

- ***When To File Form 4361 - Including "New Faith" Opportunity***

The application for Exemption from Self-Employment Tax, Form 4361, must be filed by the due date (April 15th) of your tax return, including extensions, for the **second tax year** in which you had net self-employment **earnings of $400 or more** from services as a minister (which includes parsonage allowance and/or parsonage provided). **A timely filed Form 4361 will be approved**.

Example of timing: you had net earnings of $5,000 in 1998 and $38,000 in 1999, the deadline for filing Form 4361 would be April 15th, 2000. The two years need not be consecutive. If a minister had net earnings of $700 in 1992, less than $400 in 1993 through 1998, and $4,000 in 1999, the deadline for filing Form 4361 would be April 15th, 2000.

It is very important for a minister who wishes to become exempt from social security to be aware of the date his/her ministry begins. In the absence of a formal ordination, licensing or commissioning, it is the **date a church called or hired** you as their pastor and gave you the authority to perform substantially all of the religious duties that your tax status as a minister begins.

Here is a very important court definition of a "duly ordained, commissioned, or licensed" minister. In J.M. Ballinger, U.S. Court of Appeals, 10th Circuit, No. 82-1928, 3/7/84, it was stated, *"Not all churches or religions have a formally ordained ministry, whether because of the nature of their beliefs, the lack of a denominational structure or a variety of other reasons. Courts are not in a position to determine the merits of various churches... We interpret Congress' language providing an exemption for any individual who is 'a duly ordained, commissioned, or licensed minister of a church' to mean that* ***the triggering event is the assumption of the duties and functions of a minister****."*

When a minister **changes faith** he is allowed a new window of opportunity to acquire an opposition to social security. If a minister changes employment from one autonomous (self-governing) church to another or one denomination to another, he can claim opposition to social security and timely file Form 4361 by the due date of the second tax year in which he has earnings of $400 or more from the new faith. **The date of hire** at the new church begins a new time period of making a choice. No formal re-ordination or re-licensing is necessary.

This provision **will not** be available to the minister employed by a denomination that appoints a minister to a different church within the denomination. This provision **will not** be available to a minister who has previously filed an untimely Form 4361 and had his application disapproved.

In filling out a "new faith" Form 4361, enter the new date of hire in Box 3 and enter the year of hire as the first year on line 5.

A few years ago IRS directed personnel in their departments that approve or disapprove Form 4361 applications to recognize minister's applications after they had changed faiths and acquired an opposition to public insurance. We have communicated with one service center that said they had no knowledge of this provision and sought help from the national IRS office on the issue. The Form 4361 that they had denied was resubmitted and finally approved. A **summary** of the **two tax court cases** that have brought about the ability for a minister to have more than one "window" of time to acquire an opposition to social security follows:

J.M. Ballinger, U.S. Court of Appeals, 10th Circuit, No 82-1928, 3/7/84: Taxpayer was ordained as a minister of the First Missionary Baptist Church, on November 22, 1969. He became minister of the Maranatha Church in September, 1973. He received net earnings from the ministry in excess of $400 during 1973, 1974 and 1975. On March 8, 1977 he incorrectly filed Form 4029 instead of Form 4361. It was disapproved by the IRS because he was not a member of a religious order described in Sec. 1402(g). On May 2, 1978 he was re-ordained by the Maranatha Church. On July 7, 1978 he filed the correct Form 4361 showing May 2, 1978 as the beginning of his ministry. The IRS initially approved the application. Upon discovery that Rev. Ballinger had first been ordained in 1969 and hired by Maranatha Church in September, 1973, the IRS revoked the exemption. Had Rev. Ballinger filed Form 4361 by April 15, 1975, the judges stated that it would have been a different case. The three judge panel said, *"The statute makes no distinction between a first ordination and subsequent ordinations. Courts are not in a position to determine the merits of various churches nor an individual's conversion from one church to another. Nor can we hold that an individual who has a change of belief* ***accompanied*** *by a change to another faith is not entitled to the exemption."*

James B. Hall, U.S. Court of Appeals, 10th Circuit, No 93-9027, 7/19/94: Same court ten years later upheld their decision and the three judge panel said, *"We anticipated a case like this when we decided Ballinger v. Commissioner."* Taxpayer was ordained as a deacon in the United Methodist Church in 1979 and earned more than $400 per year from his ministerial services in both 1980 and 1981. Taxpayer's activities as a deacon made him potentially eligible to apply for a 1402(e) exemption. At that time, however, the taxpayer was not religiously or conscientiously opposed to the acceptance of public insurance, thus he was not eligible and did not apply for an exemption. He left the ministry and spent five years as an engineer. Taxpayer was ordained by the Community Church and began a new ministry and accepted a new belief in opposition to public insurance. Rev. Hall applied for exemption in the first tax year immediately following his second ordination and the commencement of his new ministry. It was initially denied as untimely (after April 15, 1982.) The lower Tax Court affirmed this denial. The judges said, "We ultimately concluded that the statute *"permits all ministers who oppose public insurance on religious grounds to qualify and, as we interpret the statute, permits ministers who change churches to qualify."*

They also stated,"We are not concerned that our decision will open the floodgates for conniving Elmer Gantrys to dupe the Internal Revenue Service and opt out of the social security system without a sincere religious objection."

Having timely filed his Form 4361, taxpayer's exemption from social security was approved.

• *Exemption is Retroactive to Beginning of Ministry*

An approved Form 4361 is retroactive back to the date your ministry or change of faith began. If you paid social security for the first year of your ministry or change of ministry and have chosen to file Form 4361 during the second year, you can receive a refund of the first year's social security payment. To get a refund file Form 1040X as a claim within the three year statute of limitations. Attach a photocopy of your approved Form 4361 to Form 1040X. **The IRS does not automatically send** social security refunds.

• *How To File Form 4361 and Attachments*

For efficient processing of your exemption application it is important to include all of the required attachments and information.

Attach proof of the beginning of your ministry: a copy of your certificate for ordination, license, commissioning or a letter from the church who hired you verifying the date you were hired as their minister.

Extra statement required for applicants without ordination certificate: If your church or denomination both ordains and licenses ministers, Form 4361, line 6, requires that you attach a copy of the by-laws stating that a licensed or employed minister is invested with the authority to perform substantially all of the duties of the church or denomination. If no such by-laws exist, then type the following statement on your church's letterhead, have a person in authority sign it, and attach it to your application:

> *"Our church/denomination does not have specific by-laws regarding the powers of ordained, licensed, commissioned or employed ministers. We do give the same authority to perform all of the ecclesiastical duties to our licensed, commissioned or employed ministers as we do to those who are ordained."*

Notify church: The ordaining, licensing or commissioning body of your church must be informed that you are conscientiously opposed to or because of religious principles you are opposed to the acceptance of public insurance benefits based on ministerial service. In the absence of a formal ordination, licensing or commissioning, it is the church that hired you that you must notify. When you sign Form 4361 you are certifying (line 7) that you have performed this notification. Individual opposition is sufficient for a minister to be exempt; it does not matter that the position of the employer is different.

Prove your church is a church: You must establish that the organization that gave you the authority to do ministerial services **is a church**. The IRS requires the exemption applicant to establish or prove that the church that ordained them or "the equivalent thereof" is a religious organization described in **Sec. 501(c)(3)** and also in **Sec. 170(b)(1)(A)(i).**

IRS Publication 78, published quarterly, lists organizations, denominations or churches that have filed Form 1023 requesting exempt status. If your church is a part of a major denomination, your church will be under its group exempt status. If the church that ordained you or "the equivalent thereof" is independent or autonomous and voluntarily filed Form 1023 and received a determination letter, it is listed in IRS Publication 78. **Attach a copy of their determination letter to your Form 4361.** Churches are not required to file and submit the information requested on Form 1023. Form 8718 must accompany the Form 1023 and requires a **$500** fee to be paid to the IRS.

If the church on your application has not voluntarily filed Form 1023, you must provide proof that it is a church with your Form 4361. The service center to which you send your Form 4361 will accept the following types of information from you to establish that the church is a church:

1. On church stationery provide the name of organization, address, and Employer Identification Number. Make this statement, "We are a religious organization described in Sec. 501(c)(3) and also in Sec. 170(b)(1)(A)(i)." Include a description of the characteristics that qualify the organization as a church such as regular worship, evangelism and membership. The statement should be signed by someone authorized to represent the church.
2. If your church is incorporated attach copies of the organization's creating instrument and a copy of the constitution and bylaws.
3. Provide copies of church bulletins, newsletters, photos of the church (steeple) and members, etc., to show the regular times of worship and other activities that are typical of a church.

● *How To Send Your Form 4361*

Make photocopies of the completed Form 4361 for your records and keep in two or three safe places. Send **three** signed copies with the attached documents we have discussed by **Certified Mail** to your IRS Service Center so that you can prove that it was timely filed. **Send your Form 4361 separate from your income tax returns.**

The Service Center will send it to the Social Security department to examine. Then it goes to Washington to see if your church is listed in Publication 78 or to verify your attached proof.

Watch For Letter: The Secretary of Health and Human Services has the responsibility of communicating with the applicant to further verify that the applicant understands the grounds (basis) for exemption and is seeking the exemption on those grounds. Discussion in the committee reports suggested that the communication would be in person or by telephone. Fortunately applicants receive a letter instead. The letter asks for your signature again, verifying that you understand the grounds under which you filed Form 4361. **The letter must be returned to the IRS within 90 days** or the effective date of the exemption will not begin until it is received by the IRS.

Eventually it goes back to your Service Center, and they send a copy back to you marked **"approved"**. The process can take several months. If you fail to get an approved copy back in 6 or 8 months, call IRS and ask that they put a tracer on it. Applications sometimes get lost and need to be refiled.

- ***Put Your Approved Copy In Several Safe Places***

Once you receive your "**APPROVED COPY**" from the IRS—copy it, protect it, and treat it as a valuable document. We recommend making several copies. Give a copy to your tax accountant. If your approved copy has been misplaced or lost, request a copy from the Social Security Administration, Office of Central Records Operations, Metro West Building, 300 North Green Street, Baltimore, MD 21201.

- ***What If You Timely Filed, But Have Never Received An Approved Copy From IRS***

Ministers who failed to receive their "Approved Copy" of Form 4361 should take steps to obtain one. Often during an audit event they are unable to prove their exempt status and are billed for social security in the audit report. Common reasons for not receiving the "Approved Copy" are (1) minister moved before receiving approval; (2) application got lost in the mail or in the processing system; (3) original application lacked complete information and was denied because of lack of information. **Good News** is anytime there is proof that Form 4361 was timely filed, it can be resurrected! By resubmitting a new Form 4361, containing correct original information, with a letter stating the history and proof of timely filing, we have been successful in obtaining for several clients an "Approved Copy" effective back to the original date ministry began. Any social security tax assessed can then be canceled or refunded.

Social Security & the Religious Sects Opposed to Insurance

A completely different set of rules apply to members of religious orders. **Sec. 1402(g)** allows any self-employed member of a religious order that opposes both private and public insurance to file **Form 4029** and be exempt from social security regardless of his work activity (farming, construction, etc.). Since November 10, 1988, **Form 4029** can be filed at any time. This exemption is a statement that the individual is opposed to both **public and private insurance** and **is an actual waiver** of ever receiving any benefits from social security. It is necessary that the religious order has a history and a plan to provide for the members when they become dependent through disability or old age. **It is also necessary that the order was organized before 1950.** New religious orders described in Sec. 1402(g) cannot be formed. If a member ceases to be a member of the order their exemption is revoked. Members who have filed Form 4029 for exemption from social security and have made contributions to a private retirement annuity revoke their exemption and will have to pay back-years' social security tax according to Revenue Ruling 77-88. According to Private Letter Ruling 8741002, funding of an IRA through a CD in a bank did not constitute insurance and, thus, did not disqualify the taxpayer from exemption. However, earnings exempt from Social Security under Sec. 1402(g) are not eligible earnings from which to make an IRA contribution.

Because Revenue Ruling 77-88 has been taken out of context and often thought to apply to **Sec. 1402(e)** for ministers who have filed Form 4361, we feel it is important for you to know that it does not apply to ministers. Ministers who have filed Form 4361 are opposed to **only public** insurance and must provide their own alternative to social security. They most certainly **can** and **should have a private investment plan for retirement needs**.

Social Security and the Lay Employee

A religious worker who does not qualify for dual-status tax treatment must be treated as a lay employee of the employer for social security and medicare tax purposes. He does not have an individual choice of being exempt or subject to social security.

Prior to 1984, a not-for-profit religious organization as described in Sec. 501(c)(3) had been automatically exempt from withholding social security from their employees and matching it with their share. So an organization that wished to remain exempt from withholding social security for all its employees did not have to file any form. Prior to 1984, if an organization and its employees desired to be covered by social security, they had to file Form SS-15.

Since January 1, 1984, the Social Security Amendments Act of 1983 extended social security coverage **on a mandatory** basis to all lay employees of not-for-profit organizations.

Electing Churches—Form 8274

The Tax Reform Act of 1984 provided for an election by a church or qualified church-controlled organization that is **opposed for religious reasons** to the payment of social security taxes not to be subject to such taxes. (Sec. 3121(w)) The election merely **transfers** the social security liability **from the church to the employee.**

The electing church is required to withhold income tax and to report the compensation paid to each employee who earns **more than $100.00** on Form W-2. The electing church should withhold additional amounts of income tax so their employees will have an adequate amount of tax prepaid to cover the cost of the social security to be computed on their Schedule SE. Form 941, with the box on Line 8 marked, is the correct quarterly report for an electing church. The electing church **must communicate** to their employees their responsibility to compute and pay their own social security on their Form 1040, Schedule SE. In Chapter Six we show a filled out example of Form 941 and W-2's for an electing church. The memo "Electing church employee to pay social security on Schedule SE" is what we recommend to include on Form W-2, Box 14.

● *When To Make The Election—Form 8274*

Existing church employers, as of October 1, 1984, had until October 31, 1984 to file Form 8274. If your church was not aware of how to become an electing church and does not timely file the election, there is no recourse. To become an "electing church," file Form 8274 (two copies) before the first date on which a quarterly employment tax return would otherwise be due. **Example:** a church established on October 1, 1999, with an employee, would need to file Form 8274 by January 31, 2000.

If an electing church fails to provide the required Form W-2's for two years and fails to furnish the information upon request by the IRS, the IRS will revoke the election. The Tax Reform Act of 1986 **made it easy for electing churches to revoke their election**. By simply filing a Form 941 on or before its due date for the first quarter for which the revocation is to be effective, accompanied by payment in full of the social security taxes that would be due for the quarter, the election is revoked.

Employees of "electing churches" do not qualify to claim exemption from paying social security by filing Form 4361. The wages subject to social security on Schedule SE are the wages in Box 1 of their Form W-2 plus any Sec. 403(b) or 401(k) voluntary contributions. Such wages from an electing church can not be reduced by losses from other self-employment activity or unreimbursed employee business expenses. (Sec. 3121(b)(8); 3121(w)) (IRS Publication 557, page 9)

How To Do Correction For Wrong Treatment

Are you a dual-status minister but your employer **wrongly treated you as an employee for social security purposes**? When, according to the regulations, you are to be treated as self-employed for social security purposes, **dual-status tax treatment is mandatory**. For your employer to withhold and match social security is in error. This can be corrected for all three "open" years that we are allowed to amend returns. The rates for 1996, 1997, 1998 and 1999 have been the same: 15.3% withheld and matched for employees and 15.3% for the self-employed.

Even though it is advisable to correct the wrong treatment of the minister's status, there has not been an underpayment or overpayment of tax liability. Some employers may choose to correct the wrong treatment for the current and future years.

We want to give adequate information for making corrections if you choose to correct the open years. The amount of social security matched by the employer is not required to be credited or paid to the employee. The social security withheld from the employee's salary must be paid back to the employee. If the employer chooses to allow their matched portion to be credit for their employee, it must be counted as extra salary on the W-2c in the year of the correction.

As a self employed minister you can deduct your unreimbursed employee business expenses from your social security base.

- ***Two Ways To Handle The Corrections***

1. When the employer is willing to count their matching portion as extra salary for the minister:
   a. Prepare 941c and an amended 941 to reflect the changes made. You will not be requesting a refund on the 941c.
   b. Prepare W-2c and W-3c showing matching portion added to "Wages, tips, other compensation" as additional salary.
   c. Include total amount of social security withheld and matched as income tax withheld in "federal income tax withheld."
   d. Prepare minister's Form 1040X. The minister will have credit on his 1040X for the total social security amount withheld and matched. Depending on the level of his total income, he may have a small refund or owe a small amount of additional tax, plus interest on the balance.
2. When the employer wishes to keep their matching portion:
   a. Prepare 941c and an amended 941 to reflect the changes made and claim a credit on the next quarter's 941 or file Form 843 to claim a refund for the employer's matching portion.
   b. Prepare W-2c and W-3c showing original salary in "Wages, tips, other compensation."
   c. Include amount of social security withheld as income tax withholding in "federal income tax withheld."
   d. Prepare minister's Form 1040X. The minister will have partial credit on his 1040X for social security computed on Schedule SE and will incur interest on the balance owed.

It is important when making changes to your federal Form 1040 to remember to amend your state income tax return when it is affected. **Do not hesitate to seek** professional accounting help in preparing corrections to payroll reports. The staff at **Worth Tax & Financial Service** is available to prepare payroll reports, W-2's, and corrections for organizations.

Should the Minister's Spouse be on the Payroll?

No one will dispute the fact that a minister's spouse works many hours for the church and usually receives no paycheck. To establish a salary, it is necessary that there is a true employer/employee relationship. The amount of the salary should be reasonable and paid on the basis of time spent in working for the employer. Employed ministers **should not personally pay** their spouse a salary. It is not allowed under the "assignment of income" portion of tax law according to Sec. 61 and Revenue Ruling 74-32.

- ***Benefits – When Both Spouses Have Earned Income***

When both spouses have income from salaries it qualifies them for claiming Child Care Credit on Form 2441 for babysitting expenses incurred while both are at work. Babysitting expense **is never to be treated as an "employee business expense."**

Travel and professional expenses can be justified for both employed spouses. For a husband and wife to both be receiving a salary and conducting bona fide business activities, travel away from home expenses, auto travel, entertainment, etc., are able to be claimed.

At retirement the ability to receive two semi-retired salaries and be within the social security earnings limitation can be very advantageous. A history of both spouses having earnings before retirement is wise. To establish a salary for your spouse at retirement time would cause the Department of Social Security to notice the absence of your spouse's earnings before your retirement.

Since 1997 the maximum IRA deduction for a married couple filing jointly increased from $2,250 to $4,000, up to $2,000 each as long as their combined compensation is at least that much. Therefore the advantage of both spouses having earned income has been canceled by a good change in the IRA rules.

Estimated Tax, Form 1040ES

It is necessary for all taxpayers to "prepay" their income tax and their social security tax. An employee has tax withheld from each paycheck and "prepaid" by the employer each quarter. **Withholding by the employer of a dual-status minister is optional.** The dual-status minister is generally required to "prepay" tax by making quarterly payments based on an estimate of the amount of tax he expects to owe for the year. The current year's estimate is to be calculated at the time you prepare the previous year's tax return and the first installment of ¼ of the total is due on **April 15th**. Other due dates are **June 15th, September 15th, and January 15th**. Instead of paying the final January 15th installment, you may elect to file your return early, by January 31st, and pay any tax due with the return.

If you or your spouse are an employee and earn other wages from which tax is withheld, you may be able to arrange to have enough withheld to cover your combined tax liability. To claim less exemptions or allowances at the other job is usually more convenient than to make quarterly payments. It makes no difference **how you prepay your tax liability,** either **estimated payments** or **adequate withholding** will meet the requirements. An estimate is exactly what the word means. No one can predict the correct amount of tax a year in advance. If you anticipate no tax or **less than $1000** for the year, no estimate is necessary. If circumstances change during the year you may always amend or change your estimate and increase or decrease the quarterly payments.

Underpayment Penalties

You may be charged a penalty for not paying enough estimated tax or for not making the payments on time. The amount of underpayment penalty is the same as the rate of interest the IRS charges on late payments and it is announced each quarter. For individuals (other than high-income individuals) the penalty does not apply if **each required payment is timely** and the total tax paid is based on:

1. 90% of the total tax liability due on the return for the current year (income tax, social security tax, early withdrawal penalties, alternative minimum tax, etc.) or;
2. 100% of the total tax liability shown on the return for the preceding year, commonly referred to as a **safe harbor estimate,** (if your tax liability is expected to increase, you can pre-pay as much as the year before's liability in timely installments and plan to pay any remaining balance with the return on April 15th and not incur a penalty), or
3. 90% of the tax figured by annualizing the taxable income and adjusted self-employment income received for the months ending before the due date of the installment.

High income individuals with Adjusted Gross Income over $150,000 ($75,000 for married separate) for the preceding tax year may avoid estimated tax penalty by basing estimated taxes on 110% of their prior year's tax or 90% of the current year's tax.

File your estimated tax on **Form 1040ES** and keep in mind that the estimate includes income tax and social security and medicare tax.

Waiver of Penalty

A waiver of penalty is available if you did not make a payment because of a casualty, disaster, or other unusual circumstance. Also, a waiver may be claimed if you retired (after reaching age 62) or became disabled during the tax year a payment was due or during the preceding tax year and your underpayment was not due to willful neglect. To claim the waiver, follow the instructions given on Form 2210 or in IRS Publication 505, page 41.

Optional Withholding Agreement

A withholding agreement can be made between an employer and a dual-status minister. It is to be a written agreement. A Form W-4 can be prepared with the amount to be withheld each pay period entered on line 6 rather than claiming any allowances on line 5. The employer should withhold enough **income tax** to prepay the minister's total income tax and social security and medicare tax liability. Form W-2 will show the amount that has been withheld in Box 2.

Retirement Planning For Religious Workers

All religious workers should establish retirement plans to **supplement** social security income during retirement. Dual-status ministers who have become exempt from social security must have a disciplined savings plan for retirement to take the place of social security. **It would be foolish to become exempt from social security and do nothing to provide for one's needs in retirement.**

We want to present some ideas and information that will make it possible to have the option to retire or semi-retire. Financial planning for retirement has been neglected by many religious workers. We can blame low compensation, busy work schedules, and even a hopeful expectation that the Lord will return before retirement, but the fact is many ministers and religious workers can not afford to retire.

Investments that are diversified are the best way to plan for meeting your needs during retirement. Through mutual funds it is possible to invest regular amounts in a diversified portfolio. The principle of investing regularly and over a long time horizon results in amazing compound growth. Investments in common stocks or stock funds have historically outperformed savings in fixed income investments. **You should never feel it is too late** to begin an investment plan. Most Americans do not begin to save regularly until the children are raised and the mortgage is nearly paid. The increase in life expectancy creates a greater need for investment planning and at the same time allows a longer time for the magic of compounding to function.

Let us give you an example of **the magic of compounding.** If you began investing at age 25 and invested $150 a month for 40 years and had a 10% rate of return, you would be a millionaire at age 65. If you began investing at age 45 and invested $1,316.88 a month for 20 years and had a 10% rate of return, you would also be a millionaire at age 65.

Mutual Funds

Over meaningful time spans of 10 years or more, well-managed stock funds have nearly always done better–often much better–than the U.S. market as a whole. The growth of an investment in a mutual fund comes from two sources: income dividends and capital appreciation. While there have been times when the value of an investment in mutual funds have declined, over the years such an investment has produced much better results than savings deposits. There is no doubt that a savings account or certificate of deposit is a good place to put money you want to keep in reserve for short-term needs. Over the long pull they have not been the best place for your **investment** dollars–the larger sums that must be kept hard at work to build for your future and protect you against inflation.

Investing in the stock market can be confusing if you do not have much time to devote to it. Some publications would encourage you to try to "time" the market and to trade often. Most of us do not have the time to be watching the daily changes in the market place. Even investment professionals cannot always "buy low and sell high." Those who "buy high and sell low" become discouraged and often discontinue investing. A better strategy for investing is to invest regular amounts into a family of mutual funds and let your investment compound over a long period of time. This strategy is often called "dollar cost averaging."

A well managed mutual fund must charge the investors for management costs. Some mutual funds have "loads" or commissions up front or at the time of your investment. Other mutual funds advertised in the Wall Street Journal and financial magazines are "no load" or without a commission at the time of the investment. Generally, the "no load" funds have a higher annual management fee than the "loaded" funds. Some funds have a back end "load" if you do not own the fund long enough. **Before you make any investment in a mutual fund, you will be given a prospectus that fully explains the fees that particular fund will charge.** Choosing a "no load" mutual fund could actually end up costing more over the life of an investment because the annual management fees are charged on the compounded value of the investment. "Loaded" mutual funds typically have much lower annual management fees. "Loaded" mutual funds are marketed through registered representatives and having received a commission at the time of your investment, they are willing to answer your questions and help you monitor your investments.

Life Insurance

Life insurance is an important part of your portfolio because it provides risk protection for your family. One purpose of life insurance is to replace your earnings should you die prematurely. The amount of your debt, the ability of your spouse to earn a living, the age and number of dependent children are a few of the factors to consider in determining how much life insurance coverage you should have. There is no easy formula to use to decide whether it is best to have a term life policy or a universal life policy or a whole life policy. The facts and circumstances of your individual needs can be evaluated by an insurance professional. It is possible to combine life insurance protection and mutual fund investing within a variable life policy. Upon your death, life insurance benefits are not taxable to your beneficiaries on their Form 1040. However, the amount of benefits are to be included in your taxable estate and could cause estate tax.

Annuities

An annuity is a product of life insurance companies that is a contract which promises to pay you for the rest of your life in exchange for a stated cost of premium. A fixed annuity is invested in interest bearing investments and usually has a better rate of return than a bank certificate of deposit. A variable annuity is invested in the capital market through a group of mutual funds. An annuity's earnings are reinvested and are tax deferred, or not currently taxed. If you are receiving social security benefits, and you have a high adjusted gross income that causes a portion of your social security to be taxed, an unqualified annuity is a good tax planning tool.

At age 65 you can annuitize the investment through several options. If you annuitize an annuity, and die early, the insurance company wins; if you live beyond life expectancy, you win. The option of choosing joint life is usually a good choice. The option of choosing a refund feature means that your named beneficiary will receive any remainder of principal in your contract upon your death.

An annuity does not have to be annuitized. It is possible to allow the contract to compound and grow and be passed on to your beneficiary. The value will not be subject to probate expense. However, as the contract passes to your appointed beneficiary, the profit or gain in the contract will be taxable on your beneficiary's Form 1040.

Because annuities have an "end load" or cost if you take more than the allowed minimum withdrawal during the first six or seven years of the investment, they should never be used as a short term investment. The taxable portion of withdrawals before age 59½ or disability do incur the 10% penalty assessed by the IRS. The taxable portion of withdrawals are also subject to regular tax.

Unqualified and Qualified Plans

Investments and annuities are available in unqualified plans and qualified plans. An unqualified plan means that the cost or premium is not subtracted from your taxable income. Qualified investment plans have the added advantage of "sheltering" the cost or contribution to the plan from current tax. To establish a qualified investment or annuity, it is usually a simple procedure of signing an extra document that establishes a custodian for the plan. **Chapter One** has a more complete discussion concerning TSAs and IRAs.

Tax Sheltered Account or 403(b) Plan

Tax Sheltered Accounts are available to public school employees and employees of tax-exempt organizations. TSAs are the basic funding vehicle for retirement plans established by tax-exempt employers. This code section deals with two different methods of funding.

Forfeitable Contributions (employee loses if not vested) can be made by the **employer** to a Sec. 403(b) account on the behalf of its employees. The cost to establish and administer this type of Sec. 403(b) employer plan causes it to not be cost effective for an employer with a small number of employees. An employer's plan can be established to accept both forfeitable contributions by the employer and non-forfeitable contributions made by the employee through a salary reduction plan or just forfeitable contributions.

Non-Forfeitable Contributions (employee is always 100% vested) can be made for the **employee** to a Sec. 403(b) account established by the employer for voluntary salary reduction contributions. Contributions to a TSA account by a dual-status minister **are not** subject to social security and medicare tax. However, contributions to a TSA account by a lay employee **are** subject to social security and medicare tax withholding.

A Sec. 403(b) retirement plan can be established to accept only **non-forfeitable** voluntary contributions from one or several employees. Quite often employers will establish Sec. 403(b) plans that only allow salary reduction non-forfeitable voluntary contributions because **they are quick to establish and involve very little cost of administration.** Employees of not-for-profit organizations who change employers from time to time like the "portability" of a Sec. 403(b) non-forfeitable type of plan.

Mutual fund companies have qualified Sec. 403(b) plans that allow investment in the capital market. Insurance companies have qualified Sec. 403(b) plans that allow investment in either a fixed or a variable annuity.

● ***Retired Ministers & Parsonage Designation***

A **retired minister** receiving an otherwise taxable distribution from a qualified Sec. 401(a), Sec. 403(b), Sec. 408(k), 408(p) or Sec. 414(e) plan may have a **"parsonage allowance"** designated by the former employer or denominational pension board. It is possible for 100% of the retirement income to be non-taxable to the extent it is used for parsonage expenses. (Revenue Ruling 63-156) We have found language in the Department of Labor Regulations under ERISA that seem to consider either type of contribution to Sec. 403(b) **(forfeitable and non-forfeitable) to be considered as an employer's plan and eligible for parsonage allowance designation.** (Labor Regs. 2520.3-2(f)(3))

However, distributions from an IRA or a Keogh retirement plan are fully taxable and cannot be designated as non-taxable housing.

Individual Retirement Account

A qualified tax shelter that we are all familiar with is the Individual Retirement Account or the IRA. You can set up and make contributions to an IRA if you received taxable compensation during the year and have not reached age 70½ by the end of the year.

You can establish an IRA that is invested in mutual funds. You can establish an IRA with an insurance company that is an annuity contract. You can establish an IRA with a bank that is invested in a Certificate of Deposit. **IRAs** are now **flexible** and have the capability of being **qualified or non-qualified.** Beginning in 1998, active participation in an employer-sponsored plan by one spouse will not prevent the non-participating spouse from making a deductible contribution to an IRA unless their AGI reaches the phaseout level between $150,000 and $160,000. You can choose to designate contributions to an IRA as "non-deductible" on Form 8606 in a year that you have no tax liability.

Beginning in 1998, the Roth IRA, a new form of IRA, is available. Contributions are unqualified or non-deductible in the year of the contribution. Their earnings will accumulate tax free and qualified distributions will be tax free. Total individual contributions to all IRAs for a tax year cannot exceed $2,000. We feel this will be a wonderful choice for the non-tax paying minister's retirement planning. A Roth IRA invested in a mutual fund will capture the long term growth of the capital market. Qualified distributions are those made after a 5 year period, and in addition, made after age 59½, after death to a beneficiary, after becoming disabled or distributed to pay for "qualified first time home buyer expenses."

When Should You Have A Qualified Plan?

When you have an income tax liability, it is good tax planning to consider making contributions to a sheltered or qualified retirement plan. Even when you have no income tax liability you may wish to contribute to a Sec. 403(b) retirement plan and reduce your social security base if you are a dual-status minister. In any year you have **no income tax** liability and if you are exempt from paying social security liability (Form 4361), it would be best to invest in a Roth IRA or an unqualified investment.

Tax Planning for the Retired or Semi-retired Minister

Between the ages of 62 and 70, most ministers consider the possibility of semi-retirement. **Between age 62 and 65**, an employer can pay salary and parsonage value and/or allowance up to the limitation shown below and the minister will receive all of his social security benefits. If his earned income is more than the limitation his social security benefits will be reduced by $1 for each $2 of extra earned income. **Between age 65 and 70**, an employer can pay salary and parsonage value and/or allowance up to the limitation shown below and the minister will receive all of his social security benefits. If his earned income is more than the limitation, his social security benefits will be reduced by $1 for each $3 of extra earned income. **At age 70**, when the earnings limitation ends, you can earn $1,000,000 and still draw your full social security benefits! The amount of the limitation is adjusted for inflation every year and is announced in October.

We encourage you to read earlier in this chapter the section entitled, **"Should the Minister's Spouse be on the Payroll?"**

Sign up and receive all benefits available to you. Retired ministers receiving social security benefits while continuing to earn a salary **no longer** have to submit an "Annual Report of Earnings" to Social Security. Social Security will obtain the information from your tax return. Always have your tax advisor examine any Social Security proposed adjustments, often they add your wages from Form 1040, line 7 and your Schedule SE earnings in error.

The amount of earnings a person can receive, before it affects the amount of social security benefits available, are as follows:

	1998	1999	2000
Age 62 to 65	$ 9,120	$ 9,600	$10,080
Age 65 to 70	$14,500	$15,500	$17,000

Public Law 104-121 reflects the following earnings limit increases for ages 65 to 70: 2001 - $25,000; 2002 - $30,000. (Ages 62-65 remain unchanged but will be adjusted by the inflation factor each year.)

Definition of Earned Income

Salary and the value of a home provided and/or the parsonage allowance **ARE** considered "earned income" by social security.

Fringe benefits, an accountable employee business expense reimbursement plan, and non-forfeitable contributions to a salary-reduction TSA **ARE NOT** "earned income" and can be provided in addition to $10,080/$17,000 salary and housing limitation.

Income from pensions, interest, dividends, rents and sale of property **ARE NOT** earned income. You can receive **unlimited** amounts of such **non-earned income** and still receive all of your social security benefits.

Social Security Benefits are Sometimes Taxed

Social security benefits you receive may be taxable in some instances. You will receive Form SSA-1099 showing the total benefits paid to you during the year and the amount of any social security benefits you repaid during the year. For the first threshold of $32,000 ($25,000 for single) the maximum amount of your social security benefits that can be taxable is 50%. For the second threshold of $44,000 ($34,000 for single) the maximum amount of your social security benefits that can be taxable is 85%. The worksheet provided with Form 1040 helps you compute the "modified adjusted gross income", which for the first threshold is 50% of your social security benefits, plus other taxable income, plus tax-exempt interest, less adjustments. If this amount is less than the threshold of $32,000 ($25,000 for single) none of your benefits will be taxed. It is important for married taxpayers to file a joint return. The threshold for married separate returns is -0-. Married separate returns would cause unnecessary tax.

Is Your Social Security Earnings Record Correct?

Because of a new law requiring that all Americans receive an annual statement of potential Social Security benefits, beginning October 1, 1999, the Social Security Administration is launching the largest customized mailing ever undertaken by a Federal agency. They will send a four page annual Social Security Statement to 125 million workers, throughout the year. Workers will automatically receive their statements about three months before their birth month.

It is very important to examine your statement and correct any errors in your account. Anyone can get a copy of their statement by either calling and requesting one or logging onto the internet. Social Security's web site's address is: **http://www.ssa.gov**

Dual-status ministers often experience mistakes in their social security earnings record. The amount of earnings on Form 1040, line 7, is often combined with the social security base on Schedule SE. This mistake can lead to an overstatement of your earnings. If the amount of earnings on Form 1040, line 7, is recorded as your earnings and the parsonage allowance is omitted, your earnings will be understated. Ministers who begin to receive social security benefits while continuing to work often experience problems receiving correct amounts.

CHAPTER FIVE

Overseas Missionaries and Religious Orders

Missionaries Serving Overseas

Missionaries who are U.S. citizens serving overseas in a foreign country are subject to the same U.S. income tax laws as those living in the U.S. All income, worldwide, must be reported on their Form 1040. However, they may qualify for the $74,000 (Increases to $76,000 in 2000) foreign earned income exclusion provided in Sec. 911. Missionaries are considered to be performing ministerial duties when evangelizing, conducting worship, teaching, etc. They are to be treated as dual-status ministers. You may want to re-read Chapter Two for our detailed discussion defining dual-status and the special tax treatment for those who qualify.

When a dual-status minister, serving as a missionary overseas, has an "approved" Form 4361 and is exempt from social security, he is to write "Exempt—Form 4361" on the self-employment line, Form 1040, page 2. Depending upon your age, disability coverage under social security discontinues after becoming exempt if you do not have enough quarters of credit. Overseas missionaries have difficulty obtaining comparable life and disability insurance coverages. If you are considering an overseas ministry, you may wish to choose being covered by social security.

Missionaries who do secular jobs (carpenters, physicians, nurses, pilots, cooks, mechanics, etc.), are regular lay employees. When employed by an American employer they are subject to withholding and matching of social security and medicare tax. When employed by a foreign employer they are subject to that country's equivalent of social security, if they have one.

- ***Statement For Claiming Benefits of Section 911***

Lay employees eligible for the foreign earned income exclusion should sign and submit Form 673 to their employer. It permits the employer to not withhold federal income tax on foreign wages.

- ***Effect of Sec. 911 Foreign Earned Income Exclusion on TSA and IRA Contributions***

According to Reg. 1.403(b)-1(e)(2), foreign earned income counts as includible compensation if an employee wishes to make contributions to a TSA.

According to Reg. 1.219-1(c)(1), for IRA purposes, compensation does not include foreign earned income and/or housing that is excluded from income and contributions to an IRA are not allowed.

- ***Social Security and Binational Agreements***

U.S. Citizens living and working outside of the United States as dual-status ministers are subject to social security regardless of whether their employer is American or foreign. When they are employed by a foreign church or not-for-profit organization or they are independent contractors, they may also be subject to that country's equivalent of social security. The United States has entered into **agreements** with several foreign countries to coordinate social security coverage and taxation. Under these agreements, if your country has entered into one, dual coverage and dual contributions (taxes) for the same work are eliminated.

Independent contractors doing secular jobs, living and working outside of the United States, are subject to social security. The agreements usually eliminates double coverage and double tax for them also.

IRS Publication 54, page 9, gives a list of countries and additional information. We also have copies of the agreements and you may call and ask to consult with our agreement specialist.

- ***Form TD F 90-22.1***

"Report of Foreign Bank and Financial Accounts" should be filed for all missionaries who have a savings or checking account overseas which exceeds $10,000 in aggregate value at any time during the calendar year. The Form TD F 90-22.1 is to be filed **separately** from the Form 1040. It is due by June 30th and is to be sent to: U.S. Department of the Treasury, P.O. Box 32621, Detroit, MI 48232-0621.

Bona Fide Residency and Physical Presence Rules

To qualify for Sec. 911 foreign earned income exclusion and/or foreign housing exclusion, the missionary must be able to satisfy the requirements of either bona fide residency or be physically present in a foreign country or countries for a total of at least 330 days during any period of 12 consecutive months.

To be considered a bona fide resident of a foreign country, you must have intentions to remain overseas for an indefinite stay and to give evidence by words and acts as to the length and nature of your stay. You will not be treated as a bona fide resident of a foreign country if you have made a statement to the authorities of that country that you are not a resident and have been held not subject to its income tax. To establish your bona fide residency in a foreign country you must reside there for an uninterrupted period **which includes an entire tax year**. If you use the calendar year as your tax year, your entire tax year is the period beginning January 1 and ending December 31. The term "uninterrupted period" refers to your bona fide residence and not to your physical presence. Temporary absence for vacations or business trips is allowable.

The physical presence test does not apply to the type of residence you establish, to your intentions about returning, or to the nature and purpose of your stay overseas. It is concerned only with how long you stay in a foreign country or countries. If, during a period of 12 consecutive months, you are physically present in a foreign country 330 full days (approximately 11 months), you meet the physical presence test. ANY period of 12 consecutive months may be used. If 12 months during the middle of the overseas stay contains 330 days of physical presence, you will satisfy the requirement and be able to be exempt for the whole stay overseas.

Discussion of Form 2555 and Form 2555-EZ

The **IRS Publication 54** and **Form 2555 and Form 2555-EZ for 1999** returns will be available after the first of the year. Please obtain your copy from IRS and study it carefully. Form 2555-EZ can be filed if you are a U.S. citizen or resident alien; your income from earned wages/salaries in a foreign country is less than $74,000; you are filing a calendar year return that covers a 12-month period; there are no adjustments to your income such as ½ of self-employment tax deduction; and you are not filing a Schedule C with expenses.

- ***Foreign Earned Income Exclusion***

Exclusion has been available since 1982. The Tax Relief Act of 1997 provides an increase in the threshold. (See table below.) Individuals meeting either the bona fide residency test or the physical presence test, could elect to exclude foreign earned income at the following annual rates:

1987 through 1997	$70,000
1998	$72,000
1999	**$74,000**
2000	$76,000
2001	$78,000
2002 and later years	$80,000

The foreign earned income exclusion **is voluntary**. Generally, your initial choice of the exclusion on Form 2555 must be filed with a timely filed return (including extensions), a return amending a timely filed return, or a late filed return (determined without regard to any extensions) filed within one year from the original due date of the return. The amending of Reg. 1.911-7 now provides a fourth time to make a valid election. If no federal tax is owed after taking into account the foreign earned income exclusion or housing cost amount, an election may be made at anytime later than the times provided above whether or not the IRS has discovered the failure to make the election. The change applies to taxable years beginning after December 31, 1981. This provision had made it very important for missionaries to timely file their initial tax returns. The $75,000/$80,000 exclusion in 1982 and 1983 was denied a taxpayer, an American citizen, who worked abroad and failed to file timely returns. (William J. Faltesek, Docket No. 48522-86, 6-6-89)

Once you choose to exclude your foreign earned income, that choice remains in effect for that year and all later years unless you revoke it. If you revoke your choice for any tax year, you cannot claim the exclusion again for your next 5 tax years without the approval of the IRS. The government charges a fee for this request. In Private Letter Ruling 9625060, 3/28/96, a taxpayer, having revoked his foreign earned income exclusion election for 1993 and 1994 because taxes were higher in the United Kingdom **was granted** permission to re-elect the foreign earned income exclusion for 1995. He had moved to Hong Kong and their tax rate was less than the United Kingdom. Several other private letter rulings have been submitted to the IRS requesting to re-elect Sec. 911 exclusion. They have all received a positive response.

- ***Foreign Housing Exclusion***

In addition to the foreign earned income exclusion, you can separately claim an exclusion or a deduction from gross income for your housing amount if your tax home is in a foreign country and you qualify under either the bona fide residence test or the physical presence test.

For missionaries who earn considerably less than the $74,000 foreign earned income exclusion, it is not advisable for them to choose the foreign housing exclusion. In addition to a complex computation, **if chosen,** the foreign housing exclusion **must be used first** and fully before using the foreign earned income exclusion. In any year that a missionary earns over $74,000, he can initially choose and apply the foreign housing exclusion on a timely filed return by completing the appropriate section on Form 2555. The two exclusions available can be separately chosen and separately revoked. By attaching a statement to the return or an amended return for the first year that you do not wish to claim the exclusion(s), you can revoke either choice for any tax year.

Sec. 911 foreign housing exclusion is unique, and very different from Sec. 107 housing for ministers and Sec. 119 housing. Any year your income exceeds $74,000, take the time to study IRS Publication 54, pages 19-20. Being able to use the foreign earned income exclusion first makes your Form 2555 less complicated.

- ***Vacation Computation***

According to Revenue Ruling 76-191, while home in the U. S., (unless on vacation ONLY), income earned is usually taxable on your federal return. Vacation time earned during the last year preceding your leave can be considered eligible Sec. 911 exclusion. If your mission gives you 6 months vacation (without work) for a four year term, one-fourth, or 45 days is eligible for the exclusion. If you are working and traveling on deputation all of your furlough, all of your leave would be taxable.

To determine the amount of U. S. income you should count the number of days in the U.S., subtract the vacation days, divide the result by 365 days, then multiply that percentage times the annual salary. For a missionary, who usually works a 7 day week, you would count 7 days for each week.

Example:

Days in U.S.	75 days
Less vacation	(21 days)
	54 days
54 ÷ 365 =	14.79%

Taxable income for U.S. – $35,500 X 14.79% = **$5,250.45**

Moving Expense — Overseas

- ***Foreign Moves - Form 3903F***

If you move to a new principal place of work outside the United States and its possessions, it is a "foreign move." If all or part of the income you earn at the new foreign location is excluded under the foreign earned income exclusion, the part of the moving expense that is allocable to the excluded income is not deductible.

Since 1993, both "what" and "where" to deduct moving expenses changed. Qualified moving expenses are an above-the-line deduction subtracted from gross income in arriving at adjusted gross income under Sec. 62(a). More detailed discussion is included in Chapter One.

Qualified moving expenses **are now limited** to the reasonable cost of:

1. Moving household goods and personal effects from the former residence to the new residence; and
2. Traveling, including lodging during the period of travel, from the former residence to the new place of residence. **No meals allowed.**

A special moving rule applies to Form 3903-F: The costs of moving household goods is expanded to include the reasonable expenses of moving household goods and personal effects to and from storage and of storing them for all or part of the time the new workplace continues to be your principal workplace. If you moved in an earlier year and are claiming only storage fees during your absence from the United States, you can simply enter the allowable amount on the moving deduction line, Form 1040, page 1. Next to the amount write "Storage Fees."

- ***Non-Foreign Move—Form 3903***

A move from a foreign country to the U.S. is not a foreign move. The regular moving deduction rules apply. If you permanently retire and your principal place of work and former home were outside the U.S. and its possessions, you do not have to satisfy the 39 work week requirement. You may deduct the move back to the U.S., subject to all of the other requirements and limitations of Form 3903.

When and Where To File As An Overseas Missionary

There is an automatic extension of two months to June 15th for any U.S. citizen with **both their tax home and their abode** outside the U.S. on April 15th. This is an extension of time to file only, tax liability has to be paid by April 15th. If you take advantage of the automatic extension, you are required to attach a statement to your return showing you were residing outside the U.S. on the due date of your return. If additional time is required the regular automatic 4 month extension, Form 4868, can be filed by June 15th for an extra two months of extension.

File Form 2555 or Form 2555-EZ with Form 1040 and send to:

INTERNAL REVENUE SERVICE CENTER
Philadelphia, PA 19255-0207

- ***Special Extensions Of Time For Filing***

A new missionary arriving in an overseas country anytime during the year cannot file Form 2555 or Form 2555-EZ the first year and claim the foreign earned income exclusion. However, after he has established his bona fide residence or met the physical presence test, all of his income is eligible for the special tax treatment from the **date of his arrival.** There are two ways to handle the problem of filing:

1. **File Form 2350** by the due date of your return, requesting an extension of filing your return until after establishing foreign residence. It is necessary to pay any anticipated tax on U.S. income with Form 2350. Then, within 30 days after meeting the residency requirements, file your return along with a copy of the approved Form 2350.
   a. An earlier first year return can often be filed by satisfying the physical presence rules.
   b. After satisfying the bona fide residency rules, it is best to switch to bona fide resident because it does not have to be re-established after a furlough or vacation back in the U.S.
2. (Not the best choice!) File the current year's return and pay tax on all income, including income earned abroad. After meeting the residency requirements, file Form 1040X and Form 2555 or Form 2555-EZ within one year of the due date of the original return to claim a refund of taxes on earnings while overseas.

Independent Missionaries

If a missionary has a sponsoring mission or church, it is correct for that organization to treat the missionary as an employee under the "common law rules." Missionaries who perform ministerial duties and are employed by a foreign mission board or an integral agency of a church are entitled to dual-status treatment. Missionaries who do secular jobs (carpenters, physicians, mechanics, etc.), are regular employees subject to withholding and matching of social security and medicare tax.

When a missionary does not have a sponsoring mission or church, the total gross income may include substantial funds for ministry projects. Entering large expenditures and building projects as Schedule C deductions creates a very high audit exposure. Should an independent missionary be choosen for an audit, foreign IRS personnel are apt to be inexperienced concerning typical ministry endeavors. The experience can become costly, difficult, frustrating and time consuming.

We have included further instructions and recommendations for handling independent religious workers in Chapter Six.

Religious Orders — Two Types

Protestant Religious Orders Described in Sec. 1402(c)(4)

The idea of non-integral agency protestant ministries adopting the status of "religious order" was popular in the late 70's and early 80's. Some were advised to change their by-laws and declare their organization to be a "religious order." The Social Security Amendments Act of 1983, and the mandatory application of social security coverage to employees of not-for-profit organizations made the idea flourish. In order to avoid the cost of withholding and matching social security, several non-integral agency protestant ministries began claiming the status of "religious order." So many requests for determination were received by IRS that they put a freeze on responding to them. During 1985 the IRS responded with letters stating that the question of what constitutes a religious order was under intensive study by the Service and that they would not be able to respond to the requests until their study was completed.

During 1991, IRS issued **Revenue Procedure 91-20, IRB 1991-10**. It sets forth guidelines that will be used by IRS in determining whether an organization is a religious order for federal employment tax purposes. IRS has identified from previous court cases the following characteristics:

1. The organization is described in Sec. 501(c)(3) of the Code.
2. The members of the organization vow to live under a strict set of rules requiring moral and spiritual self-sacrifice and dedication to the goals of the organization at the expense of their material well-being.
3. The members of the organization, after successful completion of the organization's training program and probationary period, make a long-term commitment to the organization (normally more than two years).
4. The organization is, directly or indirectly, under the control and supervision of a church or convention or association of churches, or is significantly funded by a church or convention or association of churches.
5. The members of the organization normally live together as part of a community and are held to a significantly stricter level of moral and religious discipline than that required of lay church members.
6. The members of the organization work or serve full-time on behalf of the religious, educational, or charitable goals of the organization.
7. The members of the organization participate regularly in activities such as public or private prayer, religious study, teaching, care of the aging, missionary work, or church reform or renewal.

Being a 501(c)(3) organization is required. If most of the above characteristics are true, the organization will be treated as a religious order. Considering all the facts and circumstances about an organization it is not necessary that all of the above characteristics be true. In the absence of one or more of the above characteristics, Rev. Proc. 91-20 says that the IRS will contact the organization and carefully consider their views about their status.

We are aware of and have read the IRS's favorable private letter rulings granting Sec. 1402(c)(4) status of religious order to two different organizations during 1992. Several organizations have received favorable private letter rulings affirming their status of a "religious order." (Private Letter Rulings 9322009, 9418012, 9434015, 9448017 and 9630011)

If a non-integral agency ministry wrongly claims the status of a "religious order," the underpayment of payroll taxes could be so overwhelming that the ministry could find it hard to survive. IRS indicates by publishing Rev. Proc. 91-20, that they have a new awareness of this area of tax law.

- ***Information Returns and Proper Tax Treatment for Sec. 1402(c)(4) Religious Orders***

The proper form to report the income paid to a member of a "religious order" is Form W-2. The practice of **issuing Form 1099** to employee-members **is incorrect**. To qualify as an "independent contractor" or a "non-employee" of a religious order would be impossible, due to the amount of control a religious order has over its members.

1. Member, ordained or "the equivalent thereof," doing duties of the ministry. Tax treatment is the same as a dual-status minister, eligible for parsonage allowance, self-employed for

social security purposes and **must timely file Form 4361 to be exempt from social security.** Withholding of income tax is optional, Form W-2 is the proper form to show taxable salary.

2. Member, lay employee of order, performing services required by the order are not eligible for parsonage allowance. Earnings are treated as self-employment for social security purposes and **must timely file Form 4361 to be exempt from social security.** Withholding of income tax is optional, Form W-2 is the proper form to show taxable salary.
3. Non-member lay employees are automatically covered by social security, cannot become exempt, and are to receive a regular Form W-2 with income tax withholding.

Religious Orders Described in Sec. 1402(g)

Sec. 1402(g) describes Religious Orders that are opposed to both private and public insurance. Examples of such orders are the Amish, Quakers and Catholic Monastic Orders. The term "religious order" is not well defined in IRS Code or regulations. In a 1969 tax court case, Eighth Street Baptist Church, Inc. v. U.S., 295 F.Supp. 1400 (D.Kan. 1969), the judge cited Webster's dictionary as his best source of a definition to determine that Eighth Street Baptist Church was not a religious order. Sec. 1402(g)(1)(E) gives the fact that a religious order or sect has to have been in existence at all times since December 31, 1950. In a court case for the year of 1976, a taxpayer argued that this provision was unconstitutional under the first amendment since it discriminates against religious sects not established prior to December 31, 1950. The judge stated that Congress has great latitude in limiting the exemptions by any general standards, (TC Memo 1980-284, Glen A. Ross, Docket No. 3593-79). Sec. 1402(g)(1)(D) states that a religious order must have for a substantial period of time been making reasonable provisions for its dependent members.

- ***Information Returns and Proper Tax Treatment for Sec. 1402(g) Religious Orders***

1. Member, employee working for the order, doing duties required by the order, receives no salary, and has no income tax or social security tax liability, does not have to file any forms.
2. Member, working outside of the order, earnings are given to the order, and duties are the kind that are ordinarily performed by members of the order and they are required to be exercised on the behalf of the religious order as its agent. Examples in Publication 517 indicate that being instructed to be a secretary qualified and being instructed to be a lawyer did not. According to Revenue Ruling 84-13, a psychologist did not qualify either.
   a. If duties qualify, the earnings are not taxable to member and there are no tax liabilities.
   b. If duties do not qualify, even though the order receives the salary, the earnings are taxable to member and subject to federal income tax withholding and social security tax withholding and matching.
3. Member, working outside of the order, self employed doing secular work, profits are subject to regular income tax and self-employment tax. An exemption is available from self-employment tax by filing **Form 4029 at any time.** To be able to file for this exemption, the member must be conscientiously opposed to accepting benefits of **any private or public insurance and waive all rights to ever receive any social security benefits.**
4. Since 1988, members or member partnerships who have filed Form 4029 and are exempt from social security, can employ other members who have also filed Form 4029 and be exempt from withholding and matching social security tax on their wages. An exempt employer will be required to withhold income tax and prepare Form W-2 for exempt employees.
5. Non-member lay employees are automatically covered by social security, cannot become exempt, and are to receive a regular Form W-2 with income tax and social security tax withholding and matching.

CHAPTER SIX

Completed Payroll Reports

Now we are ready for the practical application of all the information presented in the preceding chapters! Though the tax laws are complex and every employer/employee relationship is unique, the examples shown in this Chapter are for the purpose of teaching the simplest approach to designing the best compensation package. **Regardless of what creative label** the employer might call money or property "paid" to an employee, **it is taxable if a section of the Internal Revenue Code does not exclude it.** Generally, the employee will be taxed on all remuneration that is not a qualified ***fringe benefit*** (Chapter One), ***parsonage allowance*** (Chapter Two), or ***reimbursement for professional*** expenses under an accountable plan (Chapter Three). Tax law excludes these categories of a compensation package from federal income tax. Fringe benefits and an accountable reimbursement plan for professional expenses are also excluded from social security and medicare tax.

Our payroll sheets are designed with extra columns for parsonage allowance and TSAs and a section to keep a record of an accountable reimbursement plan. This is a tell and show chapter. You will benefit greatly by studying the filled out sample payroll sheets and reports at the end of the chapter.

Steps in Establishing a Compensation Package

1. **Establish the fringe benefits that will be provided.** The cost of group medical insurance, contributions to a qualified pension plan, premiums for up to $50,000 group term life insurance, etc., generally are to be paid by the employer directly to the companies providing the plans. The employer provided qualified fringe benefits are not to be included on the payroll record, quarterly reports, or in the W-2 at year end.
2. **Establish an accountable reimbursement plan for auto and professional employee business expenses.** Establish a written reimbursement plan for each employee using the suggested wordings in Chapter Three. Employees must "adequately account" their professional expenses to the employer.

   The tax benefits to be gained by establishing an accountable reimbursement plan should convince employers to bear the burden of the "cost of doing ministry business." An employer should be willing to reimburse their employees for all auto and professional expenses over and above their salary. Employers who initially adjust the employee's salary and adopt a "fixed limit", according to two Private Letter Rulings (9822044 and 199916011,) can prior to the start of a calendar year determine the amount the "fixed limit" will be in the succeeding year. Computing the "fixed limit" annually is a welcome relief.

   If the employer provides an auto for an employee, they must have a written plan and follow the IRS regulations to determine how much to include in the employee's income for personal use. Employee must maintain and submit a log of business miles to his employer or 100% of the value will be reportable on Form W-2.
3. **Determine the amount of the cash salary.** You may wish to obtain a copy of "compensation guidelines" provided by denominational handbooks or other organizations.
4. **Designate an adequate portion of salary as parsonage allowance in advance for the dual-status minister.** When a church or integral agency of a church owns the house in which the minister lives, they must designate a portion of his cash compensation as parsonage allowance for the additional home expenses he personally incurs. When a church or integral agency of a church does not provide the home and the minister owns his own home, they must designate a portion of his cash compensation as parsonage allowance for the whole cost of providing the home. Use the "Suggested Wordings" in Chapter Two. The amount of **designated housing allowance**, divided by the number of pay periods is shown on the payroll record as a subtraction and **is not to be shown** as taxable compensation on

the **941 quarterly reports or W-2 at year end**. The minister is responsible to show any unused portion as income on his Form 1040, line 21.

When an employer provides housing and utilities for a lay employee that satisfies all three conditions of Sec. 119, the value is not to be shown on the payroll report, 941 quarterly reports, or W-2 at year end. It is free from federal income tax, social security, and medicare tax. When one of the tests is not satisfied, the value of housing and utilities provided is subject to income tax, social security, and medicare tax and is to be shown as taxable compensation on the payroll reports. In our payroll example below we illustrate Joseph Mop, the janitor, being provided Sec. 119 housing.

Dual-Status Minister - Rev. Snodgrass' Compensation Package

Fringe Benefits Provided:		
Hospital Insurance Premiums	$ 5,520	
Group Term Life Insurance Premiums	$ 420	
Total Cash Compensation		$32,400
*Parsonage Allowance Designated		($18,000)
Contributions to Salary Reduction 403(b) Retirement		($ 2,400)
Taxable Salary on W-2		**$12,000**

* Rev. Snodgrass owns his own home. **The $18,000 parsonage allowance is not to be shown in Box 1 of his W-2.** As we illustrate on his tax return in Chapter 7, he is responsible to show the unused portion of $1,517 as income on Form 1040, line 21. (When the parsonage is owned by the church employer, do not include its value in Box 1 of his W-2.) Rev. Snodgrass will include the $18,000 parsonage allowance on his Schedule SE for social security purposes unless he has an approved Form 4361 exemption.

Mission Community Church adopted an unlimited professional expense reimbursement plan. Upon submitting adequate records to his employer, he received separate checks each month in the amount of his auto and professional expenses of $9,988.

Calculation for Amount of Paycheck: The contributions to the 403(b) retirement will be paid directly to a mutual fund or insurance company by the employer. $32,400 less $2,400 = $30,000 divided by the number of paydays in the year. Our sample payroll sheet illustrates semimonthly pay periods:

$30,000 ÷ 24 = **$1,250.00** per pay check.

Lay Employee - Joseph Mop's Compensation Package

Value of Home & Utilities Provided (Sec. 119)	$ 5,700	
Fringe Benefits Provided:		
Hospital Insurance Premiums	$ 3,970	
Group Term Life Insurance Premiums	$ 276	
Total Cash Compensation		$21,600
Contributions to Salary Reduction 403(b) Retirement		($ 1,200)
Taxable Salary on W-2		**$20,400**

Mission Community Church adopted an unlimited professional expense reimbursement policy for Joseph Mop. Upon submitting adequate records to his employer, he received separate checks each month in the amount of his actual auto and professional expenses, total of $968.25 for the year.

Calculation for Amount of Paycheck: The contributions to the 403(b) retirement will be paid directly to a mutual fund or insurance company by the employer. $21,600 less $1,200 = $20,400 divided by the number of paydays in the year. Our sample payroll sheet illustrates semimonthly pay periods:

$20,400 ÷ 24 = **$ 850.00** per pay check.

Organizations Must File Information Returns!

Gone are the days when an employer can get by with handing the minister a piece of paper stating the amount of money paid for his services during the year. The following quotes and facts are provided with the hope that not-for-profit employers will take heed, ***do what the law requires and avoid*** the frustration of penalties and problems with the IRS.

Who is An Employer?

It is very important that a not-for-profit organization practice responsible payroll accounting in a **business-like manner**. Individuals to whom you make payments for services rendered are not to be given the "choice" of their status treatment. The correct reporting to the IRS of payments for services rendered is very well documented in IRS Publications. Employers have often suffered the consequence of listening to inaccurate opinion or counsel. IRS Publication 15-A "Employer's Supplemental Tax Guide", page 7, states:

> *"Many nonprofit organizations are exempt from income tax. Although they do not have to pay income tax themselves, they must still withhold income tax from the pay of their employees. However, there are special social security, Medicare, and Federal unemployment (FUTA) tax rules that apply to the wages they pay their employees."*

In Chapter One, we discussed fully the "common law rules" that are to be used to determine if an individual who has been paid for services rendered is an employee or an independent contractor. According to **Sec. 3509**, employers who wrongly treat an employee as a non-employee **are liable** for income tax that should have been withheld and the employee's portion of social security tax and medicare tax.

In Chapter One we also discussed the "statutory employee" definition. It is a status limited to four occupational groups and **a status that is not available** for either dual-status ministers or lay employees of a church or organization.

Who Is An Employee?

Payment to janitors, secretaries, paid babysitters, etc., for services rendered, are generally employees when the "common law rules" are applied. **Payment of $100 or more in a year** to a lay employee is subject to withholding and matching of social security and medicare tax. (IRS Publication 15-A, page 7) This threshold of $100 for non-for-profit employers is different than for-profit employer's threshold of $50 per quarter. You must carefully study federal employment tax rules and timely file payroll reports and **Form W-2's**. The sample payroll reports in this chapter will guide you.

Who Is An Independent Contractor?

Payment to guest musicians, evangelists, skilled contractors, and others who provide occasional services usually qualify for "independent contractor" status. At the time of payment for services rendered, have each person provide their social security number on a Form W-9. You are required to prepare **Form 1099** for each "independent contractor" that you paid **$600** or more during the year. Form 1099's are not required for payments to corporations.

Payments to evangelists and guest speakers can be designated as parsonage allowance in advance and you may reimburse them for adequately accounted travel expense receipts. At the time of payment for the engagement have them fill out a Form W-9. **Designated parsonage allowance and reimbursements are not to be shown on Form 1099.** Report the remaining taxable honorarium on Form 1099 if it is $600 or more for the year. If an evangelist or musical group is employed by a corporation, and the check is written to the corporation, a Form 1099 is not required.

Suggestion: There are two types of work most churches pay to have performed, janitorial and yard work, that can be planned to be non-employee engagements. To hire services that advertise in the yellow pages or the classified ads, perform the services for the general public and provide their own equipment, etc., would allow the preparation of Form 1099 and no payroll taxes to be withheld. Most lay staff positions must be correctly treated as employees.

Informational Return Penalties

IRS's emphasis on informational reporting affects everyone, not just not-for-profit corporations. **Computer cross-matching of all informational returns with individuals' tax returns** gives the IRS the ability to detect unreported income. Since 1982 there have been penalties for failure to submit W-2's and 1099's to the IRS. Information return penalties include failure to file an information return, failure to file information returns correctly and on time, failure to file paper forms that are machine readable (must be typed with black ink), and failure to file on magnetic media if filing more than 250 Form W-2's or 50 Form 1099's. For your reading pleasure, the IRS has 123 different tax codes dealing with penalties they can assess various taxpayers! Their current emphasis is on **correct and timely information**. The penalty for failure to file information returns is provided for in **Sec. 6652.**

Sec. 6721 imposes a penalty for any failure to file an information return on time, any failure to include all information required to be shown on the return, or for the inclusion of incorrect information. The amount of the penalty is based on how late the return is filed or when the failure is corrected. If corrected by the 30th day after the due date, the penalty is $15 a return, maximum of $75,000 a year. If filed or corrected more than 30 days late but by August 1, the penalty is $30 a return, maximum of $150,000 a year. If filed after August 1st of any year, the penalty is $50 a return, maximum of $250,000 a year.

Willful Or Intentional Disregard

Willful or intentional disregard causes very severe penalties. An example of a longstanding penalty for intentional disregard of doing payroll taxes from **Sec. 6672, is the 100% penalty.**

> *"Any person required to collect, truthfully account for, and pay over any tax imposed by this title who willfully fails to collect such tax, or truthfully account for and pay over such tax, or willfully attempts in any manner to evade or defeat any such tax or the payment thereof, shall, in addition to other penalties provided by law, be liable to a penalty* ***equal to the total*** *amount of the tax evaded, or not collected, or not accounted for and paid over."*

Late payment penalties and interest are in addition to the above penalties. **Trustees or treasurers** of not-for-profit organizations, whether paid or volunteer, **can be held responsible when** the organization fails to pay the taxes.

It is unfortunate that such severe penalties exist. **It is very important** for an employer to **fulfill the informational return filing requirements** rather than having to go before the board or congregation and ask for funds to be raised to pay penalties and interest that could have been avoided by filing timely returns. A summary judgement was ordered on June 29, 1999 for $5,319,750.27, plus interest and other penalty additions that have accrued after July 26, 1998, in United States v. Indianapolis Baptist Temple, KTC 1999-37 and KTC 1999-396. The debt is the result of not filing and paying payroll tax obligations for the years spanning 1987 through 1992.

Attitude Towards the IRS Should Be One of Cooperation

We recommend that the attitude of any organization towards the IRS or its agents should be one of cooperation. If your organization was not aware of your obligation to withhold income tax and withhold and match social security and medicare tax, it is our position that for all wages paid within the three year statute of limitations, late reports should be filed and taxes paid. It is possible to write a letter and claim "reasonable cause" and lack of knowledge, rather than unwillingness, and have the IRS forgive some or all of the penalties. There will always be interest assessed on the late payments.

To be uncooperative would cause the IRS to suspect your church to be a fraudulent one. Avoid being considered as a "tax protest" church. There are those who are not religious or not actually ministers but become "ordained" by mail and establish not-for-profit churches in their homes for the purpose of "tax avoidance" or "tax protest." As in Tweeddale v Commissioner, 92 T.C. 501, the judge said, "Petitioner was not a lone cowboy riding off on a wild stallion. He paid $1,200 for a set of documents constituting the plan or arrangement, purporting to establish a tax-exempt church with himself as a tax-exempt minister.....a totally merit less claim he abandoned on the eve of trial. Moreover, the organizer of this scheme went to jail for tax crimes as a result of it." The judge cited United States v. Daly, 756 F.2d 1076 (5th Cir. 1985). Daly, who did not himself file Basic Bible Church returns, formed the Basic Bible Church chapters to have the appearance of religious organizations while disseminating information on how to file returns so as to hamper IRS investigation and detection of the tax scheme. The judge further said, "We are bone-tired of seeing the Court's time, respondent's resources, and the national treasury wasted in litigating these phony vow of poverty cases."

If you are aware of anyone involved in this type of "tax protest," ask the IRS for Form 211, report them, and be eligible for up to 10% of tax collected as a reward from the IRS!

How To Prepare Information Returns

The employer is responsible for filing informational reports, not the employee. However, **we recommend that the minister take an active part** in helping the treasurer prepare and timely file required reports. Treasurers hold a very responsible position; consider paying them wages for carrying out their duties. When a new person assumes the responsibility, be sure they are properly informed and taught the importance of timely and correctly filed payroll reports.

Do not hesitate to seek professional accounting help in preparing the informational returns. **The staff at Worth Tax & Financial Service is available** to prepare payroll reports and W-2's for employers.

We would encourage the careful reading and study of the following:

IRS Publication 15, "Employer's Tax Guide"

IRS Publication 15-A, "Employers Supplemental Tax Guide," contains information for exempt organizations and the "common law guidelines"

IRS Publication 393, "1999 Federal Employment Tax Forms," which provide line by line instructions for preparing Forms W-2 and W-3.

These employer publications are automatically sent to you each year. They are sent to all new organizations that file for an identification number. Preprinted 941's and Federal Tax Deposit coupons are also automatically sent to employers. If you need any type of tax forms, call the IRS toll-free number listed in your phone book and they will provide them free. If you have access to the internet, connect to **http://www.irs.gov/prod/forms_pubs/index.html.** IRS publications and forms are available to be downloaded and printed with Adobe Reader! **Efficient :+)**

We will teach you how to prepare the proper payroll forms by example. Rev. Snodgrass and Joseph Mop are employed by Mission Community Church. We have used their sample "compensation packages," shown earlier in this chapter, to prepare the reports. Refer to them often as we give you step by step instructions.

Obtain A Federal Identification Number

Does your organization or church have one? The bank where you have your organization's checking account has required you to furnish them with a Federal Identification Number. It looks like this: 00-0000000, nine digits. It is a Federal Identification Number for federal reports, and is not your state incorporation number or sales tax exempt number.

New churches and existing churches without a number should request one by filing Form SS-4. Call the IRS at the phone number for your state shown on Form SS-4 and be assigned an identification number at the time of your call. After you are assigned a number, mail or fax the completed SS-4 to the IRS. Or send the request to your IRS Service Center and they will assign your church a number in a short period of time.

Withhold Required Taxes

IRS Publication 15-A contains information for employees of exempt organizations. It is important to understand that dual-status ministers and lay employees are treated differently for withholding purposes.

Lay Employees

Their income **IS** subject to income tax withholding and each lay employee must fill out a Form W-4. The status and number of allowances claimed will determine how much income tax is to be withheld. **IRS Publication 15** contains the tables showing how much income tax is required to be withheld. **IRS Publication 15-A** contains the tables showing a combination of income tax, social security tax, and medicare tax withholding.

Joseph Mop's W-4 shows he is married and wishes to claim "0" allowance. Turn to page 46 of IRS Publication 15 (1999) and find his semimonthly pay of $850.00 on the left-hand column. Under the "0" allowance column we see the proper amount to withhold is **$87.00**. As in our sample payroll sheet for Joseph Mop, our payroll software uses the tables for the Percentage Method of withholding and calculated $87.15 withholding.

Their income **IS** subject to social security and medicare tax withholding and matching. 1999 combined rate to be withheld for employees was 7.65%. Employers pay an additional 7.65% when they file Form 941. The rate for 2000 remains the same. **The 7.65% combined rate is made up of 6.2% rate for social security tax and 1.45% rate for medicare.**

The only exception to the above paragraph is for **electing churches**, who have filed **Form 8274** and are exempt **because of religious reasons**, Sec. 3121(w). The election merely **transfers** the social security liability **from the church to the employee**. Churches who desire to be an electing church must file two copies of Form 8274 after they hire employees, but before the first date on which a quarterly employment tax return is due. (See more detailed discussion in Chapter Four.)

Lay employees of churches that have filed Form 8274 are subject to paying social security at the 1999 self-employed rate of 15.3% (less adjustments) on their personal return.

Dual-Status Ministers

Their income **IS NOT** subject to withholding income tax according to Sec. 3401(a)(9). The dual-status minister is to "prepay" his taxes by filing Form 1040ES, Estimated Tax for Individuals. When a dual-status minister prepays his taxes on Form 1040ES, we recommend that he does not prepare Form W-4 for the employer.

Their income **IS NOT** subject to withholding and matching for social security and medicare tax purposes. Sec. 1402(a)(8), an **exception** to the normal employer/employee common law rules, states that the dual-status minister is to be treated as self-employed for social security purposes. A dual-status minister who is conscientiously opposed to or because of religious principles opposed to the acceptance of public insurance based on ministerial service can timely file Form 4361 and become exempt from social security. This is discussed fully in Chapter Four. When the employer is a church or integral agency of a church, **it is NEVER correct** to treat a dual-status minister, doing the duties of a minister, **as an employee** for social security and medicare tax purposes.

- ***Optional Withholding***

When an employer and a dual-status minister agree to optional withholding as the means for prepaying the minister's tax liability, he should prepare a Form W-4. Entering the amount to be withheld each pay period on line 6 will satisfy the requirement that the agreement be written. (Status and number of allowances on line 5 should be left blank.) We recommend that the dual-status minister "estimate" his total tax liability—income tax, social security, and medicare tax; divide it by the number of pay periods (24 if paid semimonthly) and have the employer "withhold" that amount each payday as **federal income tax withholding**. The amount withheld will be shown as a credit in Box 2 of Form W-2.

This option would take the place of the dual-status minister prepaying his taxes on Form 1040ES. Rev. Snodgrass estimated he needed $3,840.00 prepaid and had $160.00 withheld each payday.

$$\$3,840.00 \div 24 = \$160.00$$

His other choice would have been to personally pay 4 estimated tax payments of $960.00 on **Form 1040ES.**

Independent Religious Workers

When an independent religious worker **does not** have a sponsoring mission or church, the total gross income may include substantial funds for ministry projects. Entering large expenditures and building projects as Schedule C deductions creates a very high audit exposure. Should an independent minister/missionary be chosen for an audit, foreign IRS personnel are apt to be inexperienced concerning typical ministry endeavors. The communication between the taxpayer and the IRS agent can be difficult, frustrating, and time consuming.

The **ideal solution** to the Schedule C problem for the independent religious worker is **to establish an employer/employee relationship with a church** in the U.S.

Every independent religious worker or missionary needs to find a supporting organization or church to be willing to function as his/her employer. A carefully planned compensation plan with fringe benefits, designated parsonage allowance, an accountable reimbursement plan, and salary will provide the best tax advantages and **reduce audit exposure.** A church checking account should be set up with the religious worker having signature privileges. **The religious worker then advises all of his/her supporters to make their checks payable to the church.** As the religious worker pays for "work projects" and employee business expenses, they become legitimate church ministry expenses of the organization. Copies of all of the financial transactions and detailed receipts should be submitted to the sponsoring church.

The income the religious worker receives for his personal salary is recorded on a payroll record and included on the church's quarterly Form 941 and a **Form W-2 at year end**. The religious worker's uncomplicated Form 1040 will reflect only his true personal earnings. If the religious worker qualifies for dual-status treatment, he will be responsible for his own social security on Schedule SE the same as any dual-status minister employed by a church or integral agency of a church. If he does not qualify for dual-status treatment, the support received can be used to provide the necessary social security and medicare tax withholding and matching.

Prepare a Payroll Sheet for each Employee

Employers are responsible for accurate recording of the salary, deductions, and net pay for each individual employee. Computers are wonderful replacements of manual payroll! Most payroll software programs will allow modifications to handle the dual-status minister and the employee of "an electing church."

We have created and have available manual "Payroll Sheets" that contain extra columns needed to show parsonage allowance and TSAs and provides a section to keep a record of the professional business expense reimbursements.

1. Begin entering a paycheck on the "Payroll Sheet" by entering the total cash salary (including parsonage allowance) in the "total" column in the middle. Also enter in this column: a bonus or love gift, salary to offset social security cost, any taxable fringe benefits, etc., as they are paid to the employee.
2. The columns to the right of the "total" column allow you to show income tax, social security tax, medicare tax, state income tax, and local income tax deductions. A dual-status minister who "prepays" his federal taxes on Form 1040ES and state taxes on the appropriate state forms will not use these columns.
3. A column to the left of the "total" column allows you to subtract parsonage allowance for the dual-status minister. The parsonage allowance of $18,000 for Rev. Snodgrass is divided by 24 to arrive at the semimonthly amount of $750.00.
4. A column to the left of the "total" column allows you to subtract contributions to a Tax Sheltered Account. TSA contributions are subject to social security and medicare tax withholding and matching for the lay employee according to Revenue Ruling 65-208. They are not subject to social security on Schedule SE for the dual-status employee according to Revenue Ruling 68-395. The total contribution is to be entered as a memo on Form W-2, Box 13.
5. Use the right hand section to record the checks written to reimburse an employee for adequately accounted employee business expenses. Study Chapter Three and **be sure you have adopted a written reimbursement plan** that satisfies the IRS Regulation 1.62-2 that became effective 1-1-91.

Chart of Where to Show Transactions

Study of our "**Chart of Where to Show Transactions**", shown on page 95. It will guide you as to what portions of the compensation package you are required to include and what portions you are not required to include on the payroll reports. The payroll sheet's "total" column, for each employee, should include any item from the chart with a "yes" in the "taxable income" column.

- ***Use A Blank "Payroll Sheet" As A Summary***

It is important that your "payroll sheets," Form 941's (all four quarters), and the W-2's at year end **reconcile or balance.** Use a blank "Payroll Sheet" as a summary of monthly or quarterly totals if you have several employees. IRS's computer will automatically bill additional tax or inquire as to the reason if there are errors. It is our experience that it takes **a LONG TIME to correct payroll report problems.**

Make Payroll Tax Deposits as Required

The amount of payroll taxes you owe determines the frequency of deposits. You owe these taxes when you pay the wages. There are penalties for making late deposits. When you make a payroll tax deposit with Form 8109, the bank electronically transmits your payment to the IRS Service Center that day.

There are two deposit schedules—monthly or semiweekly—for determining when you deposit taxes. The IRS will notify you each November whether you are a monthly or semiweekly depositor for the coming calendar year. This determination is made based on the aggregate amount of employment taxes reported during a "look back" period. The regulations define a look back period as the twelve-month period ending on the preceding June 30th.

Combine federal income tax withheld with total amount of social security and medicare tax to be paid (15.3%) to determine total liability for each period.

- ***Underpayment of Deposits Penalty***

It is important to make timely deposits for payroll taxes. The applicable percentage of penalty for late payment in Sec. 6656 is (1) 2% if not more than 5 days late, (2) 5% if not more than 15 days late, and (3) 10% if more than 15 days late. It is possible to have the penalty waived if it occurs during the 1st quarter that a deposit was required.

- ***$1,000 Rule, Since July 1, 1998 (threshold increased from $500)***

If an employer accumulates less than $1,000 tax liability for the quarter, no deposit is needed and payment can be made with the tax return for the quarter. Form 941, line 17, is to be left blank.

- ***Monthly Rule***

An employer is a monthly depositor if the aggregate amount of employment taxes reported for the look back period is $50,000 or less. A monthly depositor must deposit employment taxes for payments made during a calendar month by the 15th day of the following month.

- ***Semiweekly Rule***

An employer is a semiweekly depositor if the aggregate amount of employment taxes reported for the look back period is more than $50,000. Under the semiweekly deposit rule, those paying wages on Wednesday, Thursday, and/or Friday must deposit employment taxes by the next Wednesday, while those paying wages on Saturday, Sunday, Monday, and/or Tuesday are required to deposit employment taxes on the following Friday.

If the total accumulated tax reaches $100,000 or more on any given day, it must be deposited by the next banking day.

- ***How To Make A Deposit***

Use the Federal Tax Deposit Coupons, Form 8109, to make the deposits if you are a monthly depositor. Write the amount due on the coupon, indicate it is 941 tax liability and which quarter is being paid. Write the check, paid to the order of your bank, and take it to the bank and ask for a receipt.

The Electronic Federal Tax Payment System (EFTPS) requires all employers with $50,000 annual payroll tax after July 1, 1999, to make electronic deposits. When you are required to make deposits by EFT and fail to do so, you are subject to a 10% penalty. All employers are encouraged to voluntarily participate.

Mission Community Church's Form 941 for the 4th quarter shows the monthly liabilities on line 17, Monthly Summary Record of Federal Tax Liability section. **We computed the monthly liabilities as follows:**

Joseph's Social Security tax - $1,800.00 X 12.4%=	$ 223.20
Joseph's Medicare Tax - $1,800.00 X 2.9% =	52.20
Rev. Snodgrass' Federal Tax	320.00
Joseph's Federal Tax	174.30
October Total	**$ 769.70**
Joseph's taxable wage - $1,800.00 X 12.4% =	$ 223.20
Joseph's Medicare Tax - $1,800.00 X 2.9% =	52.20
Rev. Snodgrass' Federal Tax	320.00
Joseph's Federal Tax	174.30
November Total	**$ 769.70**
Joseph's taxable wage - $1800.00 X 12.4 =	$ 223.20
Joseph's Medicare Tax - $1800.00 X 2.9% =	52.20
Rev. Snodgrass' Federal Tax	320.00
Joseph's Federal Tax	174.30
December Total	**$ 769.70**

Prepare Quarterly Reports

- ***Form 941 - Instructions With Social Security***

LINE 2 will include taxable salaries of both dual-status ministers and lay employees from the extreme left-hand column of the "Payroll Sheets".

LINE 3 Enter the income tax you withheld and all optional withholding for dual-status employees.

LINE 6a will only include taxable salaries (including TSA contributions) of lay employees. In our 1999 example, the employee's withheld social security tax of 6.2% and the employer's matching portion 6.2% is combined for a total tax of 12.4%. The 2000 rate will be the same.

LINE 7a will only include taxable salaries (including TSA contributions) of lay employees. In our 1999 example, the employee's withheld medicare tax of 1.45% and the employer's matching portion 1.45% is combined for a total tax of 2.9%. The 2000 rate will be the same.

LINE 15 undeposited taxes due must be less than $1,000 or you will be billed up to a 10% penalty for not making a payroll tax deposit at your local bank.

- ***Form 941 - Instructions Without Social Security - Filed Form 8274***

If an existing church filed Form 8274 by October 31, 1984 (a new church by the first date on which a quarterly tax return would be due), and for religious reasons became exempt from withholding and matching social security, they should use **Form 941 and mark the box** provided on line 8. Their employees will be liable for paying social security and medicare tax at the combined rate of 15.3% (less adjustments) on their personal Schedule SE for 1999.

LINE 2 will include taxable salaries of both dual-status ministers and lay employees from the extreme left-hand column of the "Payroll Sheet".

LINE 3 Enter the income tax you withheld, all optional withholding for dual-status employees and additional withholding for lay employees' social security liability.

LINE 6a Leave blank - does not apply to electing churches.

LINE 7a Leave blank - does not apply to electing churches.

LINE 8 Mark the check box

LINE 15 undeposited taxes due must be less than $1,000 or you will be billed up to a 10% penalty for not making a deposit at your local bank.

- ***Due Dates for Quarterly Reports***

January, February, and March .... due on April 30th
April, May, and June .... due on July 31st
July, August, and September .... due on October 31st
October, November, and December ... due on January 31st.

- ***When 941 Reports Are Not Necessary***

Employers who withhold income tax on wages, or who must pay social security or Medicare tax, must file Form 941 quarterly. If there is no liability, the IRS does not require you to file Form 941. When a church employer has only dual-status employees and are not withholding income tax, no quarterly Form 941 is required. IRS computers are programmed to look at lines 3, 6a, and 7 and cross match tax liabilities with the annual Form W-3.

Always report the taxable salaries for a dual-status employee on Form W-2 annually.

Prepare Year End Reports

Form W-3 and Copy A of all Form W-2's are to be sent to the Social Security Administration. All Forms W-2 and W-3 are processed at the Wilkes-Barre Data Operations Center. Since Copy A is imaged and character recognized by machines, **they must be typed with black ink.** Do not use script type and make no white outs or strike overs. Make all dollar entries without the dollar sign and comma but with the decimal point (00000.00). Show the cents portion of the money amounts. Specific line by line instructions are given in IRS Publication 393 for the preparation of the W-3 and the W-2's. If a box **does not apply,** instructions say to **leave it blank.** A dual-status minister's W-2 **must not** have any entry in **Boxes 3, 4, 5, and 6.** If the tax liability figures on the W-3 do not reconcile with the tax liability figures that have been reported quarterly on the 941, you will receive a computer print-out from the IRS asking why they are different and a billing of tax liability they think you owe.

Form 941's, Line 2 wages should = W-2's, Box 1 (but are not cross-matched by IRS)
Form 941's, Line 3 tax should = W-2's, Box 2
Form 941's, Line 6a wages should = W-2's, Box 3
Form 941's, Line 6b tax should = W-2's, Box 4 X 2
Form 941's, Line 7a wages should = W-2's, Box 5
Form 941's, Line 7b tax should = W-2's, Box 6 X 2 (odd cents okay)

Year-end reports are to be prepared by January 31st. Employees are to be given their W-2 copies by January 31st. You have until February 28th to actually send Copy A of the W-2 to the Social Security Administration. Some employers have given a W-2 to their employee, then failed to send Copy A to the Social Security Administration. **Please send Copy A to the government** so they can cross match it with your employees' returns. Avoid "failure to file" penalties!

We feel it will be helpful to list a few of the entries that are typical for religious workers. Enter appropriate codes using capital letters, leave one space blank after the code and enter the dollar amount on the same line. Use decimal points but not dollar signs or commas.

Box 13: C 230 ($230 premium for over $50,000 group term life insurance)
D 1200 ($1,200 elective deferral to 401(k) plan)
E 1200 ($1,200 elective deferral to 403(b) plan)
L 3100 ($4,000 reimbursement for 10,000 miles @ 40¢, enter $900 in Box 1 @31¢)
P 825 ($825 reimbursement for qualified moving expenses)
S 1200 ($1,200 salary reduction contributions to 408(p) SIMPLE plan)
No Entry ($3,100 reimbursement for 10,000 miles @ 31¢)
No Entry (All reimbursements with accountable plan at IRS rates or actual)

Box 14: You may use this box for any other information you want to give your employee. Please label each item. Examples are parsonage allowance designated, moving expenses paid, or reminder for employee of an electing church to pay S.S. on Form SE.

Box 10: Show total amount of dependent care benefits paid or incurred by you for your employee.

Box 12: Show total value of taxable fringe benefits, that are also shown in Box 1, as taxable, such as value of personal use of employer owned auto.

State Tax Withholding

Call your State Department and ask for materials and instructions for withholding the proper amount of state tax for your employees. Some states require that you withhold state tax for the dual-status minister as well as the lay employee.

Unemployment Taxes

Not-for-profit employers are not subject to Federal Unemployment Taxes. IRS Publication 15-A, page 7, states this fact. Most states do not require not-for-profit employers to pay state unemployment tax. Consult with your state unemployment office to be sure.

Workmen's Compensation Insurance

Most states require not-for-profit employers to provide Workmen's Compensation Insurance coverage for all employees. Consult with an insurance professional in your state to be sure.

Form I-9 - Employment Eligibility Verification

The Immigration Reform and Control Act of 1986 requires all employers to examine the applicant's documents proving identity and eligibility to work in the United States and complete Form I-9 **before hiring the applicant**. The law says that we cannot hire an alien if we know that the alien is not authorized to work in the U.S. The Form I-9 is not an IRS form, but can be obtained from the U.S. Department of Justice, Immigration and Naturalization Service (INS), Washington, D.C. 20402.

The employer keeps Form I-9 for possible audit. Fines for non-compliance are from $100 to $1,000 per employee for failure to maintain the necessary paperwork. Fines for hiring illegal aliens are from $250 to $10,000 per individual illegally employed.

New Hire Reporting Requirements

Since October 1,1997, within a few business days of a new employee's date of hire (20 days in Indiana), all employers are to submit to their state unemployment department a report containing the following information: (1) the new employee's name, address and social security number; and (2) the employer's name, address and federal tax identification number. The employer may submit the report by conveying to the department a copy of the new employee's W-4 form or an alternative scannable W-4.

How To Correct Information Returns

The IRS provides Form W-2c, Form W-3c and Form 941C as the means of correcting mistakes on previously filed information returns. It is important to correct returns when you discover a mistake. There are detailed line by line instructions for you to follow in their preparation.

Annual Form 1096 and Form 1099's

Prepare Form 1096 and Form 1099's for payments to evangelists, musicians and contractors whom you paid more than $600. They are required to be given to the recipients by January 31 and sent to your IRS Service Center by February 28th. You may be required to prepare and file Form 1099-INT for interest of $10 or more paid on bonds or loans from individuals. You may be required to prepare and file Form 1099 Misc for rents paid.

Chart of Where to Show Transactions

For a dual-status employee, leave Form W-2, Boxes 3 and 5 blank.

	Type of Transaction	*Taxable Income Box 1, W-2	Lay Employee FICA & Medicare Box 3 & 5, W-2	**Dual-Status Sch. SE Line 2	Show on Sch. C	Not to be shown anywhere	Deducted on Form 1040
INCOME	Salary, Dual-status minister	Yes		Yes			
	Soc. Security paid by employer, dual-status	Yes		Yes			
	Salary, Lay employee	Yes	Yes				
	Salary, Lay employee of electing church	Yes	No	***Yes			
	Bonus or gift from employer	Yes	Yes	Yes			
	Professional income			Yes	Yes		
	Gift from relative, etc	No	No	No		Yes	
FRINGES	Employer qualified pension-401a,SEP,403b	No	No	No		Yes	
	Premium for $50,000 term life insurance	No	No	No		Yes	
	Premium for over $50,000 term life insurance	Yes	Yes	Yes			
	Permanent life, employee's beneficiary	Yes	Yes	Yes			
	Medical insurance paid by employer	No	No	No		Yes	
	Qualified medical reimbursement plan	No	No	No		Yes	
	Qualified moving reimbursement	No	No	No		Yes	
	Nonqualified moving reimbursement	Yes	Yes	Yes			
	Employee TSA, 403(b) lay employee	No	Yes				
	Employee TSA, 403(b) dual-status	No		No			
ADJ	Employee payments to an IRA						1040, Ln. 23
	Self-employed Keogh payments						1040, Ln. 29
	Unreimbursed qualified moving						1040, Ln. 26
HOUSING	Value of home provided, dual-status	No		Yes			
	Parsonage Allowance, dual-status	No		Yes			
	Value of home provided, lay employee (Sec.119 qualifications met)	No	No				
	Value of home provided, lay employee (Sec. 119 qualifications not met)	Yes	Yes				
PROF EXP	Auto reimbursement	No	No	No		Yes	
	Employer provided auto, personal use	Yes	Yes	Yes			
	Travel and professional reimbursement	No	No	No		Yes	
	Expense allowance without adequate accounting to employer	Yes	Yes	Deduct			Sch. A, Ln. 20
	Unreimbursed business expenses			Deduct			Sch. A, Ln. 20

* Amounts in this column are to be shown in left-hand column of payroll sheets, line 2 of Form 941, and Box 1 of W-2.

** If a dual-status employee is exempt because he has filed Form 4361, then he is to disregard the column for Social Security and write "Exempt—Form 4361" on the self-employment line of Form 1040, Page 2.

*** Lay employees of electing church report wage on Section B, Part I, Line 5a of Sch. SE

EMPLOYEE'S EARNINGS RECORD

YEAR 1999 DATE HIRED ______ DATE TERMINATED ______

NAME H. James Snodgrass
ADDRESS 2309 E. Smith Street
CITY South Bend STATE IN ZIP 46617
SOCIAL SECURITY NUMBER 483-12-0000

FILING STATUS
MARRIED X SINGLE ______
FEDERAL–NUMBER OF EXEMPTIONS N/A
STATE–NUMBER OF EXEMPTIONS N/A

UNORDAINED ☐
ORDAINED ☒
PARSONAGE DESIGNATED $18,000

Quarter	Month	Payroll Period Ending	*Taxable Salary & Allowances	Parsonage	TSA	Total	Federal W/H Tax	Social Security Tax	Medicare Tax	State W/H Tax	Local W/H Tax	Net Pay	Reimbursement Check	Reimbursement Miles	Reimbursement Amount
FIRST QUARTER	JAN	1	500.00	750.00	100.00	1350.00	160.00			30.00	2.50	1057.50			
		15	500.00	750.00	100.00	1350.00	160.00			30.00	2.50	1057.50			
		Monthly	1000.00	1500.00	200.00	2700.00	320.00			60.00	5.00	2115.00	1075	1842	671.67
	FEB	1	500.00	750.00	100.00	1350.00	160.00			30.00	2.50	1057.50			
		15	500.00	750.00	100.00	1350.00	160.00			30.00	2.50	1057.50			
		Monthly	1000.00	1500.00	200.00	2700.00	320.00			60.00	5.00	2115.00	1080	2231	1307.86
	MAR	1	500.00	750.00	100.00	1350.00	160.00			30.00	2.50	1057.50			
		15	500.00	750.00	100.00	1350.00	160.00			30.00	2.50	1057.50			
		Monthly	1000.00	1500.00	200.00	2700.00	320.00			60.00	5.00	2115.00	1085	2269	1234.56
		Quarterly	3000.00	4500.00	600.00	8100.00	960.00			180.00	15.00	6345.00			
TOTAL TO DATE			3000.00	4500.00	600.00	8100.00	960.00			180.00	15.00	6345.00			
SECOND QUARTER	APR	1	500.00	750.00	100.00	1350.00	160.00			30.00	2.50	1057.50			
		15	500.00	750.00	100.00	1350.00	160.00			30.00	2.50	1057.50			
		Monthly	1000.00	1500.00	200.00	2700.00	320.00			60.00	5.00	2115.00	1093	1732	851.32
	MAY	1	500.00	750.00	100.00	1350.00	160.00			30.00	2.50	1057.50			
		15	500.00	750.00	100.00	1350.00	160.00			30.00	2.50	1057.50			
		Monthly	1000.00	1500.00	200.00	2700.00	320.00			60.00	5.00	2115.00	1097	1388	625.15
	JUNE	1	500.00	750.00	100.00	1350.00	160.00			30.00	2.50	1057.50			
		15	500.00	750.00	100.00	1350.00	160.00			30.00	2.50	1057.50			
		Monthly	1000.00	1500.00	200.00	2700.00	320.00			60.00	5.00	2115.00	1104	1673	952.07
		Quarterly	3000.00	4500.00	600.00	8100.00	960.00			180.00	15.00	6345.00			
TOTAL TO DATE			6000.00	9000.00	1200.00	16200.00	1920.00			360.00	30.00	12690.00			
THIRD QUARTER	JULY	1	500.00	750.00	100.00	1350.00	160.00			30.00	2.50	1057.50			
		15	500.00	750.00	100.00	1350.00	160.00			30.00	2.50	1057.50			
		Monthly	1000.00	1500.00	200.00	2700.00	320.00			60.00	5.00	2115.00	1110	1558	756.65
	AUG	1	500.00	750.00	100.00	1350.00	160.00			30.00	2.50	1057.50			
		15	500.00	750.00	100.00	1350.00	160.00			30.00	2.50	1057.50			
		Monthly	1000.00	1500.00	200.00	2700.00	320.00			60.00	5.00	2115.00	1116	2652	1064.35
	SEPT	1	500.00	750.00	100.00	1350.00	160.00			30.00	2.50	1057.50			
		15	500.00	750.00	100.00	1350.00	160.00			30.00	2.50	1057.50			
		Monthly	1000.00	1500.00	200.00	2700.00	320.00			60.00	5.00	2115.00	1123	1227	513.34
		Quarterly	3000.00	4500.00	600.00	8100.00	960.00			180.00	15.00	6345.00			
TOTAL TO DATE			9000.00	13500.00	1800.00	24300.00	2880.00			540.00	45.00	19035.00			
FOURTH QUARTER	OCT	1	500.00	750.00	100.00	1350.00	160.00			30.00	2.50	1057.50			
		15	500.00	750.00	100.00	1350.00	160.00			30.00	2.50	1057.50			
		Monthly	1000.00	1500.00	200.00	2700.00	320.00			60.00	5.00	2115.00	1130	1332	694.86
	NOV	1	500.00	750.00	100.00	1350.00	160.00			30.00	2.50	1057.50			
		15	500.00	750.00	100.00	1350.00	160.00			30.00	2.50	1057.50			
		Monthly	1000.00	1500.00	200.00	2700.00	320.00			60.00	5.00	2115.00	1137	1578	797.08
	DEC	1	500.00	750.00	100.00	1350.00	160.00			30.00	2.50	1057.50			
		15	500.00	750.00	100.00	1350.00	160.00			30.00	2.50	1057.50			
		Monthly	1000.00	1500.00	200.00	2700.00	320.00			60.00	5.00	2115.00	1143	1397	519.09
		Quarterly	3000.00	4500.00	600.00	8100.00	960.00			180.00	15.00	6345.00			
TOTAL TO DATE			12000.00	18000.00	2400.00	32400.00	3840.00			720.00	60.00	25380.00		20879	9988.00

*Amount to be shown on Form 941, Line 2 and Form W-2, Box 1. Carefully study Chapter Six in "Income Tax Guide for Ministers and Religious Workers".

EMPLOYEE'S EARNINGS RECORD

YEAR 1999 DATE HIRED ______ DATE TERMINATED ______

NAME Joseph Mop
ADDRESS 1621 E. Jones Street
CITY South Bend STATE IN ZIP 46617
SOCIAL SECURITY NUMBER 403-19-0000

FILING STATUS
MARRIED X SINGLE ______
FEDERAL–NUMBER OF EXEMPTIONS 0
STATE–NUMBER OF EXEMPTIONS 0

UNORDAINED ☒
ORDAINED ☐
PARSONAGE DESIGNATED $ ______

Quarter / Month	Payroll Period Ending	*Taxable Salary & Allowances	Parsonage	TSA	Total	Federal W/H Tax	Social Security Tax	Medicare Tax	State W/H Tax	Local W/H Tax	Net Pay	Reimbursement Check	Reimbursement Miles	Reimbursement Amount
FIRST QUARTER – JAN	1	850.00		50.00	900.00	87.15	55.80	13.05	28.90	4.25	660.85			
	15	850.00		50.00	900.00	87.15	55.80	13.05	28.90	4.25	660.85			
	Monthly	1700.00		100.00	1800.00	174.30	111.60	26.10	57.80	8.50	1321.70	1076	210	91.06
FEB	1	850.00		50.00	900.00	87.15	55.80	13.05	28.90	4.25	660.85			
	15	850.00		50.00	900.00	87.15	55.80	13.05	28.90	4.25	660.85			
	Monthly	1700.00		100.00	1800.00	174.30	111.60	26.10	57.80	8.50	1321.70	1081	229	86.41
MAR	1	850.00		50.00	900.00	87.15	55.80	13.05	28.90	4.25	660.85			
	15	850.00		50.00	900.00	87.15	55.80	13.05	28.90	4.25	660.85			
	Monthly	1700.00		100.00	1800.00	174.30	111.60	26.10	57.80	8.50	1321.70	1086	189	89.77
	Quarterly	5100.00		300.00	5400.00	522.90	334.80	78.30	173.40	25.50	3965.10			
TOTAL TO DATE		5100.00		300.00	5400.00	522.90	334.80	78.30	173.40	25.50	3965.10			
SECOND QUARTER – APR	1	850.00		50.00	900.00	87.15	55.80	13.05	28.90	4.25	660.85			
	15	850.00		50.00	900.00	87.15	55.80	13.05	28.90	4.25	660.85			
	Monthly	1700.00		100.00	1800.00	174.30	111.60	26.10	57.80	8.50	1321.70	1094	174	70.46
MAY	1	850.00		50.00	900.00	87.15	55.80	13.05	28.90	4.25	660.85			
	15	850.00		50.00	900.00	87.15	55.80	13.05	28.90	4.25	660.85			
	Monthly	1700.00		100.00	1800.00	174.30	111.60	26.10	57.80	8.50	1321.70	1098	154	91.58
JUNE	1	850.00		50.00	900.00	87.15	55.80	13.05	28.90	4.25	660.85			
	15	850.00		50.00	900.00	87.15	55.80	13.05	28.90	4.25	660.85			
	Monthly	1700.00		100.00	1800.00	174.30	111.60	26.10	57.80	8.50	1321.70	1105	298	106.42
	Quarterly	5100.00		300.00	5400.00	522.90	334.80	78.30	173.40	25.50	3965.10			
TOTAL TO DATE		10200.00		600.00	10800.00	1045.80	669.60	156.60	346.80	51.00	7930.20			
THIRD QUARTER – JULY	1	850.00		50.00	900.00	87.15	55.80	13.05	28.90	4.25	660.85			
	15	850.00		50.00	900.00	87.15	55.80	13.05	28.90	4.25	660.85			
	Monthly	1700.00		100.00	1800.00	174.30	111.60	26.10	57.80	8.50	1321.70	1111	154	99.25
AUG	1	850.00		50.00	900.00	87.15	55.80	13.05	28.90	4.25	660.85			
	15	850.00		50.00	900.00	87.15	55.80	13.05	28.90	4.25	660.85			
	Monthly	1700.00		100.00	1800.00	174.30	111.60	26.10	57.80	8.50	1321.70	1117	120	54.80
SEPT	1	850.00		50.00	900.00	87.15	55.80	13.05	28.90	4.25	660.85			
	15	850.00		50.00	900.00	87.15	55.80	13.05	28.90	4.25	660.85			
	Monthly	1700.00		100.00	1800.00	174.30	111.60	26.10	57.80	8.50	1321.70	1124	184	73.36
	Quarterly	5100.00		300.00	5400.00	522.90	334.80	78.30	173.40	25.50	3965.10			
TOTAL TO DATE		15300.00		900.00	16200.00	1568.70	1004.40	234.90	520.20	76.50	11895.30			
FOURTH QUARTER – OCT	1	850.00		50.00	900.00	87.15	55.80	13.05	28.90	4.25	660.85			
	15	850.00		50.00	900.00	87.15	55.80	13.05	28.90	4.25	660.85			
	Monthly	1700.00		100.00	1800.00	174.30	111.60	26.10	57.80	8.50	1321.70	1131	145	78.50
NOV	1	850.00		50.00	900.00	87.15	55.80	13.05	28.90	4.25	660.85			
	15	850.00		50.00	900.00	87.15	55.80	13.05	28.90	4.25	660.85			
	Monthly	1700.00		100.00	1800.00	174.30	111.60	26.10	57.80	8.50	1321.70	1138	129	66.33
DEC	1	850.00		50.00	900.00	87.15	55.80	13.05	28.90	4.25	660.85			
	15	850.00		50.00	900.00	87.15	55.80	13.05	28.90	4.25	660.85			
	Monthly	1700.00		100.00	1800.00	174.30	111.60	26.10	57.80	8.50	1321.70	1144	139	60.31
	Quarterly	5100.00		300.00	5400.00	522.90	334.80	78.30	173.40	25.50	3965.10			
TOTAL TO DATE		20400.00		1200.00	21600.00	2091.60	1339.20	313.20	693.60	102.00	15860.40		2125	968.25

*Amount to be shown on Form 941, Line 2 and Form W-2, Box 1. Carefully study Chapter Six in "Income Tax Guide for Ministers and Religious Workers".

Example, Nonelecting Church

Form **941** (Rev. January 1999) Department of the Treasury Internal Revenue Service

Employer's Quarterly Federal Tax Return

▶ See separate instructions for information on completing this return.
Please type or print.

Enter state code for state in which deposits were made ONLY if different from state in address to the right (see page 2 of instructions). ▶ ☐

Name, Trade name, if any: Mission Community Church
Address and ZIP code: 1620 E. Jones Street, South Bend, IN 46617
Date quarter ended: 12/31/99
EIN: 35-2938279

OMB No. 1545-0029 | T | FF | FD | FP | I | T

If address is different from prior return, check here ▶ ☐ IRS Use

If you do not have to file returns in the future, check here ▶ ☐ and enter date final wages paid ▶
If you are a seasonal employer, see **Seasonal employers** on page 1 of the instructions and check here ▶ ☐

Line	Description		Amount
1	Number of employees in the pay period that includes March 12th ▶	1	
2	Total wages and tips, plus other compensation	2	8100.00
3	Total income tax withheld from wages, tips, and sick pay	3	1482.90
4	Adjustment of withheld income tax for preceding quarters of calendar year	4	
5	Adjusted total of income tax withheld (line 3 as adjusted by line 4 -- see instructions)	5	1482.90
6	Taxable social security wages — 6a 5400.00 x 12.4% (.124) =	6b	669.60
	Taxable social security tips — 6c 0.00 x 12.4% (.124) =	6d	0.00
7	Taxable Medicare wages and tips — 7a 5400.00 x 2.9% (.029) =	7b	156.60
8	Total social security and Medicare taxes (add lines 6b, 6d, and 7b). Check here if wages are not subject to social security and/or Medicare tax ▶ ☐	8	826.20
9	Adjustment of social security and Medicare taxes (see instructions for required explanation) Sick Pay $ ___ ± Fractions of Cents $ ___ ± Other $ ___ =	9	
10	Adjusted total of social security and Medicare taxes (line 8 as adjusted by line 9 -- see instructions)	10	826.20
11	**Total taxes** (add lines 5 and 10)	11	2309.10
12	Advance earned income credit (EIC) payments made to employees	12	
13	Net taxes (subtract line 12 from line 11). **If $1000 or more, this must equal line 17, column (d) below (or line D of Schedule B (Form 941))**	13	2309.10
14	Total deposits for quarter, including overpayment applied from a prior quarter	14	2309.10
15	**Balance due** (subtract line 14 from line 13). See instructions	15	0.00
16	**Overpayment**, if line 14 is more than line 13, enter excess here ▶ $ ___ and check if to be: ☐ Applied to next return OR ☐ Refunded.		

- **All filers:** If line 13 is less than $1000, you need not complete line 17 or Schedule B (Form 941).
- **Semiweekly schedule depositors:** Complete Schedule B (Form 941) and check here ▶ ☐
- **Monthly schedule depositors:** Complete line 17, columns (a) through (d), and check here ▶ ☒

17 Monthly Summary of Federal Tax Liability. Do not complete if you were a semiweekly schedule depositor.

(a) First month liability	(b) Second month liability	(c) Third month liability	(d) Total liability for quarter
769.70	769.70	769.70	2309.10

Sign Here — Under penalties of perjury, I declare that I have examined this return, including accompanying schedules and statements, and to the best of my knowledge and belief, it is true, correct, and complete.
Signature ▶ Print Your Name & Title ▶ Date ▶

For Privacy Act and Paperwork Reduction Act Notice, see instructions. Form **941** (Rev. 1-99)

CAA 9 9411 B999411 NTF 20314 GLD 1679

DO NOT STAPLE

a Control number: 33333	For Official Use Only ▶ OMB No. 1545-0008	1 Wages, tips, other compensation: 32400.00	2 Federal income tax withheld: 5931.60
b Kind of Payer: 941 ☒ Military ☐ 943 ☐ CT-1 ☐ Hshld. emp. ☐ Medicare govt. emp. ☐		3 Social security wages: 21600.00	4 Social security tax withheld: 1339.20
c Total number of Forms W-2: 2	d Establishment number	5 Medicare wages and tips: 21600.00	6 Medicare tax withheld: 313.20
e Employer identification number: 35-2938279		7 Social security tips	8 Allocated tips
f Employer's name: Mission Community Church		9 Advance EIC payments	10 Dependent care benefits
1620 E. Jones Street, South Bend, IN 46617		11 Nonqualified plans	12 Deferred compensation: 3600.00
		13	
g Employer's address and ZIP code		14	
h Other EIN used this year		15 Income tax withheld by third-party payer	
i Employer's state I.D. no.			
Contact person	Telephone number ( )	Fax number ( )	E-mail address

Under penalties of perjury, I declare that I have examined this return and accompanying documents, and, to the best of my knowledge and belief, they are true, correct, and complete.

Signature ▶ Title ▶ Date ▶

Form **W-3 Transmittal of Wage and Tax Statements 1999** Department of the Treasury Internal Revenue Service

Send this entire page with the entire Copy A page of Forms W-2 to the Social Security Administration. Photocopies are NOT acceptable.
Do not send any remittance (cash, checks, money orders, etc.) with FORMS W-2 and W-3.

Example, Nonelecting Church

a Control number: 22222 | Void ☐ | For Official Use Only ► OMB No. 1545-0008

b Employer identification number: 35-2938279

c Employer's name, address, and ZIP code:
Mission Community Church
1620 E. Jones Street
South Bend, IN 46617

d Employee's social security number: 483-12-0000

e Employee's name (first, middle initial, last): H. James Snodgrass

2309 E. Smith Street
South Bend, IN 46617

f Employee's address and ZIP code

1 Wages, tips, other compensation	12000.00	2 Federal income tax withheld	3840.00
3 Social security wages		4 Social security tax withheld	
5 Medicare wages and tips		6 Medicare tax withheld	
7 Social security tips		8 Allocated tips	
9 Advance EIC payment		10 Dependent care benefits	
11 Nonqualified plans		12 Benefits included in box 1	
13 See instrs. for box 13	E 2400.00	14 Other	Ordained - Not included above 18000.00 Parsonage Allowance

15 Statutory employee ☐ Deceased ☐ Pension plan ☒ Legal rep. ☐ Deferred compensation ☒

16 State	Employer's state I.D. no.	17 State wages, tips, etc.	18 State income tax	19 Locality name	20 Local wages, tips, etc.	21 Local income tax
IN		12000.00	720.00	St.Joe	12000.00	60.00

Form **W-2** Wage and Tax Statement 1999

Department of the Treasury—Internal Revenue Service

For Privacy Act and Paperwork Reduction Act Notice, see separate instructions.

Copy A For Social Security Administration—Send this entire page with Form W-3 to the Social Security Administration; photocopies are **not** acceptable.

Cat. No. 10134D

a Control number: 22222 | Void ☐ | For Official Use Only ► OMB No. 1545-0008

b Employer identification number: 35-2938279

c Employer's name, address, and ZIP code:
Mission Community Church
1620 E. Jones Street
South Bend, IN 46617

d Employee's social security number: 403-19-0000

e Employee's name (first, middle initial, last): Joseph Mop

1621 E. Jones Street
South Bend, IN 46617

f Employee's address and ZIP code

1 Wages, tips, other compensation	20400.00	2 Federal income tax withheld	2091.60
3 Social security wages	21600.00	4 Social security tax withheld	1339.20
5 Medicare wages and tips	21600.00	6 Medicare tax withheld	313.20
7 Social security tips		8 Allocated tips	
9 Advance EIC payment		10 Dependent care benefits	
11 Nonqualified plans		12 Benefits included in box 1	
13 See instrs. for box 13	E 1200.00	14 Other	

15 Statutory employee ☐ Deceased ☐ Pension plan ☒ Legal rep. ☐ Deferred compensation ☒

16 State	Employer's state I.D. no.	17 State wages, tips, etc.	18 State income tax	19 Locality name	20 Local wages, tips, etc.	21 Local income tax
IN		20400.00	693.60	St.Joe	20400.00	102.00

Form **W-2** Wage and Tax Statement 1999

Department of the Treasury—Internal Revenue Service

For Privacy Act and Paperwork Reduction Act Notice, see separate instructions.

Copy A For Social Security Administration—Send this entire page with Form W-3 to the Social Security Administration; photocopies are **not** acceptable.

Cat. No. 10134D

Do NOT Cut, Staple, or Separate Forms on This Page — Do NOT Cut, Staple, or Separate Forms on This Page

Example, Electing Church (Filed Form 8274)

Form **941** (Rev. January 1999) Department of the Treasury Internal Revenue Service

Employer's Quarterly Federal Tax Return

▶ See separate instructions for information on completing this return.
Please type or print.

Enter state code for state in which deposits were made ONLY if different from state in address to the right (see page 2 of instructions). ▶ ☐

Name, Trade name, if any: Mission Community Church
Address and ZIP code: 1620 E. Jones Street, South Bend, IN 46617
Date quarter ended: 12/31/99
EIN: 35-2938279

OMB No. 1545-0029
T
FF
FD
FP
I
T

If address is different from prior return, check here ▶ ☐ — IRS Use

If you do not have to file returns in the future, check here ▶ ☐ and enter date final wages paid ▶
If you are a seasonal employer, see **Seasonal employers** on page 1 of the instructions and check here ▶ ☐

Line	Description			Box	Amount
1	Number of employees in the pay period that includes March 12th ▶	1			
2	Total wages and tips, plus other compensation			2	8100.00
3	Total income tax withheld from wages, tips, and sick pay			3	2245.89
4	Adjustment of withheld income tax for preceding quarters of calendar year			4	
5	Adjusted total of income tax withheld (line 3 as adjusted by line 4 -- see instructions)			5	2245.89
6	Taxable social security wages	6a	0.00 × 12.4% (.124) =	6b	0.00
	Taxable social security tips	6c	0.00 × 12.4% (.124) =	6d	0.00
7	Taxable Medicare wages and tips	7a	0.00 × 2.9% (.029) =	7b	0.00
8	Total social security and Medicare taxes (add lines 6b, 6d, and 7b). Check here if wages are not subject to social security and/or Medicare tax ▶ ☒			8	0.00
9	Adjustment of social security and Medicare taxes (see instructions for required explanation) Sick Pay $ ____ ± Fractions of Cents $ ____ ± Other $ ____ =			9	
10	Adjusted total of social security and Medicare taxes (line 8 as adjusted by line 9 -- see instructions)			10	0.00
11	**Total taxes** (add lines 5 and 10)			11	2245.89
12	Advance earned income credit (EIC) payments made to employees			12	
13	Net taxes (subtract line 12 from line 11). **If $1000 or more, this must equal line 17, column (d) below (or line D of Schedule B (Form 941))**			13	2245.89
14	Total deposits for quarter, including overpayment applied from a prior quarter			14	2245.89
15	**Balance due** (subtract line 14 from line 13). See instructions			15	0.00

16 **Overpayment**, if line 14 is more than line 13, enter excess here ▶ $ ____
and check if to be: ☐ Applied to next return OR ☐ Refunded.

- **All filers:** If line 13 is less than $1000, you need not complete line 17 or Schedule B (Form 941).
- **Semiweekly schedule depositors:** Complete Schedule B (Form 941) and check here ▶ ☐
- **Monthly schedule depositors:** Complete line 17, columns (a) through (d), and check here ▶ ☒

17 **Monthly Summary of Federal Tax Liability.** Do not complete if you were a semiweekly schedule depositor.

(a) First month liability	(b) Second month liability	(c) Third month liability	(d) Total liability for quarter
748.63	748.63	748.63	2245.89

Sign Here Under penalties of perjury, I declare that I have examined this return, including accompanying schedules and statements, and to the best of my knowledge and belief, it is true, correct, and complete.
Signature ▶ Print Your Name & Title ▶ Date ▶

For Privacy Act and Paperwork Reduction Act Notice, see Instructions. Form **941** (Rev. 1-99)

CAA 9 9411 B999411 NTF 20314 GLD 1679

DO NOT STAPLE

a Control number: 33333 — For Official Use Only ▶ OMB No. 1545-0008

b Kind of Payer: 941 ☒ Military ☐ 943 ☐ CT-1 ☐ Hshld. emp. ☐ Medicare govt. emp. ☐

1 Wages, tips, other compensation	32400.00	2 Federal income tax withheld	8983.56
3 Social security wages		4 Social security tax withheld	
5 Medicare wages and tips		6 Medicare tax withheld	
7 Social security tips		8 Allocated tips	
9 Advance EIC payments		10 Dependent care benefits	
11 Nonqualified plans		12 Deferred compensation	3600.00
13		14	
15 Income tax withheld by third-party payer			

c Total number of Forms W-2: 2
d Establishment number:
e Employer identification number: 35-2938279
f Employer's name: Mission Community Church
1620 E. Jones Street
South Bend, IN 46617
g Employer's address and ZIP code
h Other EIN used this year
i Employer's state I.D. no.

Contact person | Telephone number ( ) | Fax number ( ) | E-mail address

Under penalties of perjury, I declare that I have examined this return and accompanying documents, and, to the best of my knowledge and belief, they are true, correct, and complete.

Signature ▶ Title ▶ Date ▶

Form **W-3 Transmittal of Wage and Tax Statements** 1999 — Department of the Treasury Internal Revenue Service

Send this entire page with the entire Copy A page of Forms W-2 to the Social Security Administration. Photocopies are NOT acceptable.
Do not send any remittance (cash, checks, money orders, etc.) with FORMS W-2 and W-3.

Example, Electing Church (Filed Form 8274)

a Control number	22222	Void ☐	For Official Use Only ► OMB No. 1545-0008
b Employer identification number: 35-2938279		1 Wages, tips, other compensation: 12000.00	2 Federal income tax withheld: 3840.00
c Employer's name, address, and ZIP code: Mission Community Church, 1620 E. Jones Street, South Bend, IN 46617		3 Social security wages	4 Social security tax withheld
		5 Medicare wages and tips	6 Medicare tax withheld
		7 Social security tips	8 Allocated tips
d Employee's social security number: 483-12-0000		9 Advance EIC payment	10 Dependent care benefits
e Employee's name (first, middle initial, last): H. James Snodgrass		11 Nonqualified plans	12 Benefits included in box 1
2309 E. Smith Street, South Bend, IN 46617		13 See instrs. for box 13: E 2400.00	14 Other: Ordained - Not included above 18000.00 Parson-age Allowance
f Employee's address and ZIP code		15 Statutory employee ☐ Deceased ☐ Pension plan ☒	Legal rep. ☐ Deferred compensation ☒

16 State	Employer's state I.D. no.	17 State wages, tips, etc.	18 State income tax	19 Locality name	20 Local wages, tips, etc.	21 Local income tax
IN		12000.00	720.00	St.Joe	12000.00	60.00

Form **W-2 Wage and Tax Statement 1999**

Department of the Treasury—Internal Revenue Service

For Privacy Act and Paperwork Reduction Act Notice, see separate instructions.

Copy A For Social Security Administration—Send this entire page with Form W-3 to the Social Security Administration; photocopies are **not** acceptable.

Cat. No. 10134D

a Control number	22222	Void ☐	For Official Use Only ► OMB No. 1545-0008
b Employer identification number: 35-2938279		1 Wages, tips, other compensation: 20400.00	2 Federal income tax withheld: 5143.56
c Employer's name, address, and ZIP code: Mission Community Church, 1620 E. Jones Street, South Bend, IN 46617		3 Social security wages	4 Social security tax withheld
		5 Medicare wages and tips	6 Medicare tax withheld
		7 Social security tips	8 Allocated tips
d Employee's social security number: 403-19-0000		9 Advance EIC payment	10 Dependent care benefits
e Employee's name (first, middle initial, last): Joseph Mop		11 Nonqualified plans	12 Benefits included in box 1
1621 E. Jones Street, South Bend, IN 46617		13 See instrs. for box 13: E 1200.00	14 Other: Electing church employee to pay social security on Sch. SE
f Employee's address and ZIP code		15 Statutory employee ☐ Deceased ☐ Pension plan ☒	Legal rep. ☐ Deferred compensation ☒

16 State	Employer's state I.D. no.	17 State wages, tips, etc.	18 State income tax	19 Locality name	20 Local wages, tips, etc.	21 Local income tax
IN		20400.00	693.60	St.Joe	20400.00	102.00

Form **W-2 Wage and Tax Statement 1999**

Department of the Treasury—Internal Revenue Service

For Privacy Act and Paperwork Reduction Act Notice, see separate instructions.

Copy A For Social Security Administration—Send this entire page with Form W-3 to the Social Security Administration; photocopies are **not** acceptable.

Cat. No. 10134D

Do NOT Cut, Staple, or Separate Forms on This Page — Do NOT Cut, Staple, or Separate Forms on This Page

Note: Joseph Mop's W-2, Box 2 above includes $3,051.96 additional federal withholdings to coveself-employment tax liability that he will incur as an employee of anelecting church. The Form 941 on the previous page reflects $762.99 ($3,051.96 X ¼) additional federal withholdings on line 3 for the 4th quarter.

Completed Income Tax Return

A typical problem with the actual tax forms filled out seems to be the most practical way to further explain the tax law as it applies to the minister. So study the following information about Rev. Snodgrass and how it is to be shown on the tax forms.

To illustrate that **$876.00 difference** in tax liability resulted from Rev. Snodgrass having an accountable reimbursement plan, we have prepared his return both ways. The proration of unreimbursed employee business expenses, according to the Dalan Case is also illustrated. His W-2 would show **$21,988** without reimbursement, and as shown in Chapter Six, **$12,000** with reimbursement.

Facts of the Problem

Rev. H. James Snodgrass and Mary T., live at 2309 E. Smith St., South Bend, Indiana 46617. Rev. Snodgrass' S.S.# is 483-12-0000; Mary's S.S.# is 483-15-0000. They have three children, Ruth, Thomas and Samuel, ages 17,15 & 12. Children under 17 qualify for the new Child Tax Credit.

Rev. Snodgrass is pastor of Mission Community Church and Mrs. Snodgrass is a nurse at a local hospital. Mary's wage on her W-2 is **$35,278** with **$4,008** federal tax withheld, $2,187 social security tax, $512 medicare tax, **$728** State tax and **$176** Local tax withheld. Combine his salary of **$12,000/$21,988** and her salary of **$35,278** on line 7, Form 1040.

During the year Rev. Snodgrass received **$690** professional income from weddings and funerals. In earning this income, Rev. Snodgrass spent **$114** for booklets & **$11** for Schedule C tax prep fee.

The Snodgrasses own their own home (purchased 6-10-86) and they make payments of $743 a month. Their interest was **$8,081** and principal payments were **$835**. Real estate taxes were **$1,182**. Insurance was **$340**, and repairs were **$793**. They bought a new couch & chair for **$849**, and a new TV & VCR for **$560**. Decorator items (oval rug for living room) cost **$463**. Utilities and personal phone were **$2,738**. Miscellaneous household expenses Mary kept a record of came to **$642**.

Professional expenses are as follows: Tuition for class at seminary **$345**, Office Supplies **$86**, Religious Materials **$327**, Subscriptions **$132**, Home entertainment meals **$381**. He purchased **$649** worth of books this year and also bought a fax machine for **$529**. Rev. Snodgrass was reimbursed for the depreciation factor (**$236**) for prior year purchases and chose Sec. 179 expensing for this year's purchases. Travel expenses are as follows: Lodging **$363**, Meals away from home **$257**, Tips for meals **$48**, Cleaning while away from home **$22**. Local transportation expenses are as follows: Parking **$11**, Tolls **$34**. The total year's reimbursement for professional and travel expenses was **$3,420** as shown on the payroll sheet.

Business auto mileage from his log book was **20,879** miles. Total miles driven for the year was **26,945**. The church reimbursed mileage allowance of **32½¢/31¢** a mile during the year for a total of **$6,568**. Actual expenses amount to less than 32½¢/31¢ per mile for reimbursement. The return showing non-reimbursed expenses shows the actual expenses for each auto on "Worksheet for Form 2106." Without reimbursement, vehicle #1 is computed by actual method as required, and vehicle #2 is computed by optional which is slightly better. Details of their auto trade are shown on the "Auto Basis Worksheets."

Itemized deductions are as follows: Medical expenses were not greater than 7.5% of AGI. Additional State tax last spring of **$152**, Real Estate Tax is used again **$1,182**, personal property tax on the family auto of **$78**, personal property tax of **$456** on vehicle #2 must be deducted on Schedule A as taxes. He can not use auto interest of $639 on Schedule A (vehicle #1 $158 & vehicle #2 $481). Interest on home is used again **$8,081**. Personal interest of $753 can not be used. Contributions were to Mission Community Church **$5,308**, Central Bible College **$200**. Total tax return preparation fee **$128/177** less Schedule C portion - $11= **$117/166**, Nursing license **$135**, Uniforms, shoes, nylons and cost of cleaning them **$375**.

Due to the fact a minister is self-employed for social security purposes, we are able to use the business percentage of personal property tax, auto interest **$845** and business portion of tax preparation fee **$40/89** as a reduction of S.S. base.

Study the completed forms on the following pages to see how the Snodgrass return is prepared.

Without Accountable Reimbursement Plan

Form 1040 Department of the Treasury—Internal Revenue Service
U.S. Individual Income Tax Return 1999 (99) IRS Use Only—Do not write or staple in this space.

For the year Jan. 1–Dec. 31, 1999, or other tax year beginning , 1999, ending , OMB No. 1545-0074

Label (See instructions on page 18.) **Use the IRS label.** Otherwise, please print or type.

Your first name and initial: H. James	Last name: Snodgrass	Your social security number: 483 12 0000
If a joint return, spouse's first name and initial: Mary T.	Last name: Snodgrass	Spouse's social security number: 483 15 0000
Home address (number and street). If you have a P.O. box, see page 18.: 2309 E. Smith Street	Apt. no.	▲ IMPORTANT! ▲ You **must** enter your SSN(s) above.
City, town or post office, state, and ZIP code. If you have a foreign address, see page 18.: South Bend, IN 46617		

Presidential Election Campaign (See page 18.)

	Yes	No
Do you want $3 to go to this fund?		X
If a joint return, does your spouse want $3 to go to this fund?		X

Note. Checking "Yes" will not change your tax or reduce your refund.

Filing Status (Check only one box.)

1. ☐ Single
2. ☒ Married filing joint return (even if only one had income)
3. ☐ Married filing separate return. Enter spouse's social security no. above and full name here. ▶
4. ☐ Head of household (with qualifying person). (See page 18.) If the qualifying person is a child but not your dependent, enter this child's name here. ▶
5. ☐ Qualifying widow(er) with dependent child (year spouse died ▶ 19). (See page 18.)

Exemptions

6a ☒ **Yourself.** If your parent (or someone else) can claim you as a dependent on his or her tax return, **do not** check box 6a.
b ☒ **Spouse**

No. of boxes checked on 6a and 6b: 2

c Dependents:

(1) First name Last name	(2) Dependent's social security number	(3) Dependent's relationship to you	(4) ✓ if qualifying child for child tax credit (see page 19)
Ruth A Snodgrass	483 13 0000	Child	☐
Thomas A Snodgrass	485 14 0000	Child	☒
Samuel A Snodgrass	486 15 0000	Child	☒

If more than six dependents, see page 19.

No. of your children on 6c who: • lived with you 3; • did not live with you due to divorce or separation (see page 19); Dependents on 6c not entered above

d Total number of exemptions claimed — Add numbers entered on lines above ▶ 5

Income

Attach Copy B of your Forms W-2 and W-2G here. Also attach Form(s) 1099-R if tax was withheld. If you did not get a W-2, see page 20. Enclose, but do not staple, any payment. Also, please use Form 1040-V.

7	Wages, salaries, tips, etc. Attach Form(s) W-2. 21,988 + 35,278	7	57,266
8a	**Taxable** interest. Attach Schedule B if required	8a	
b	**Tax-exempt** interest. DO NOT include on line 8a [8b]		
9	Ordinary dividends. Attach Schedule B if required	9	
10	Taxable refunds, credits, or offsets of state and local income taxes (see page 21)	10	
11	Alimony received	11	
12	Business income or (loss). Attach Schedule C or C-EZ	12	565
13	Capital gain or (loss). Attach Schedule D if required. If not required, check here ▶ ☐	13	
14	Other gains or (losses). Attach Form 4797	14	
15a	Total IRA distributions [15a] b Taxable amount (see page 22)	15b	
16a	Total pensions and annuities [16a] b Taxable amount (see page 22)	16b	
17	Rental real estate, royalties, partnerships, S corporations, trusts, etc. Attach Schedule E	17	
18	Farm income or (loss). Attach Schedule F	18	
19	Unemployment compensation	19	
20a	Social security benefits [20a] b Taxable amount (see page 24)	20b	
21	Other income. List type and amount (see page 24) Excess Pars. Allow.	21	1,517
22	Add the amounts in the far right column for lines 7 through 21. This is your **total income** ▶	22	59,348

Adjusted Gross Income

23	IRA deduction (see page 26)	23			
24	Student loan interest deduction (see page 26)	24			
25	Medical savings account deduction. Attach Form 8853	25			
26	Moving expenses. Attach Form 3903	26			
27	One-half of self-employment tax. Attach Schedule SE	27	2,156		
28	Self-employed health insurance deduction (see page 28)	28			
29	Keogh and self-employed SEP and SIMPLE plans	29			
30	Penalty on early withdrawal of savings	30			
31a	Alimony paid b Recipient's SSN ▶	31a			
32	Add lines 23 through 31a			32	2,156
33	Subtract line 32 from line 22. This is your **adjusted gross income** ▶			33	57,192

For Disclosure, Privacy Act, and Paperwork Reduction Act Notice, see page 54. Cat. No. 11320B Form **1040** (1999)

Form 1040 (1999) Page **2**

Tax and Credits

34	Amount from line 33 (adjusted gross income)			34	57,192
35a	Check if: ☐ **You** were 65 or older, ☐ Blind; ☐ **Spouse** was 65 or older, ☐ Blind. Add the number of boxes checked above and enter the total here ▶ 35a				
b	If you are married filing separately and your spouse itemizes deductions or you were a dual-status alien, see page 30 and check here ▶ 35b ☐				
36	Enter your **itemized deductions** from Schedule A, line 28, **OR standard deduction** shown on the left. **But** see page 30 to find your standard deduction if you checked any box on line 35a or 35b **or** if someone can claim you as a dependent			36	22,024
37	Subtract line 36 from line 34			37	35,168
38	If line 34 is $94,975 or less, multiply $2,750 by the total number of exemptions claimed on line 6d. If line 34 is over $94,975, see the worksheet on page 31 for the amount to enter			38	13,750
39	**Taxable income.** Subtract line 38 from line 37. If line 38 is more than line 37, enter -0-			39	21,418
40	**Tax** (see page 31). Check if any tax is from a ☐ Form(s) 8814 b ☐ Form 4972 ▶			40	3,214
41	Credit for child and dependent care expenses. Attach Form 2441	41			
42	Credit for the elderly or the disabled. Attach Schedule R	42			
43	Child tax credit (see page 33)	43	1,000		
44	Education credits. Attach Form 8863	44			
45	Adoption credit. Attach Form 8839	45			
46	Foreign tax credit. Attach Form 1116 if required	46			
47	Other. Check if from a ☐ Form 3800 b ☐ Form 8396 c ☐ Form 8801 d ☐ Form (specify)	47			
48	Add lines 41 through 47. These are your **total credits**			48	1,000
49	Subtract line 48 from line 40. If line 48 is more than line 40, enter -0- ▶			49	2,214

Standard Deduction for Most People — Single: $4,300; Head of household: $6,350; Married filing jointly or Qualifying widow(er): $7,200; Married filing separately: $3,600

Other Taxes

50	Self-employment tax. Attach Schedule SE	50	4,312
51	Alternative minimum tax. Attach Form 6251	51	
52	Social security and Medicare tax on tip income not reported to employer. Attach Form 4137	52	
53	Tax on IRAs, other retirement plans, and MSAs. Attach Form 5329 if required	53	
54	Advance earned income credit payments from Form(s) W-2	54	
55	Household employment taxes. Attach Schedule H	55	
56	Add lines 49 through 55. This is your **total tax** ▶	56	6,526

Payments

57	Federal income tax withheld from Forms W-2 and 1099	57	7,848		
58	1999 estimated tax payments and amount applied from 1998 return	58			
59a	**Earned income credit.** Attach Sch. EIC if you have a qualifying child	59a			
b	Nontaxable earned income: amount ▶ and type ▶				
60	Additional child tax credit. Attach Form 8812	60			
61	Amount paid with request for extension to file (see page 48)	61			
62	Excess social security and RRTA tax withheld (see page 48)	62			
63	Other payments. Check if from a ☐ Form 2439 b ☐ Form 4136	63			
64	Add lines 57, 58, 59a, and 60 through 63. These are your **total payments** ▶			64	7,848

Refund

65	If line 64 is more than line 56, subtract line 56 from line 64. This is the amount you **OVERPAID**	65	1,322
66a	Amount of line 65 you want **REFUNDED TO YOU** ▶	66a	1,322
b	Routing number ▶ c Type: ☐ Checking ☐ Savings		
d	Account number		
67	Amount of line 65 you want **APPLIED TO YOUR 2000 ESTIMATED TAX** ▶ [67]		

Have it directly deposited! See page 48 and fill in 66b, 66c, and 66d.

Amount You Owe

68	If line 56 is more than line 64, subtract line 64 from line 56. This is the **AMOUNT YOU OWE**. For details on how to pay, see page 49 ▶	68	
69	Estimated tax penalty. Also include on line 68 [69]		

Sign Here

Under penalties of perjury, I declare that I have examined this return and accompanying schedules and statements, and to the best of my knowledge and belief, they are true, correct, and complete. Declaration of preparer (other than taxpayer) is based on all information of which preparer has any knowledge.

Joint return? See page 18. Keep a copy for your records.

Your signature	Date	Your occupation: Minister	Daytime telephone number (optional) ( )
Spouse's signature. If a joint return, BOTH must sign.	Date	Spouse's occupation: Nurse	

Paid Preparer's Use Only

Preparer's signature	Date	Check if self-employed ☐	Preparer's SSN or PTIN
Firm's name (or yours if self-employed) and address			EIN
			ZIP code

Form **1040** (1999)

Without Accountable Reimbursement Plan

SCHEDULES A&B (Form 1040)
Department of the Treasury Internal Revenue Service (99)

Schedule A—Itemized Deductions

(Schedule B is on back)

▶ Attach to Form 1040. ▶ See Instructions for Schedules A and B (Form 1040).

OMB No. 1545-0074 | 1999 | Attachment Sequence No. 07

Name(s) shown on Form 1040: H. James & Mary T. Snodgrass | Your social security number: 483 : 12 : 0000

Medical and Dental Expenses		**Caution.** Do not include expenses reimbursed or paid by others.				
	1	Medical and dental expenses (see page A-1)	1			
	2	Enter amount from Form 1040, line 34. [2]				
	3	Multiply line 2 above by 7.5% (.075)	3			
	4	Subtract line 3 from line 1. If line 3 is more than line 1, enter -0-			4	
Taxes You Paid (See page A-2.)	5	State and local income taxes 728+176+720+60+152	5	1,836		
	6	Real estate taxes (see page A-2)	6	1,182		
	7	Personal property taxes	7	534		
	8	Other taxes. List type and amount ▶	8			
	9	Add lines 5 through 8			9	3,552
Interest You Paid (See page A-3.)	10	Home mortgage interest and points reported to you on Form 1098	10	8,081		
	11	Home mortgage interest not reported to you on Form 1098. If paid to the person from whom you bought the home, see page A-3 and show that person's name, identifying no., and address ▶	11			
Note. Personal interest is not deductible.	12	Points not reported to you on Form 1098. See page A-3 for special rules	12			
	13	Investment interest. Attach Form 4952 if required. (See page A-3.)	13			
	14	Add lines 10 through 13			14	8,081
Gifts to Charity If you made a gift and got a benefit for it, see page A-4.	15	Gifts by cash or check. If you made any gift of $250 or more, see page A-4	15	5,508		
	16	Other than by cash or check. If any gift of $250 or more, see page A-4. You **MUST** attach Form 8283 if over $500	16			
	17	Carryover from prior year	17			
	18	Add lines 15 through 17			18	5,508
Casualty and Theft Losses	19	Casualty or theft loss(es). Attach Form 4684. (See page A-5.)			19	
Job Expenses and Most Other Miscellaneous Deductions	20	Unreimbursed employee expenses—job travel, union dues, job education, etc. You **MUST** attach Form 2106 or 2106-EZ if required. (See page A-5.) ▶ Nursing 510; Form 2106 9,103 Less IRC 265 Limitation -3,752	20	5,861		
	21	Tax preparation fees	21	166		
(See page A-5 for expenses to deduct here.)	22	Other expenses—investment, safe deposit box, etc. List type and amount ▶	22			
	23	Add lines 20 through 22	23	6,027		
	24	Enter amount from Form 1040, line 34. [24] 57,192				
	25	Multiply line 24 above by 2% (.02)	25	1,144		
	26	Subtract line 25 from line 23. If line 25 is more than line 23, enter -0-			26	4,883
Other Miscellaneous Deductions	27	Other—from list on page A-6. List type and amount ▶			27	
Total Itemized Deductions	28	Is Form 1040, line 34, over $126,600 (over $63,300 if married filing separately)? ☒ **No.** Your deduction is not limited. Add the amounts in the far right column for lines 4 through 27. Also, enter this amount on Form 1040, line 36. ☐ **Yes.** Your deduction may be limited. See page A-6 for the amount to enter. ▶			28	22,024

For Paperwork Reduction Act Notice, see Form 1040 instructions. Cat. No. 11330X **Schedule A (Form 1040) 1999**

SCHEDULE C-EZ (Form 1040)
Department of the Treasury Internal Revenue Service (99)

Net Profit From Business

(Sole Proprietorship)

▶ Partnerships, joint ventures, etc., must file Form 1065 or 1065-B.
▶ Attach to Form 1040 or Form 1041. ▶ See instructions on back.

OMB No. 1545-0074 | 1999 | Attachment Sequence No. 09A

Name of proprietor: H. James Snodgrass | Social security number (SSN): 483 : 12 : 0000

Part I General Information

You May Use Schedule C-EZ Instead of Schedule C Only If You:

- Had business expenses of $2,500 or less.
- Use the cash method of accounting.
- Did not have an inventory at any time during the year.
- Did not have a net loss from your business.
- Had only one business as a sole proprietor.

And You:

- Had no employees during the year.
- Are not required to file **Form 4562,** Depreciation and Amortization, for this business. See the instructions for Schedule C, line 13, on page C-3 to find out if you must file.
- Do not deduct expenses for business use of your home.
- Do not have prior year unallowed passive activity losses from this business.

A Principal business or profession, including product or service: Honorariums
B Enter code from pages C-8 & 9 ▶ 813000
C Business name. If no separate business name, leave blank.
D Employer ID number (EIN), if any
E Business address (including suite or room no.). Address not required if same as on Form 1040, page 1.
City, town or post office, state, and ZIP code

Part II Figure Your Net Profit

Line	Description	Box	Amount
1	**Gross receipts. Caution:** *If this income was reported to you on Form W-2 and the "Statutory employee" box on that form was checked, see **Statutory Employees** in the instructions for Schedule C, line 1, on page C-2 and check here* ▶ ☐	1	690
2	**Total expenses.** If more than $2,500, you **must** use Schedule C. See instructions	2	125
3	**Net profit.** Subtract line 2 from line 1. If less than zero, you **must** use Schedule C. Enter on **Form 1040, line 12,** and ALSO on **Schedule SE, line 2.** (Statutory employees **do not** report this amount on Schedule SE, line 2. Estates and trusts, enter on Form 1041, line 3.)	3	565

Part III Information on Your Vehicle. Complete this part **ONLY** if you are claiming car or truck expenses on line 2.

4 When did you place your vehicle in service for business purposes? (month, day, year) ▶ ____/____/____

5 Of the total number of miles you drove your vehicle during 1999, enter the number of miles you used your vehicle for:

a Business ________ b Commuting ________ c Other ________

6 Do you (or your spouse) have another vehicle available for personal use? ☐ Yes ☐ No

7 Was your vehicle available for use during off-duty hours? ☐ Yes ☐ No

8a Do you have evidence to support your deduction? ☐ Yes ☐ No

b If "Yes," is the evidence written? ☐ Yes ☐ No

For Paperwork Reduction Act Notice, see Form 1040 instructions. Cat. No. 14374D **Schedule C-EZ (Form 1040) 1999**

Without Accountable Reimbursement Plan

Form **2106** — Department of the Treasury, Internal Revenue Service (99)

Employee Business Expenses

▶ See separate instructions.

▶ Attach to Form 1040.

OMB No. 1545-0139 — **1999** — Attachment Sequence No. **54**

Your name	Occupation in which you incurred expenses	Social security number
H. James Snodgrass	Ministry	483 : 12 : 0000

Part I — Employee Business Expenses and Reimbursements

STEP 1 Enter Your Expenses		Column A Other Than Meals and Entertainment	Column B Meals and Entertainment
1 Vehicle expense from line 22c or line 29. (Rural mail carriers: See instructions.)	1	6,026	
2 Parking fees, tolls, and transportation, including train, bus, etc., that **did not** involve overnight travel or commuting to and from work	2	45	
3 Travel expense while away from home overnight, including lodging, airplane, car rental, etc. **Do not** include meals and entertainment	3	385	
4 Business expenses not included on lines 1 through 3. **Do not** include meals and entertainment	4	2,304	
5 Meals and entertainment expenses (see instructions)	5		
6 **Total expenses.** In Column A, add lines 1 through 4 and enter the result. In Column B, enter the amount from line 5	6	8,760	686

Note: *If you were not reimbursed for any expenses in Step 1, skip line 7 and enter the amount from line 6 on line 8.*

STEP 2 Enter Reimbursements Received From Your Employer for Expenses Listed in STEP 1

		Column A	Column B
7 Enter reimbursements received from your employer that were **not** reported to you in box 1 of Form W-2. Include any reimbursements reported under code "L" in box 13 of your Form W-2 (see instructions)	7		

STEP 3 Figure Expenses To Deduct on Schedule A (Form 1040)

		Column A	Column B
8 Subtract line 7 from line 6. If zero or less, enter -0-. However, if line 7 is greater than line 6 in Column A, report the excess as income on Form 1040, line 7	8	8,760	686
Note: *If **both columns** of line 8 are zero, you cannot deduct employee business expenses. Stop here and attach Form 2106 to your return.*			
9 In Column A, enter the amount from line 8. In Column B, multiply line 8 by 50% (.50). (Employees subject to Department of Transportation (DOT) hours of service limits: Multiply meal expenses by 55% (.55) instead of 50%. For more details, see instructions.)	9	8,760	343
10 Add the amounts on line 9 of both columns and enter the total here. **Also, enter the total on Schedule A (Form 1040), line 20.** (Fee-basis state or local government officials, qualified performing artists, and individuals with disabilities: See the instructions for special rules on where to enter the total.) ▶	10		9,103

For Paperwork Reduction Act Notice, see instructions. Cat. No. 11700N Form **2106** (1999)

Form 2106 (1999) Page **2**

Part II — Vehicle Expenses

Section A—General Information (You must complete this section if you are claiming vehicle expenses.)

		(a) Vehicle 1	(b) Vehicle 2
11 Enter the date the vehicle was placed in service	11	1 / 6 / 96	3 / 10 / 99
12 Total miles the vehicle was driven during 1999	12	6,630 miles	20,315 miles
13 Business miles included on line 12	13	5,320 miles	15,559 miles
14 Percent of business use. Divide line 13 by line 12	14	80.24 %	76.59 %
15 Average daily roundtrip commuting distance	15	8 miles	8 miles
16 Commuting miles included on line 12	16	320 miles	2,176 miles
17 Other miles. Add lines 13 and 16 and subtract the total from line 12	17	990 miles	2,580 miles

18 Do you (or your spouse) have another vehicle available for personal use? ☒ Yes ☐ No

19 If your employer provided you with a vehicle, is personal use during off-duty hours permitted? ☐ Yes ☐ No ☒ Not applicable

20 Do you have evidence to support your deduction? ☒ Yes ☐ No

21 If "Yes," is the evidence written? ☒ Yes ☐ No

Section B—Standard Mileage Rate (See the instructions for Part II to find out whether to complete this section or Section C.)

22a Multiply business miles driven **before** April 1, 1999, by 32½¢ (.325)	1,022 mi.	22a	332
b Multiply business miles driven **after** March 31, 1999, by 31¢ (.31)	14,537 mi.	22b	4,506
c Add lines 22a and 22b. Enter the result here and on line 1		22c	4,838

Section C—Actual Expenses

		(a) Vehicle 1		(b) Vehicle 2	
23 Gasoline, oil, repairs, vehicle insurance, etc.	23		799		
24a Vehicle rentals	24a				
b Inclusion amount (see instructions)	24b				
c Subtract line 24b from line 24a	24c				
25 Value of employer-provided vehicle (applies only if 100% of annual lease value was included on Form W-2—see instructions)	25				
26 Add lines 23, 24c, and 25	26		799		
27 Multiply line 26 by the percentage on line 14	27		641		
28 Depreciation. Enter amount from line 38 below	28		547		
29 Add lines 27 and 28. Enter total here and on line 1	29		1,188		

Section D—Depreciation of Vehicles (Use this section only if you owned the vehicle and are completing Section C for the vehicle.)

		(a) Vehicle 1		(b) Vehicle 2	
30 Enter cost or other basis (see instructions)	30	* 11,821			
31 Enter amount of section 179 deduction (see instructions)	31				
32 Multiply line 30 by line 14 (see instructions if you elected the section 179 deduction)	32	9,485			
33 Enter depreciation method and percentage (see instructions)	33	DDB½ .1152			
34 Multiply line 32 by the percentage on line 33 (see instructions)	34		** 547		
35 Add lines 31 and 34	35		547		
36 Enter the limit from the table in the line 36 instructions	36	1,775			
37 Multiply line 36 by the percentage on line 14	37		*** 712		
38 Enter the **smaller** of line 35 or line 37. Also enter this amount on line 28 above	38		547		

Form **2106** (1999)

* Ln 30-Basis determined by using Ln G of Auto Basis Worksheet 9485 ÷ 80.24%

** Ln 34 1,092 X ½ = 547 Year of sale limitation

*** Ln 37 1,424 X ½ = 712 Year of sale limitation

Without Accountable Reimbursement Plan

WORKSHEET TO BE USED WITH FORM 2106

Taxable Year: 1999

Your Name	Social Security Number	Occupation in which expenses were incurred
H. James Snodgrass	483 : 12 : 0000	Minister

☒ Ordained ☐ Licensed ☐ Commissioned ☐ Other — Filed Form 4361? ☐ Yes ☒ No

ACTUAL AUTO EXPENSES
(Complete Form 2106, Part II, Sec. A & B first)

	Vehicle 1	Vehicle 2
1. Garage rent		
2. Gas, oil, & lubrication	330	1,415
3. Repairs	200	242
4. Tires & batteries	84	
5. Insurance & auto club	161	389
6. Miscellaneous		
7. Washing and polishing	24	120
8. License (registration portion)		13
9. **TOTAL**	799	2,179

(enter on Form 2106, Part II, Section C, Line 23)

LOCAL TRAVEL EXPENSES

1. Parking	11
2. Tolls	34
3. Fares	
4. **TOTAL**	45

(Enter on Form 2106-EZ, Part II, Line 2 or Form 2106, Part I, Line 2)

OVERNIGHT TRAVEL EXPENSES

1. Auto rental, taxi, etc.	
2. Fares (air, train, bus)	
3. Parking & tolls	
4. Laundry & cleaning	22
5. Lodging	363
6. Telephone, telegraph, postage, fax	
7. Tips, other than meals	
8. **TOTAL**	385

(Enter on Form 2106-EZ, Part II, Line 3 or Form 2106, Part I, Line 3)

PROFESSIONAL EXPENSES (UNREIMBURSED)

1. Business-in-home (see attached)	
2. Education expenses	345
3. Equipment depreciation	1,414
4. Office supplies and postage	86
5. Religious materials	327
6. Sales aids	
7. Seminars and dues	
8. Subscriptions and paperbacks	132
9. Telephone	
10. Other	
11. **TOTAL**	2,304

(Enter on Form 2106-EZ, Part II, Line 4 or Form 2106, Part I, Line 4)

MEALS AND ENTERTAINMENT

1. Meals while away from home (☒ Actual ☐ Optional)	257
2. Entertainment, meals	381
3. Entertainment, other	
4. Tips for meals	48
5. **TOTAL**	686

(Enter on Form 2106-EZ, Part II, Line 5 or Form 2106, Part I, Line 5)

COMPUTATION OF PARSONAGE ALLOWANCE

Date of purchase: 6 / 10 / 87

FMV of home you own: $ 115,000

	A PROVIDED BY CHURCH	B PAID BY MINISTER
1. Value of parsonage provided by church		
2. Rent or principal payments		835
3. Taxes		1,182
4. Interest		8,081
5. Insurance		340
6. Repairs & upkeep		793
7. Furniture, appliances, etc.		1,409
8. Decorator items		463
9. Utilities		2,738
10. Miscellaneous supplies		642
11. **TOTAL**		16,483

12. Fair Rental Value Computation: Compute in year of purchase and in any year of major expense. (Homeowners only)

FRV of home	13,800
FRV of furniture	4,500
Decorator items	463
Utilities	2,738
Miscellaneous	642
Total of line 12	22,143

13. Less of Column B, line 11 or line 12	16,483
14. Amount designated	18,000
15a. If line 14 is greater than line 13, enter the difference here and as income on Form 1040, line 21; **or** 15b. If amount is included in error on W-2, enter the lesser of line 13 or line 14 as a deduction on Form 1040, line 21	1,517

COMPUTATION OF SOCIAL SECURITY BASE

(If exempt, you may omit this section. Write "Exempt-Form 4361" on the self-employment line, Form 1040, page 2.)

1. Salary from W-2	21,988
2. Parsonage provided, Column A, line 11	
3. Parsonage allowance, Column B, line 14	18,000
4. Recapture of auto depreciation	
5. Less business portion of tax preparation	(89)
6. Less business % of auto interest and personal property tax	(845)
7. Less unreimbursed employee business expense *(enter from Form 2106-EZ, line 6 or Form 2106, line 10)*	(9,103)
8. **TOTAL** *(enter on Schedule SE, Sec. A, line 2)*	29,951

Auto #1: $158 interest X 80.24% business % = $ 127

Auto #2: ($481 interest + $456 personal property tax) X 76.59% business % = $ 718

Total *(to line 6 of Computation of Social Security Base, above)* = $ 845

Without Accountable Reimbursement Plan

SCHEDULE SE (Form 1040) Department of the Treasury Internal Revenue Service	**Self-Employment Tax** ▶ See Instructions for Schedule SE (Form 1040). ▶ Attach to Form 1040.	OMB No. 1545-0074 1999 Attachment Sequence No. 17
Name of person with **self-employment** income (as shown on Form 1040) H. James Snodgrass	Social security number of person with **self-employment** income ▶	483 : 12 : 0000

Who Must File Schedule SE

You must file Schedule SE if:

- You had net earnings from self-employment from **other than** church employee income (line 4 of Short Schedule SE or line 4c of Long Schedule SE) of $400 or more, **OR**
- You had church employee income of $108.28 or more. Income from services you performed as a minister or a member of a religious order **is not** church employee income. See page SE-1.

Note: *Even if you had a loss or a small amount of income from self-employment, it may be to your benefit to file Schedule SE and use either "optional method" in Part II of Long Schedule SE. See page SE-3.*

Exception. If your only self-employment income was from earnings as a minister, member of a religious order, or Christian Science practitioner **and** you filed Form 4361 and received IRS approval not to be taxed on those earnings, **do not** file Schedule SE. Instead, write "Exempt–Form 4361" on Form 1040, line 50.

May I Use Short Schedule SE or MUST I Use Long Schedule SE?

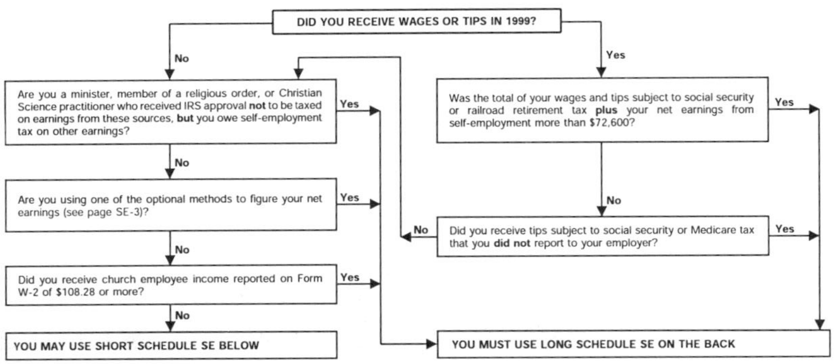

Section A—Short Schedule SE. Caution: *Read above to see if you can use Short Schedule SE.*

1	Net farm profit or (loss) from Schedule F, line 36, and farm partnerships, Schedule K-1 (Form 1065), line 15a	1	
2	Net profit or (loss) from Schedule C, line 31; Schedule C-EZ, line 3; Schedule K-1 (Form 1065), line 15a (other than farming); and Schedule K-1 (Form 1065-B), box 9. Ministers and members of religious orders, see page SE-1 for amounts to report on this line. See page SE-2 for other income to report 29,951 + 565	2	30,516
3	Combine lines 1 and 2	3	30,516
4	**Net earnings from self-employment.** Multiply line 3 by 92.35% (.9235). If less than $400, **do not** file this schedule; you do not owe self-employment tax ▶	4	28,182
5	**Self-employment tax.** If the amount on line 4 is: • $72,600 or less, multiply line 4 by 15.3% (.153). Enter the result here and on **Form 1040, line 50.** • More than $72,600, multiply line 4 by 2.9% (.029). Then, add $9,002.40 to the result. Enter the total here and on **Form 1040, line 50.**	5	4,312
6	**Deduction for one-half of self-employment tax.** Multiply line 5 by 50% (.5). Enter the result here and on **Form 1040, line 27** — 6: 2,156		

For Paperwork Reduction Act Notice, see Form 1040 instructions. Cat. No. 11358Z **Schedule SE (Form 1040) 1999**

Schedule SE (Form 1040) 1999 Attachment Sequence No. 17 Page **2**

Name of person with **self-employment** income (as shown on Form 1040)	Social security number of person with **self-employment** income ▶	

Section B—Long Schedule SE

Part I Self-Employment Tax

Note: *If your only income subject to self-employment tax is* ***church employee income,*** *skip lines 1 through 4b. Enter -0- on line 4c and go to line 5a. Income from services you performed as a minister or a member of a religious order* ***is not*** *church employee income. See page SE-1.*

A	If you are a minister, member of a religious order, or Christian Science practitioner **and** you filed Form 4361, but you had $400 or more of **other** net earnings from self-employment, check here and continue with Part I ▶ ☐		
1	Net farm profit or (loss) from Schedule F, line 36, and farm partnerships, Schedule K-1 (Form 1065), line 15a. **Note:** *Skip this line if you use the farm optional method. See page SE-3*	1	
2	Net profit or (loss) from Schedule C, line 31; Schedule C-EZ, line 3; Schedule K-1 (Form 1065), line 15a (other than farming); and Schedule K-1 (Form 1065-B), box 9. Ministers and members of religious orders, see page SE-1 for amounts to report on this line. See page SE-2 for other income to report. **Note:** *Skip this line if you use the nonfarm optional method. See page SE-3.*	2	
3	Combine lines 1 and 2	3	
4a	If line 3 is more than zero, multiply line 3 by 92.35% (.9235). Otherwise, enter amount from line 3	4a	
b	If you elected one or both of the optional methods, enter the total of lines 15 and 17 here	4b	
c	Combine lines 4a and 4b. If less than $400, **do not** file this schedule; you do not owe self-employment tax. **Exception.** If less than $400 and you had **church employee income,** enter -0- and continue ▶	4c	
5a	Enter your **church employee income** from Form W-2. **Caution:** *See page SE-1 for definition of church employee income* — 5a		
b	Multiply line 5a by 92.35% (.9235). If less than $100, enter -0-	5b	
6	**Net earnings from self-employment.** Add lines 4c and 5b	6	
7	Maximum amount of combined wages and self-employment earnings subject to social security tax or the 6.2% portion of the 7.65% railroad retirement (tier 1) tax for 1999	7	72,600 00
8a	Total social security wages and tips (total of boxes 3 and 7 on Form(s) W-2) and railroad retirement (tier 1) compensation — 8a		
b	Unreported tips subject to social security tax (from Form 4137, line 9) — 8b		
c	Add lines 8a and 8b	8c	
9	Subtract line 8c from line 7. If zero or less, enter -0- here and on line 10 and go to line 11 ▶	9	
10	Multiply the **smaller** of line 6 or line 9 by 12.4% (.124)	10	
11	Multiply line 6 by 2.9% (.029)	11	
12	**Self-employment tax.** Add lines 10 and 11. Enter here and on **Form 1040, line 50**	12	
13	**Deduction for one-half of self-employment tax.** Multiply line 12 by 50% (.5). Enter the result here and on **Form 1040, line 27** — 13		

Part II Optional Methods To Figure Net Earnings (See page SE-3.)

Farm Optional Method. You may use this method **only** if:

- Your gross farm income[1] was not more than $2,400, **or**
- Your net farm profits[2] were less than $1,733.

14	Maximum income for optional methods	14	1,600 00
15	Enter the **smaller** of: two-thirds (⅔) of gross farm income[1] (not less than zero) **or** $1,600. Also include this amount on line 4b above	15	

Nonfarm Optional Method. You may use this method **only** if:

- Your net nonfarm profits[3] were less than $1,733 and also less than 72.189% of your gross nonfarm income,[4] **and**
- You had net earnings from self-employment of at least $400 in 2 of the prior 3 years.

Caution: *You may use this method no more than five times.*

16	Subtract line 15 from line 14	16	
17	Enter the **smaller** of: two-thirds (⅔) of gross nonfarm income[4] (not less than zero) **or** the amount on line 16. Also include this amount on line 4b above	17	

[1]From Sch. F, line 11, and Sch. K-1 (Form 1065), line 15b.
[2]From Sch. F, line 36, and Sch. K-1 (Form 1065), line 15a.
[3]From Sch. C, line 31; Sch. C-EZ, line 3; Sch. K-1 (Form 1065), line 15a; and Sch. K-1 (Form 1065-B), box 9.
[4]From Sch. C, line 7; Sch. C-EZ, line 1; Sch. K-1 (Form 1065), line 15c; and Sch. K-1 (Form 1065-B), box 9.

Schedule SE (Form 1040) 1999

Without Accountable Reimbursement Plan

STATEMENT OF UNREIMBURSED EXPENSE ALLOCATION - IRC SEC. 265

Taxpayer's Name	Social Security Number	Year
H. James Snodgrass	483-12-0000	1999

TAXABLE COMPENSATION

W-2 Salary .... $ 21,988

Plus — Total

Unused Parsonage Allowance ..... $ 1,517 = $ 23,505

Plus

Recapture of Auto Depreciation .... $ ______

DIVIDED BY

GROSS COMPENSATION
(from "Worksheet to be Used with Form 2106" -

W-2 Salary .... $ 21,988

Plus — Total

Parsonage Provided .... $ ______

Plus = $ 39,988

Parsonage Allowance .... $ 18,000

Plus

Recapture of Auto Depreciation .... $ ______

=

INCLUSION RATIO

TAXABLE COMPENSATION DIVIDED BY GROSS COMPENSATION

58.78 %

COMPUTATION OF DEDUCTIBLE EMPLOYEE BUSINESS EXPENSE

1. Total Unreimbursed Clergy Business Expense (Form 2106-EZ, Line 6 or Form 2106, Line 10) ... $ 9,103
2. Inclusion Ratio (From Above) .... 58.78 %
3. Allowable Deductible Expenses to Schedule A, Line 20 (Line 1 X Line 2) .... $ 5,351
4. Expenses Disallowed (Line 1 - Line 3) .... $ 3,752

Form **8824** — Department of the Treasury, Internal Revenue Service

Like-Kind Exchanges

(and nonrecognition of gain from conflict-of-interest sales)

▶ Attach to your tax return.

OMB No. 1545-1190 — 1999 — Attachment Sequence No. 109

Name(s) shown on tax return: H. James Snodgrass — Identifying number: 483 12 0000

Part I — Information on the Like-Kind Exchange

Note: *If the property described on line 1 or line 2 is real or personal property located outside the United States, indicate the country.*

1 Description of like-kind property given up ▶ 1996 Oldsmobile

2 Description of like-kind property received ▶ 1999 Mazda 626

3 Date like-kind property given up was originally acquired (month, day, year) .... **3** 1 / 6 / 96

4 Date you actually transferred your property to other party (month, day, year) .... **4** 3 / 10 / 99

5 Date like-kind property you received was identified (month, day, year). See instructions .... **5** 3 / 10 / 99

6 Date you actually received the like-kind property from other party (month, day, year) .... **6** 3 / 10 / 99

7 Was the exchange made with a related party? If "Yes," complete Part II. If "No," go to Part III. See instructions.
a ☐ Yes, in this tax year b ☐ Yes, in a prior tax year c ☒ No

Part II — Related Party Exchange Information

8 Name of related party — Related party's identifying number

Address (no., street, and apt., room, or suite no.)

City or town, state, and ZIP code — Relationship to you

9 During this tax year (and before the date that is 2 years after the last transfer of property that was part of the exchange), did the related party sell or dispose of the like-kind property received from you in the exchange? ☐ Yes ☐ No

10 During this tax year (and before the date that is 2 years after the last transfer of property that was part of the exchange), did you sell or dispose of the like-kind property you received? .... ☐ Yes ☐ No

If both lines 9 and 10 are "No" and this is the year of the exchange, go to Part III. If both lines 9 and 10 are "No" and this is **not** *the year of the exchange, stop here. If either line 9 or line 10 is "Yes," complete Part III and report the deferred gain or (loss) from line 24 on your return this tax year* **unless** *one of the exceptions on line 11 applies. See* **Related party exchanges** *in the instructions.*

11 If one of the exceptions below applies to the disposition, check the applicable box:
a ☐ The disposition was after the death of either of the related parties.
b ☐ The disposition was an involuntary conversion, and the threat of conversion occurred after the exchange.
c ☐ You can establish to the satisfaction of the IRS that neither the exchange nor the disposition had tax avoidance as its principal purpose. If this box is checked, attach an explanation. See instructions.

Part III — Realized Gain or (Loss), Recognized Gain, and Basis of Like-Kind Property Received

Caution: *If you transferred* **and** *received* **(a)** *more than one group of like-kind properties, or* **(b)** *cash or other (not like-kind) property, see* **Reporting of multi-asset exchanges** *in the instructions.*

Note: *Complete lines 12 through 14* **only** *if you gave up property that was not like-kind. Otherwise, go to line 15.*

12	Fair market value (FMV) of other property given up	12	
13	Adjusted basis of other property given up	13	
14	Gain or (loss) recognized on other property given up. Subtract line 13 from line 12. Report the gain or (loss) in the same manner as if the exchange had been a sale	14	
15	Cash received, FMV of other property received, plus net liabilities assumed by other party, reduced (but not below zero) by any exchange expenses you incurred. See instructions	15	
16	FMV of like-kind property you received	16	14,498
17	Add lines 15 and 16	17	14,498
18	Adjusted basis of like-kind property you gave up, net amounts paid to other party, plus any exchange expenses **not** used on line 15. See instructions	18	13,093
19	**Realized gain or (loss).** Subtract line 18 from line 17	19	1,405
20	Enter the smaller of line 15 or line 19, but not less than zero	20	0
21	Ordinary income under recapture rules. Enter here and on Form 4797, line 16. See instructions	21	
22	Subtract line 21 from line 20. If zero or less, enter -0-. If more than zero, enter here and on Schedule D or Form 4797, unless the installment method applies. See instructions	22	0
23	**Recognized gain.** Add lines 21 and 22	23	0
24	Deferred gain or (loss). Subtract line 23 from line 19. If a related party exchange, see instructions	24	1,405
25	**Basis of like-kind property received.** Subtract line 15 from the sum of lines 18 and 23	25	13,093

For Paperwork Reduction Act Notice, see back of form. Cat. No. 12311A Form **8824** (1999)

Without Accountable Reimbursement Plan

STATEMENT OF DEPRECIATION AND COST RECOVERY

Attach to Schedule or Form 2106

Description of Property	N or U	Date Acquired	Cost or Other Basis	Bus. %	Business Basis	20% Bonus / Sec 179 Expensing	Salvage / Land / ITC Adj.	Adjusted Basis	Prior Dpr. or Recovery	ACRS or MACRS Class	Method Used	Life or Rec. Period	Year 19 98	%	Year 19___	%	Year 19___	%
Total Amount Expensed for Each Year (After 12/31/81)													1,178					
Library	N	1/95	533	100%	533			533	366	7	DDB½		48	8.93				
Equipment	N	8/11/95	538	100%	538			538	370	7	DDB½		48	8.93				
Library	N	1/96	400	100%	400			400	225	7	DDB½		50	12.49				
Library	N	1/98	366	100%	366			366	52	7	DDB½		90	24.49				
Fax Machine	N	2/10/99	529	100%	529	529		0					0					
Library	N	1/99	649	100%	649	649		0					0					
		TOTAL	3,015									TOTAL	1,414					

Form **4562** Department of the Treasury Internal Revenue Service (99)

Depreciation and Amortization (Including Information on Listed Property)

▶ See separate instructions. ▶ Attach this form to your return.

OMB No. 1545-0172 **1999** Attachment Sequence No. 67

Name(s) shown on return: H. James & Mary T. Snodgrass | Business or activity to which this form relates: Form 2106 | Identifying number: 483 12 0000

Part I Election To Expense Certain Tangible Property (Section 179) (Note: *If you have any "listed property," complete Part V before you complete Part I.*)

1	Maximum dollar limitation. If an enterprise zone business, see page 2 of the instructions	1	$19,000
2	Total cost of section 179 property placed in service. See page 2 of the instructions	2	1,178
3	Threshold cost of section 179 property before reduction in limitation	3	$200,000
4	Reduction in limitation. Subtract line 3 from line 2. If zero or less, enter -0-	4	0
5	Dollar limitation for tax year. Subtract line 4 from line 1. If zero or less, enter -0-. If married filing separately, see page 2 of the instructions	5	19,000

	(a) Description of property	(b) Cost (business use only)	(c) Elected cost
6	Fax Machine	529	529
	Library	649	649

7	Listed property. Enter amount from line 27	7	
8	Total elected cost of section 179 property. Add amounts in column (c), lines 6 and 7	8	1,178
9	Tentative deduction. Enter the smaller of line 5 or line 8	9	1,178
10	Carryover of disallowed deduction from 1998. See page 2 of the instructions	10	
11	Business income limitation. Enter the smaller of business income (not less than zero) or line 5 (see instructions)	11	1,178
12	Section 179 expense deduction. Add lines 9 and 10, but do not enter more than line 11	12	1,178
13	Carryover of disallowed deduction to 2000. Add lines 9 and 10, less line 12 ▶	13	0

Note: *Do not use Part II or Part III below for listed property (automobiles, certain other vehicles, cellular telephones, certain computers, or property used for entertainment, recreation, or amusement). Instead, use Part V for listed property.*

Part II MACRS Depreciation for Assets Placed in Service ONLY During Your 1999 Tax Year (Do Not Include Listed Property.)

Section A—General Asset Account Election

14 If you are making the election under section 168(i)(4) to group any assets placed in service during the tax year into one or more general asset accounts, check this box. See page 3 of the instructions ▶ ☐

Section B—General Depreciation System (GDS) (See page 3 of the instructions.)

(a) Classification of property	(b) Month and year placed in service	(c) Basis for depreciation (business/investment use only—see instructions)	(d) Recovery period	(e) Convention	(f) Method	(g) Depreciation deduction
15a 3-year property						
b 5-year property						
c 7-year property						
d 10-year property						
e 15-year property						
f 20-year property						
g 25-year property			25 yrs.		S/L	
h Residential rental property			27.5 yrs.	MM	S/L	
			27.5 yrs.	MM	S/L	
i Nonresidential real property			39 yrs.	MM	S/L	
				MM	S/L	

Section C—Alternative Depreciation System (ADS) (See page 5 of the instructions.)

(a) Classification of property	(b)	(c)	(d)	(e)	(f)	(g)
16a Class life					S/L	
b 12-year			12 yrs.		S/L	
c 40-year			40 yrs.	MM	S/L	

Part III Other Depreciation (Do Not Include Listed Property.) (See page 5 of the instructions.)

17	GDS and ADS deductions for assets placed in service in tax years beginning before 1999	17	236
18	Property subject to section 168(f)(1) election	18	
19	ACRS and other depreciation	19	

Part IV Summary (See page 6 of the instructions.)

20	Listed property. Enter amount from line 26	20	
21	**Total.** Add deductions on line 12, lines 15 and 16 in column (g), and lines 17 through 20. Enter here and on the appropriate lines of your return. Partnerships and S corporations—see instructions	21	1,414
22	For assets shown above and placed in service during the current year, enter the portion of the basis attributable to section 263A costs	22	

For Paperwork Reduction Act Notice, see page 9 of the instructions. Cat. No. 12906N Form **4562** (1999)

Without Accountable Reimbursement Plan

W 10-99

WORKSHEET TO COMPUTE AUTO BASIS

FORMULA FOR COMPUTING GAIN OR LOSS WHEN USE IS PART BUSINESS AND PART PERSONAL:

1. Odometer reading when traded *(old car)* .... 86,206 Miles
2. Odometer reading when acquired *(old car)* .... 3,280 Miles
3. Total miles driven while owned *(line 1 less line 2)* .... 82,926 Miles
4. Business miles driven while owned *(line D)* .... 67,286 Miles
5. Average business % while owned *(line 4 divided by line 3)* ...... 81.14 %
6. Purchase price of old car *(list price)* .... $ 7,890
7. Trade-in allowance towards new car or Sales price .... $(3,000)
8. **Difference** *(line 6 less line 7)* .... $ 4,890
9. Business portion *(line 8 times line 5)* .... $ 3,968
10. Gain or loss on previous trade-in *(if none, enter zero)* .... $ 0
11. Balance of lines 9 and 10 *(subtract gain or add loss)* .... $ 3,968
12. Depreciation and expensing allowed or allowable *(use worksheet below)* .... $ 3,423
13. Gain or loss on business portion .... $ 545 Gain or (Loss) *(circle one)*
    (Gain when line 12 is greater than line 11)
    (Loss when line 11 is greater than line 12)
14. Purchase price of new car .... $ 10,610 (List price) + $ 531 (Sales Tax) = $ 11,141 (Total)

DESCRIPTION OF AUTO
DATE ACQUIRED 1/6/96
YEAR 1996
MAKE Oldsmobile
(NEW) OR USED *(circle one)*

	1996 1st Year	1997 2nd Year	1998 3rd Year	1999 4th Year	5th Year	6th Year
A. Odometer reading end of year	29,260	62,320	94,390	101,020		
B. Odometer reading beginning of year	0	29,260	62,320	94,390		
C. Total miles driven during year *(A minus B)*	29,260	33,060	32,070	6,630		
D. Business miles from log	25,400	28,820	27,320	5,320		
E. Business % *(D divided by C)*	86.81%	87.17%	85.19%	80.24%	%	%
F. Multiply line 14 by E	$ 9,672	$ 9,712	$ 9,491	$ 8,940	$	$
G. Basis for depreciation .... *(Balance of line 13 and F; Subtract gain, Add loss)*	$ 10,217	$ 10,257	$ 10,036	$ 9,485	$	$

Year	Basis From (G)	(H) Expensing Sec. 179	(I) Adjusted Basis	(J) Class Life	(K) Method Used	(L) Life or RP	(M) Act Opt	(N) Depreciation Computed	(O) Depreciation Limit	(P) Depreciation Allowed	(Q) Depreciation Recapture
1996	10,217		10,217	5	DDB½	20.00	Act	2,043	2,656	2,043	
1997	10,257		10,257	5	DDB½	32.00	Act	3,282	4,271	3,282	
1998	10,036		10,036	5	DDB½	19.20	Act	1,927	2,513	1,927	
1999	9,485		9,485	5	DDB½	11.52	Act	*547	712	547	

*Half-year convention in year of trade or sale: 1,093 x ½ = 547

General Instructions:

Lines 1 through 11: Enter information from previous auto's worksheet if there has been a trade. Leave blank if newly acquired auto is the result of an outright purchase.

Line 12: Depreciation allowed or allowable is computed as follows:

Actual Depreciation or optional "factor" [see ¶ (P)] .... $ 3,423

Plus Expensing - Code Sec. 179 .... $

Total to be taken to line 12 .... $ 3,423

Line 13: If auto is sold, take Gain or Loss to Form 4797. If trade, complete form 8824.

Note!
The depreciation figure on line 12 of the General Instructions and the figures on lines 1 through 6 above were taken from a previous auto worksheet not shown in this publication.

(H) An election in year of purchase, reduce basis each year by amount claimed in year of purchase. Since 6-18-84, luxury auto rules severely limit the use of Code Sec. 179 expensing for autos.

(I) Adjusted basis - Line G minus Column (H). (Basis used for depreciation computation.)

(J) When actual expenses are used, enter "5" for autos purchased after 12-31-86.
When optional method is used, leave blank.

(K) Indicate MACRS percentage method by using "DDB".
Indicate conventions by "½" or "¼". If 40% of purchases are after 9-30, you must use mid-quarter convention.
Indicate Straight Line method by "SL".

(L) When MACRS percentage method is chosen, enter % used.
When MACRS straight line is chosen, enter 5 years.
When optional method was chosen in 1st year and you have switched to actual, enter the life chosen according to useful life.

(M) Indicate whether depreciation computation in Column (N) is actual method "A" or optional method "O". If optional, indicate whether 7, 7½, 8, 10, 10½, 11, 11½, or 12¢ rate is used. ("O-11½" or "O-12").

(N) **COMPUTE ACTUAL DEPRECIATION AS FOLLOWS:**

MACRS percentage method: After 12-31-86 - Column (I) multiplied by:

Year	Mid-year	Mid-quarter (1st)	Mid-quarter (2nd)	Mid-quarter (3rd)	Mid-quarter (4th)
1	20%	35%	25%	15%	5%
2	32%	26%	30%	34%	38%
3	19.20%	15.60%	18%	20.40%	22.80%
4	11.52%	11.01%	11.37%	12.24%	13.68%
5	11.52%	11.01%	11.37%	11.30%	10.94%
6	5.76%	1.38%	4.26%	7.06%	9.58%

MACRS straight line method: Column (I) divided by 5 years. First year is either ½ year or mid-quarter convention.

When business use is 50% or less, only 5 year straight line can be computed for autos purchased since 6-18-84.

If Code Sec. 179 expensing has been elected, add Column (H) to actual depreciation.

Since 1-1-81, if you choose actual depreciation in year of purchase, you must continue to use actual as long as you own that car.

COMPUTE OPTIONAL DEPRECIATION FACTOR AS FOLLOWS:

1980 thru 1989: Business miles up to but no more than 15,000 per year or 60,000 per auto, multiplied by 7¢ in 1980 and 1981; 7½¢ in 1982; 8¢ in 1983, 1984, and 1985; 9¢ in 1986; 10¢ in 1987; 10½¢ in 1988; 11¢ in 1989.

1990 thru 1998: All business miles multiplied by 11¢ in 1990 and 1991; 11½¢ in 1992 and 1993; 12¢ in 1994, 1995, 1996, 1997, and 1998.

1999: All business miles multiplied by 12¢.

If optional method is elected in the 1st year, it carries with it the election to exclude the auto from the MACRS method of depreciation. As "non-recovery" property, depreciation is required to be computed as straight line over the useful life in any year election is changed to actual method. As "non-recovery" property, you may choose actual or optional method each year.

(O) Luxury auto limitations for depreciation:

Date Auto Placed in Service

# of Years Owned	1-1-87 thru 12-31-88	1-1-89 thru 12-31-90	1-1-91 thru 12-31-91	1-1-92 thru 12-31-92	1-1-93 thru 12-31-93	1-1-94 thru 12-31-94	1-1-95 thru 12-31-96	1-1-97 thru 12-31-97	1-1-98 thru 12-31-98	1-1-99 thru 12-31-99
1st year	$2,560	$2,660	$2,660	$2,760	$2,860	$2,960	$3,060	$3,160	$3,160	$3,060
2nd year	$4,100	$4,200	$4,300	$4,400	$4,600	$4,700	$4,900	$5,000	$5,000	$5,000
3rd year	$2,450	$2,550	$2,550	$2,650	$2,750	$2,850	$2,950	$3,050	$2,950	$2,950
4th- 6th	$1,475	$1,475	$1,575	$1,575	$1,675	$1,675	$1,775	$1,775	$1,775	$1,775

Date Auto Placed in Service 1 / 6 / 96

Year	Amount from Table		Business %		Depr. Limit	Year	Amount from Table		Business %		Depr. Limit
1st	$ 3,060	X	86.81 %	=	$ 2,656	4th	$ 1,775	X	80.24 %	=	$ *1,424
2nd	$ 4,900	X	87.17 %	=	$ 4,271	5th	$	X	%	=	$
3rd	$ 2,950	X	85.19 %	=	$ 2,513	6th	$	X	%	=	$

* Half-year convention: 1,424 x ½ = 712

(P) Enter the smallest of Column (N) or (O). Also, enter this amount on Form 2106.

(Q) Autos purchased after 6-18-84: Depreciation Recapture or "pay back" is to be computed if an auto was more than 50% business use in year of purchase, but drops below 50% business use in any future year when a method of accelerated depreciation was used. You must include in gross income the difference between depreciation and Code Section 179 expensing claimed and the amount of depreciation recomputed at the 5 year straight line method. You must continue using 5 year straight line even if business use rises back above 50%.
When this happens, get another worksheet, figure the 5 year SL on it and use it for the rest of the auto's life. Employees enter the income on Form 1040, line 21; Ministers also include in computation for Social Security; Self employed taxpayers on Sch. C, line 6; Farmers on Sch. F, line 10.

Without Accountable Reimbursement Plan

W 10-99

WORKSHEET TO COMPUTE AUTO BASIS

FORMULA FOR COMPUTING GAIN OR LOSS WHEN USE IS PART BUSINESS AND PART PERSONAL:

1. Odometer reading when traded *(old car)* .... 101,020 Miles
2. Odometer reading when acquired *(old car)* .... 0 Miles
3. Total miles driven while owned *(line 1 less line 2)* .... 101,020 Miles
4. Business miles driven while owned *(line D)* .... 86,860 Miles
5. Average business % while owned *(line 4 divided by line 3)* ...... 85.98 %
6. Purchase price of old car *(list price)* .... $ 11,141
7. Trade-in allowance towards new car or Sales price .... $(4,338)
8. **Difference** *(line 6 less line 7)* .... $ 6,803
9. Business portion *(line 8 times line 5)* .... $ 5,849
10. Gain or loss on previous trade-in *(if none, enter zero)* .... $ 545
11. Balance of lines 9 and 10 *(subtract gain or add loss)* .... $ 6,394
12. Depreciation and expensing allowed or allowable *(use worksheet below)* .... $ 7,799
13. Gain or loss on business portion .... $ 1,405 (Gain circled) or Loss *(circle one)*
(Gain when line 12 is greater than line 11)
(Loss when line 11 is greater than line 12)
14. Purchase price of new car .... $ 18,235 (List price) + $ 695 (Sales Tax) = $ 18,930 (Total)

DESCRIPTION OF AUTO
DATE ACQUIRED 3/10/99
YEAR 1999
MAKE Mazda 626
NEW (circled) OR USED *(circle one)*

	1999 1st Year	2nd Year	3rd Year	4th Year	5th Year	6th Year
A. Odometer reading end of year	20,315					
B. Odometer reading beginning of year	0					
C. Total miles driven during year *(A minus B)*	20,315					
D. Business miles from log	15,559					
E. Business % *(D divided by C)*	76.59%	%	%	%	%	%
F. Multiply line 14 by E	$ 14,498	$	$	$	$	$
G. Basis for depreciation (Balance of line 13 and F; Subtract gain, Add loss)	$ 13,093	$	$	$	$	$

Year	Basis From (G)	(H) Expensing Sec. 179	(I) Adjusted Basis	(J) Class Life	(K) Method Used	(L) Life or RP	(M) Act Opt	(N) Depreciation Computed	(O) Depreciation Limit	(P) Depreciation Allowed	(Q) Depreciation Recapture
1999	13,093		13,093				Opt	1,867			
	Note: Actual depreciation would have been as follows:										
				5	DDB½	20.00	Act	2,619	2,420	2,420	

General Instructions:

Lines 1 through 11: Enter information from previous auto's worksheet if there has been a trade. Leave blank if newly acquired auto is the result of an outright purchase.

Line 12: Depreciation allowed or allowable is computed as follows:

Actual Depreciation or optional "factor" [see ¶ (P)] .... $______

Plus Expensing - Code Sec. 179 .... $______

Total to be taken to line 12 .... $______

Line 13: If auto is sold, take Gain or Loss to Form 4797. If trade, complete form 8824.

(H) An election in year of purchase, reduce basis each year by amount claimed in year of purchase. Since 6-18-84, luxury auto rules severely limit the use of Code Sec. 179 expensing for autos.

(I) Adjusted basis - Line G minus Column (H). (Basis used for depreciation computation.)

(J) When actual expenses are used, enter "5" for autos purchased after 12-31-86. When optional method is used, leave blank.

(K) Indicate MACRS percentage method by using "DDB". Indicate conventions by "½" or "¼". If 40% of purchases are after 9-30, you must use mid-quarter convention. Indicate Straight Line method by "SL".

(L) When MACRS percentage method is chosen, enter % used. When MACRS straight line is chosen, enter 5 years. When optional method was chosen in 1st year and you have switched to actual, enter the life chosen according to useful life.

(M) Indicate whether depreciation computation in Column (N) is actual method "A" or optional method "O". If optional, indicate whether 7, 7½, 8, 10, 10½, 11, 11½, or 12¢ rate is used. ("O-11½" or "O-12").

(N) **COMPUTE ACTUAL DEPRECIATION AS FOLLOWS:**

MACRS percentage method: After 12-31-86 - Column (I) multiplied by:

Year	Mid-year	Mid-quarter (1st)	Mid-quarter (2nd)	Mid-quarter (3rd)	Mid-quarter (4th)
1	20%	35%	25%	15%	5%
2	32%	26%	30%	34%	38%
3	19.20%	15.60%	18%	20.40%	22.80%
4	11.52%	11.01%	11.37%	12.24%	13.68%
5	11.52%	11.01%	11.37%	11.30%	10.94%
6	5.76%	1.38%	4.26%	7.06%	9.58%

MACRS straight line method: Column (I) divided by 5 years. First year is either ½ year or mid-quarter convention.

When business use is 50% or less, only 5 year straight line can be computed for autos purchased since 6-18-84.

If Code Sec. 179 expensing has been elected, add Column (H) to actual depreciation.

Since 1-1-81, if you choose actual depreciation in year of purchase, you must continue to use actual as long as you own that car.

COMPUTE OPTIONAL DEPRECIATION FACTOR AS FOLLOWS:

1980 thru 1989: Business miles up to but no more than 15,000 per year or 60,000 per auto, multiplied by 7¢ in 1980 and 1981; 7½¢ in 1982; 8¢ in 1983, 1984, and 1985; 9¢ in 1986; 10¢ in 1987; 10½¢ in 1988; 11¢ in 1989.

1990 thru 1998: All business miles multiplied by 11¢ in 1990 and 1991; 11½¢ in 1992 and 1993; 12¢ in 1994, 1995, 1996, 1997, and 1998.

1999: All business miles multiplied by 12¢.

If optional method is elected in the 1st year, it carries with it the election to exclude the auto from the MACRS method of depreciation. As "non-recovery" property, depreciation is required to be computed as straight line over the useful life in any year election is changed to actual method. As "non-recovery" property, you may choose actual or optional method each year.

(O) Luxury auto limitations for depreciation:

Date Auto Placed in Service

# of Years Owned	1-1-87 thru 12-31-88	1-1-89 thru 12-31-90	1-1-91 thru 12-31-91	1-1-92 thru 12-31-92	1-1-93 thru 12-31-93	1-1-94 thru 12-31-94	1-1-95 thru 12-31-96	1-1-97 thru 12-31-97	1-1-98 thru 12-31-98	1-1-99 thru 12-31-99
1st year	$2,560	$2,660	$2,660	$2,760	$2,860	$2,960	$3,060	$3,160	$3,160	$3,060
2nd year	$4,100	$4,200	$4,300	$4,400	$4,600	$4,700	$4,900	$5,000	$5,000	$5,000
3rd year	$2,450	$2,550	$2,550	$2,650	$2,750	$2,850	$2,950	$3,050	$2,950	$2,950
4th- 6th	$1,475	$1,475	$1,575	$1,575	$1,675	$1,675	$1,775	$1,775	$1,775	$1,775

Date Auto Placed in Service 3 / 10 / 99

Year	Amount from Table		Business %		Depr. Limit	Year	Amount from Table		Business %		Depr. Limit
1st	$ 3,060	X	76.59 %	=	$ 2,420	4th	$	X	%	=	$
2nd	$	X	%	=	$	5th	$	X	%	=	$
3rd	$	X	%	=	$	6th	$	X	%	=	$

(P) Enter the smallest of Column (N) or (O). Also, enter this amount on Form 2106.

(Q) Autos purchased after 6-18-84: Depreciation Recapture or "pay back" is to be computed if an auto was more than 50% business use in year of purchase, but drops below 50% business use in any future year when a method of accelerated depreciation was used. You must include in gross income the difference between depreciation and Code Section 179 expensing claimed and the amount of depreciation recomputed at the 5 year straight line method. You must continue using 5 year straight line even if business use rises back above 50%. When this happens, get another worksheet, figure the 5 year SL on it and use it for the rest of the auto's life. Employees enter the income on Form 1040, line 21; Ministers also include in computation for Social Security; Self employed taxpayers on Sch. C, line 6; Farmers on Sch. F, line 10.

With Accountable Reimbursement Plan

Form 1040 Department of the Treasury—Internal Revenue Service
U.S. Individual Income Tax Return 1999 (99) IRS Use Only—Do not write or staple in this space.

For the year Jan. 1–Dec. 31, 1999, or other tax year beginning , 1999, ending , OMB No. 1545-0074

Label (See instructions on page 18.) Use the IRS label. Otherwise, please print or type.

Your first name and initial: H. James	Last name: Snodgrass	Your social security number: 483 12 0000
If a joint return, spouse's first name and initial: Mary T.	Last name: Snodgrass	Spouse's social security number: 483 15 0000
Home address (number and street). If you have a P.O. box, see page 18.: 2309 E. Smith Street	Apt. no.	**IMPORTANT!** You **must** enter your SSN(s) above.
City, town or post office, state, and ZIP code. If you have a foreign address, see page 18: South Bend, IN 46617		

Presidential Election Campaign (See page 18.)

	Yes	No
Do you want $3 to go to this fund?		X
If a joint return, does your spouse want $3 to go to this fund?		X

Note. Checking "Yes" will not change your tax or reduce your refund.

Filing Status (Check only one box.)

1 [ ] Single
2 [X] Married filing joint return (even if only one had income)
3 [ ] Married filing separate return. Enter spouse's social security no. above and full name here. ▶
4 [ ] Head of household (with qualifying person). (See page 18.) If the qualifying person is a child but not your dependent, enter this child's name here. ▶
5 [ ] Qualifying widow(er) with dependent child (year spouse died ▶ 19). (See page 18.)

Exemptions

6a [X] **Yourself.** If your parent (or someone else) can claim you as a dependent on his or her tax return, **do not** check box 6a. — No. of boxes checked on 6a and 6b: 2
b [X] Spouse
c Dependents:

(1) First name Last name	(2) Dependent's social security number	(3) Dependent's relationship to you	(4) ✓ if qualifying child for child tax credit (see page 19)
Ruth A Snodgrass	483 13 0000	Child	[ ]
Thomas A Snodgrass	485 14 0000	Child	[X]
Samuel A Snodgrass	486 15 0000	Child	[X]

If more than six dependents, see page 19.

No. of your children on 6c who: • lived with you: 3; • did not live with you due to divorce or separation (see page 19); Dependents on 6c not entered above

d Total number of exemptions claimed — Add numbers entered on lines above ▶ 5

Income

Attach Copy B of your Forms W-2 and W-2G here. Also attach Form(s) 1099-R if tax was withheld. If you did not get a W-2, see page 20. Enclose, but do not staple, any payment. Also, please use Form 1040-V.

7	Wages, salaries, tips, etc. Attach Form(s) W-2. 12,000 + 35,278	7	47,278
8a	**Taxable** interest. Attach Schedule B if required	8a	
b	**Tax-exempt** interest. DO NOT include on line 8a — 8b		
9	Ordinary dividends. Attach Schedule B if required	9	
10	Taxable refunds, credits, or offsets of state and local income taxes (see page 21)	10	
11	Alimony received	11	
12	Business income or (loss). Attach Schedule C or C-EZ	12	565
13	Capital gain or (loss). Attach Schedule D if required. If not required, check here ▶ [ ]	13	
14	Other gains or (losses). Attach Form 4797	14	
15a	Total IRA distributions 15a — b Taxable amount (see page 22)	15b	
16a	Total pensions and annuities 16a — b Taxable amount (see page 22)	16b	
17	Rental real estate, royalties, partnerships, S corporations, trusts, etc. Attach Schedule E	17	
18	Farm income or (loss). Attach Schedule F	18	
19	Unemployment compensation	19	
20a	Social security benefits 20a — b Taxable amount (see page 24)	20b	
21	Other income. List type and amount (see page 24) Excess Pars. Allow.	21	1,517
22	Add the amounts in the far right column for lines 7 through 21. This is your **total income** ▶	22	49,360

Adjusted Gross Income

23	IRA deduction (see page 26)	23			
24	Student loan interest deduction (see page 26)	24			
25	Medical savings account deduction. Attach Form 8853	25			
26	Moving expenses. Attach Form 3903	26			
27	One-half of self-employment tax. Attach Schedule SE	27	2,097		
28	Self-employed health insurance deduction (see page 28)	28			
29	Keogh and self-employed SEP and SIMPLE plans	29			
30	Penalty on early withdrawal of savings	30			
31a	Alimony paid b Recipient's SSN ▶	31a			
32	Add lines 23 through 31a			32	2,097
33	Subtract line 32 from line 22. This is your **adjusted gross income** ▶			33	47,263

For Disclosure, Privacy Act, and Paperwork Reduction Act Notice, see page 54. Cat. No. 11320B Form **1040** (1999)

Form 1040 (1999) Page **2**

Tax and Credits

34	Amount from line 33 (adjusted gross income)			34	47,263
35a	Check if: [ ] **You** were 65 or older, [ ] Blind; [ ] **Spouse** was 65 or older, [ ] Blind. Add the number of boxes checked above and enter the total here ▶ 35a				
b	If you are married filing separately and your spouse itemizes deductions or you were a dual-status alien, see page 30 and check here ▶ 35b [ ]				
36	Enter your **itemized deductions** from Schedule A, line 28, **OR standard deduction** shown on the left. **But** see page 30 to find your standard deduction if you checked any box on line 35a or 35b **or** if someone can claim you as a dependent			36	17,141
37	Subtract line 36 from line 34			37	30,122
38	If line 34 is $94,975 or less, multiply $2,750 by the total number of exemptions claimed on line 6d. If line 34 is over $94,975, see the worksheet on page 31 for the amount to enter			38	13,750
39	**Taxable income.** Subtract line 38 from line 37. If line 38 is more than line 37, enter -0-			39	16,372
40	**Tax** (see page 31). Check if any tax is from a [ ] Form(s) 8814 b [ ] Form 4972 ▶			40	2,456
41	Credit for child and dependent care expenses. Attach Form 2441	41			
42	Credit for the elderly or the disabled. Attach Schedule R	42			
43	Child tax credit (see page 33)	43	1,000		
44	Education credits. Attach Form 8863	44			
45	Adoption credit. Attach Form 8839	45			
46	Foreign tax credit. Attach Form 1116 if required	46			
47	Other. Check if from a [ ] Form 3800 b [ ] Form 8396 c [ ] Form 8801 d [ ] Form (specify)	47			
48	Add lines 41 through 47. These are your **total credits**			48	1,000
49	Subtract line 48 from line 40. If line 48 is more than line 40, enter -0- ▶			49	1,456

Standard Deduction for Most People — Single: $4,300; Head of household: $6,350; Married filing jointly or Qualifying widow(er): $7,200; Married filing separately: $3,600

Other Taxes

50	Self-employment tax. Attach Schedule SE	50	4,194
51	Alternative minimum tax. Attach Form 6251	51	
52	Social security and Medicare tax on tip income not reported to employer. Attach Form 4137	52	
53	Tax on IRAs, other retirement plans, and MSAs. Attach Form 5329 if required	53	
54	Advance earned income credit payments from Form(s) W-2	54	
55	Household employment taxes. Attach Schedule H	55	
56	Add lines 49 through 55. This is your **total tax** ▶	56	5,650

Payments

57	Federal income tax withheld from Forms W-2 and 1099	57	7,848		
58	1999 estimated tax payments and amount applied from 1998 return	58			
59a	**Earned income credit.** Attach Sch. EIC if you have a qualifying child	59a			
b	Nontaxable earned income: amount ▶ and type ▶				
60	Additional child tax credit. Attach Form 8812	60			
61	Amount paid with request for extension to file (see page 48)	61			
62	Excess social security and RRTA tax withheld (see page 48)	62			
63	Other payments. Check if from a [ ] Form 2439 b [ ] Form 4136	63			
64	Add lines 57, 58, 59a, and 60 through 63. These are your **total payments** ▶			64	7,848

Refund

65	If line 64 is more than line 56, subtract line 56 from line 64. This is the amount you **OVERPAID**	65	2,198
66a	Amount of line 65 you want **REFUNDED TO YOU** ▶	66a	2,198
b	Routing number ▶ c Type: [ ] Checking [ ] Savings		
d	Account number		
67	Amount of line 65 you want **APPLIED TO YOUR 2000 ESTIMATED TAX** ▶ 67		

Have it directly deposited! See page 48 and fill in 66b, 66c, and 66d.

Amount You Owe

68 If line 56 is more than line 64, subtract line 64 from line 56. This is the **AMOUNT YOU OWE.** For details on how to pay, see page 49 ▶ 68
69 Estimated tax penalty. Also include on line 68 — 69

Sign Here

Under penalties of perjury, I declare that I have examined this return and accompanying schedules and statements, and to the best of my knowledge and belief, they are true, correct, and complete. Declaration of preparer (other than taxpayer) is based on all information of which preparer has any knowledge.

Joint return? See page 18. Keep a copy for your records.

Your signature	Date	Your occupation: Minister	Daytime telephone number (optional) ( )
Spouse's signature. If a joint return, BOTH must sign.	Date	Spouse's occupation: Nurse	

Paid Preparer's Use Only

Preparer's signature	Date	Check if self-employed [ ]	Preparer's SSN or PTIN
Firm's name (or yours if self-employed) and address			EIN
			ZIP code

Form **1040** (1999)

With Accountable Reimbursement Plan

SCHEDULES A&B (Form 1040)
Department of the Treasury Internal Revenue Service (99)

Schedule A—Itemized Deductions

(Schedule B is on back)

▶ Attach to Form 1040. ▶ See Instructions for Schedules A and B (Form 1040).

OMB No. 1545-0074 — 1999 — Attachment Sequence No. 07

Name(s) shown on Form 1040: H. James & Mary T. Snodgrass — Your social security number: 483 : 12 : 0000

Medical and Dental Expenses		**Caution.** Do not include expenses reimbursed or paid by others.				
	1	Medical and dental expenses (see page A-1)	1			
	2	Enter amount from Form 1040, line 34. [2]				
	3	Multiply line 2 above by 7.5% (.075)	3			
	4	Subtract line 3 from line 1. If line 3 is more than line 1, enter -0-			4	
Taxes You Paid (See page A-2.)	5	State and local income taxes 728+176+720+60+152	5	1,836		
	6	Real estate taxes (see page A-2)	6	1,182		
	7	Personal property taxes	7	534		
	8	Other taxes. List type and amount ▶	8			
	9	Add lines 5 through 8			9	3,552
Interest You Paid (See page A-3.)	10	Home mortgage interest and points reported to you on Form 1098	10	8,081		
	11	Home mortgage interest not reported to you on Form 1098. If paid to the person from whom you bought the home, see page A-3 and show that person's name, identifying no., and address ▶	11			
Note. Personal interest is not deductible.	12	Points not reported to you on Form 1098. See page A-3 for special rules	12			
	13	Investment interest. Attach Form 4952 if required. (See page A-3.)	13			
	14	Add lines 10 through 13			14	8,081
Gifts to Charity If you made a gift and got a benefit for it, see page A-4.	15	Gifts by cash or check. If you made any gift of $250 or more, see page A-4	15	5,508		
	16	Other than by cash or check. If any gift of $250 or more, see page A-4. You **MUST** attach Form 8283 if over $500	16			
	17	Carryover from prior year	17			
	18	Add lines 15 through 17			18	5,508
Casualty and Theft Losses	19	Casualty or theft loss(es). Attach Form 4684. (See page A-5.)			19	
Job Expenses and Most Other Miscellaneous Deductions	20	Unreimbursed employee expenses—job travel, union dues, job education, etc. You **MUST** attach Form 2106 or 2106-EZ if required. (See page A-5.) ▶ Nursing Expense 510	20	510		
	21	Tax preparation fees	21	117		
(See page A-5 for expenses to deduct here.)	22	Other expenses—investment, safe deposit box, etc. List type and amount ▶	22			
	23	Add lines 20 through 22	23	627		
	24	Enter amount from Form 1040, line 34. [24] 47,263				
	25	Multiply line 24 above by 2% (.02)	25	945		
	26	Subtract line 25 from line 23. If line 25 is more than line 23, enter -0-			26	0
Other Miscellaneous Deductions	27	Other—from list on page A-6. List type and amount ▶			27	
Total Itemized Deductions	28	Is Form 1040, line 34, over $126,600 (over $63,300 if married filing separately)? ☐ **No.** Your deduction is not limited. Add the amounts in the far right column for lines 4 through 27. Also, enter this amount on Form 1040, line 36. ☐ **Yes.** Your deduction may be limited. See page A-6 for the amount to enter. ▶			28	17,141

For Paperwork Reduction Act Notice, see Form 1040 instructions. Cat. No. 11330X Schedule A (Form 1040) 1999

SCHEDULE C-EZ (Form 1040)
Department of the Treasury Internal Revenue Service (99)

Net Profit From Business

(Sole Proprietorship)

▶ Partnerships, joint ventures, etc., must file Form 1065 or 1065-B.
▶ Attach to Form 1040 or Form 1041. ▶ See instructions on back.

OMB No. 1545-0074 — 1999 — Attachment Sequence No. 09A

Name of proprietor: H. James Snodgrass — Social security number (SSN): 483 : 12 : 0000

Part I General Information

You May Use Schedule C-EZ Instead of Schedule C Only If You:

- Had business expenses of $2,500 or less.
- Use the cash method of accounting.
- Did not have an inventory at any time during the year.
- Did not have a net loss from your business.
- Had only one business as a sole proprietor.

And You:

- Had no employees during the year.
- Are not required to file **Form 4562,** Depreciation and Amortization, for this business. See the instructions for Schedule C, line 13, on page C-3 to find out if you must file.
- Do not deduct expenses for business use of your home.
- Do not have prior year unallowed passive activity losses from this business.

A Principal business or profession, including product or service: Honorariums

B Enter code from pages C-8 & 9 ▶ 8 1 3 0 0 0

C Business name. If no separate business name, leave blank.

D Employer ID number (EIN), if any

E Business address (including suite or room no.). Address not required if same as on Form 1040, page 1.

City, town or post office, state, and ZIP code

Part II Figure Your Net Profit

Line	Description	Box	Amount
1	**Gross receipts. Caution:** *If this income was reported to you on Form W-2 and the "Statutory employee" box on that form was checked, see* ***Statutory Employees*** *in the instructions for Schedule C, line 1, on page C-2 and check here* ▶ ☐	1	690
2	**Total expenses.** If more than $2,500, you **must** use Schedule C. See instructions	2	125
3	**Net profit.** Subtract line 2 from line 1. If less than zero, you **must** use Schedule C. Enter on **Form 1040, line 12,** and ALSO on **Schedule SE, line 2.** (Statutory employees **do not** report this amount on Schedule SE, line 2. Estates and trusts, enter on Form 1041, line 3.)	3	565

Part III **Information on Your Vehicle.** Complete this part **ONLY** if you are claiming car or truck expenses on line 2.

4 When did you place your vehicle in service for business purposes? (month, day, year) ▶ ____/____/____

5 Of the total number of miles you drove your vehicle during 1999, enter the number of miles you used your vehicle for:

a Business ________ b Commuting ________ c Other ________

6 Do you (or your spouse) have another vehicle available for personal use? ☐ Yes ☐ No

7 Was your vehicle available for use during off-duty hours? ☐ Yes ☐ No

8a Do you have evidence to support your deduction? ☐ Yes ☐ No

b If "Yes," is the evidence written? ☐ Yes ☐ No

For Paperwork Reduction Act Notice, see Form 1040 instructions. Cat. No. 14374D Schedule C-EZ (Form 1040) 1999

With Accountable Reimbursement Plan

WORKSHEET TO BE USED WITH FORM 2106

Your Name	Social Security Number	Occupation in which expenses were incurred	Taxable Year
H. James Snodgrass	483 12 0000	Minister	1999

☒ Ordained ☐ Licensed ☐ Commissioned ☐ Other — Filed Form 4361? ☐ Yes ☒ No

ACTUAL AUTO EXPENSES (Complete Form 2106, Part II, Sec. A & B first)

	Vehicle 1	Vehicle 2
1. Garage rent		
2. Gas, oil, & lubrication		
3. Repairs		
4. Tires & batteries		
5. Insurance & auto club		
6. Miscellaneous		
7. Washing and polishing		
8. License (registration portion)		
9. TOTAL		

(enter on Form 2106, Part II, Section C, Line 23)

LOCAL TRAVEL EXPENSES

1. Parking	
2. Tolls	
3. Fares	
4. TOTAL	

(Enter on Form 2106-EZ, Part II, Line 2 or Form 2106, Part I, Line 2)

OVERNIGHT TRAVEL EXPENSES

1. Auto rental, taxi, etc.	
2. Fares (air, train, bus)	
3. Parking & tolls	
4. Laundry & cleaning	
5. Lodging	
6. Telephone, telegraph, postage, fax	
7. Tips, other than meals	
8. TOTAL	

(Enter on Form 2106-EZ, Part II, Line 3 or Form 2106, Part I, Line 3)

PROFESSIONAL EXPENSES (UNREIMBURSED)

1. Business-in-home (see attached)	
2. Education expenses	
3. Equipment depreciation	
4. Office supplies and postage	
5. Religious materials	
6. Sales aids	
7. Seminars and dues	
8. Subscriptions and paperbacks	
9. Telephone	
10. Other	
11. TOTAL	

(Enter on Form 2106-EZ, Part II, Line 4 or Form 2106, Part I, Line 4)

MEALS AND ENTERTAINMENT

1. Meals while away from home ☒ Actual ☐ Optional	
2. Entertainment, meals	
3. Entertainment, other	
4. Tips for meals	
5. TOTAL	

(Enter on Form 2106-EZ, Part II, Line 5 or Form 2106, Part I, Line 5)

COMPUTATION OF PARSONAGE ALLOWANCE

Date of purchase: 6 / 10 / 87
FMV of home you own: $ 115,000

	A PROVIDED BY CHURCH	B PAID BY MINISTER
1. Value of parsonage provided by church		
2. Rent or principal payments		835
3. Taxes		1,182
4. Interest		8,081
5. Insurance		340
6. Repairs & upkeep		793
7. Furniture, appliances, etc.		1,409
8. Decorator items		463
9. Utilities		2,738
10. Miscellaneous supplies		642
11. TOTAL		16,483
12. Fair Rental Value Computation: Compute in year of purchase and in any year of major expense. (Homeowners only)		
FRV of home 13,800		
FRV of furniture 4,500		
Decorator items 463		
Utilities 2,738		
Miscellaneous 642		
Total of line 12 22,143		
13. Less of Column B, line 11 or line 12		16,483
14. Amount designated		18,000
15a. If line 14 is greater than line 13, enter the difference here and as income on Form 1040, line 21; **or** 15b. If amount is included in error on W-2, enter the lesser of line 13 or line 14 as a deduction on Form 1040, line 21		1,517

COMPUTATION OF SOCIAL SECURITY BASE

(If exempt, you may omit this section. Write "Exempt-Form 4361" on the self-employment line, Form 1040, page 2.)

1. Salary from W-2	12,000
2. Parsonage provided, Column A, line 11	
3. Parsonage allowance, Column B, line 14	18,000
4. Recapture of auto depreciation	
5. Less business portion of tax preparation	(40)
6. Less business % of auto interest and personal property tax	*(845)
7. Less unreimbursed employee business expense (enter from Form 2106-EZ, line 6 or Form 2106, line 10)	
8. TOTAL (enter on Schedule SE, Sec. A, line 2)	29,115

* Auto 1 ($158 int. X 80.24% bus. %) + Auto 2 ([$481 int. + $456 P.P. tax] X 76.59 bus %) = $ 845

SCHEDULE SE (Form 1040) — **Self-Employment Tax** — OMB No. 1545-0074 — 1999

Department of the Treasury Internal Revenue Service

▶ See Instructions for Schedule SE (Form 1040).
▶ Attach to Form 1040.

Attachment Sequence No. 17

Name of person with **self-employment** income (as shown on Form 1040): H. James Snodgrass
Social security number of person with **self-employment** income ▶ 483 12 0000

Who Must File Schedule SE

You must file Schedule SE if:

- You had net earnings from self-employment from **other than** church employee income (line 4 of Short Schedule SE or line 4c of Long Schedule SE) of $400 or more, **OR**
- You had church employee income of $108.28 or more. Income from services you performed as a minister or a member of a religious order **is not** church employee income. See page SE-1.

Note: *Even if you had a loss or a small amount of income from self-employment, it may be to your benefit to file Schedule SE and use either "optional method" in Part II of Long Schedule SE. See page SE-3.*

Exception. If your only self-employment income was from earnings as a minister, member of a religious order, or Christian Science practitioner **and** you filed Form 4361 and received IRS approval not to be taxed on those earnings, **do not** file Schedule SE. Instead, write "Exempt–Form 4361" on Form 1040, line 50.

May I Use Short Schedule SE or MUST I Use Long Schedule SE?

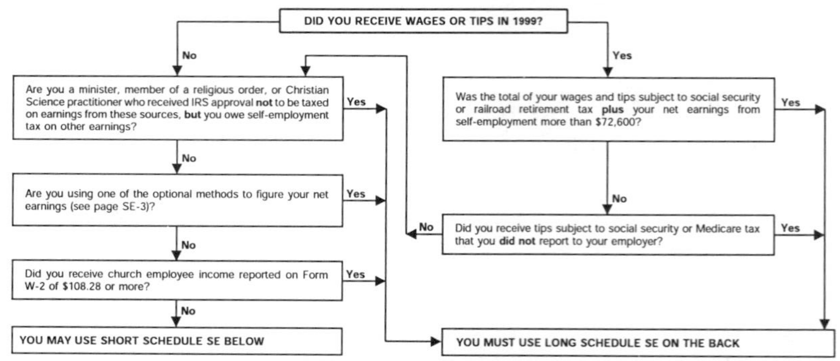

Section A—Short Schedule SE. Caution: *Read above to see if you can use Short Schedule SE.*

1	Net farm profit or (loss) from Schedule F, line 36, and farm partnerships, Schedule K-1 (Form 1065), line 15a	1	
2	Net profit or (loss) from Schedule C, line 31; Schedule C-EZ, line 3; Schedule K-1 (Form 1065), line 15a (other than farming); and Schedule K-1 (Form 1065-B), box 9. Ministers and members of religious orders, see page SE-1 for amounts to report on this line. See page SE-2 for other income to report . . . 29,115 + 565	2	29,680
3	Combine lines 1 and 2	3	29,680
4	**Net earnings from self-employment.** Multiply line 3 by 92.35% (.9235). If less than $400, **do not** file this schedule; you do not owe self-employment tax ▶	4	27,409
5	**Self-employment tax.** If the amount on line 4 is: • $72,600 or less, multiply line 4 by 15.3% (.153). Enter the result here and on **Form 1040, line 50.** • More than $72,600, multiply line 4 by 2.9% (.029). Then, add $9,002.40 to the result. Enter the total here and on **Form 1040, line 50.**	5	4,194
6	**Deduction for one-half of self-employment tax.** Multiply line 5 by 50% (.5). Enter the result here and on **Form 1040, line 27** . . . 6 — 2,097		

For Paperwork Reduction Act Notice, see Form 1040 instructions. Cat. No. 11358Z **Schedule SE (Form 1040) 1999**

☐ Prior Client

☐ New Client

CHECKLIST

INCOME TAX DATA

Year ______________

This Checklist Will Serve as a Guide in Assembling Your Tax Data and Help You to Take Advantage of All Allowable Deductions. Round Off All Figures to the Nearest Even Dollar.

TAXPAYER		SPOUSE	
Last Name		Last Name (if different)	
First Name and Initial		First Name and Initial	
Occupation	Blind?	Occupation	Blind?
Social Security Number	Birth Date	Social Security Number	Birth Date

Street Address or P.O. Box (if address to appear on return is different than shipping address, enter both.)

City	State	Zip

County of Residence (as of 12/31)	Township or City (as of 12/31)	School District Name (as of 12/31)

Home Telephone	Work Telephone
Fax and/or E-Mail	Best Time to Reach

CHECK HOW YOU WANT TO PAY.

- ☐ Send complete returns C.O.D.
- ☐ Charge to my bankcard.
- ☐ Send Invoice, hold returns until you receive payment.

CHECK HOW TO SEND:

- ☐ First Class Mail.
- ☐ United Parcel Service.

☐ American Express ☐ Discover ☐ VISA ☐ MasterCard

Expiration Month Year

Charge this order to my Charge Account as I have indicated, to be paid according to the current terms of that Account.

Signature ______________________________

(Authorized credit card signature.)

Compliments of . . .

WORTH TAX & FINANCIAL SERVICE

Home Office
Warsaw / Winona Lake, IN

LOCATION:
Just East of Bob Evans
3201 E. Center Street
Warsaw, IN 46580

MAIL TO:
P.O. Box 725
Winona Lake, IN 46590

PHONE / E-MAIL
219•267•4687
800•368•0363 Fax
bjworth@worthfinancial.com

Dependents *Must have Social Security Number*

First, Initial, Last	Date of Birth	Social Security #	Relationship	Months in Home	Full-time Student
					☐
					☐
					☐
					☐
					☐
					☐
					☐
					☐

* If dependent is 19 or over, check box if full-time student for at least 5 months of calendar year. See page 119 to list education expenses for either Hope Scholarship Credit or Lifetime Learning Credit.

Estimated Tax Paid *Send copies of canceled checks*

Quarter	Federal	Date Paid	State	Date Paid	Local	Date Paid
Prior Year Credit	$		$		$	
1st (4/15)	$		$		$	
2nd (6/15)	$		$		$	
3rd (9/15)	$		$		$	
4th (1/15)	$		$		$	
Paid with Extension	$		$		$	

Wages from W-2's *Enclose all copies of W-2 statements. If clergy, send a copy of payroll sheet.*

HW	Employer	Wage	Fed Tax	FICA	Medicare	State	Local

IRA Distributions Received *(Enclose all statements - 1099R & 5498)*

HW	Source & Type	Fed Tax	Total Amount	Value of Acc't (12/31)

Yes No

☐ ☐ Were proceeds used for expenses as a first-time home buyer? (Did not own for two years preceding purchase)

☐ ☐ Were proceeds used to pay for higher education costs? (If yes, list on page 119)

Pension & Annuity Income Received *(Enclose all statements - 1099R)*

HW	Source & Type	Fed Tax	Total Amount	Taxable Amount

	Husband	Wife
Unemployment Compensation		
Social Security Benefits		

Interest Income

Enclose all 1099 statements. Indicate H for husband, W for wife, or J for joint.

HWJ	Institution (if seller-financed mortgage, see below)	Forfeiture*	Amount

HWJ	Name	Address	Social Security #	Amount

* Penalty on early withdrawal of savings

Dividend Income

Enclose all 1099 statements and annual summaries.

HWJ	Name of Payer	Ordinary Dividends	Capital Gain Distributions	Non-Taxable Distributions

Other Income

HWJ	Source	Amount
	Alimony Received (enclose copy of divorce decree)	
	Baby Sitting	
	Director's Fees	
	Hobbies	
	Jury Duty	
	Odd Jobs	
	Partnership/Estates/S-Corporation (enclose K-1s)	
	Prizes and Awards	
	Royalties	
	State refund if you itemized last year	
	City or local refund if you itemized last year	
	Tips not reported to your employer	
	Honorariums	
	Lottery, Gambling Sch. A Losses ( )	
	Other	

Itemized Deductions

Medical

Type of Expenses	Amount
Insurance Premiums	
Medicare Premiums	
Prescriptions	
Insulin	
Doctors	
Dentists	
Chiropractors	
Hospitals	
Ambulance	
Artificial teeth	
Eye glasses	
Hearing aid	
Batteries for hearing aid	
Lab fees	
Nursing fees	
Special shoes	
X-Rays	
Medical supplies (prescription)	
Nursing home	
Air conditioning (prescription)	
Humidifier (prescription)	
Electricity for A.C. & humidifier	
Auto travel (miles)	
Transportation	
Lodging	
Other	
Amount listed above reimbursed by insurance	

Taxes

Kind of Tax	Amount
Last years paid in spring State & local taxes	
For a previous year, if you filed late, received a notice of change, or amended return. State & local taxes	
If you have purchased or sold a home or personal use property, provide a copy of closing statement. Real estate tax #1	
Real estate tax #2	
Personal property tax	
Auto excise tax	

Interest Paid

Home Interest	Amount
1st mortgage	
2nd mortgage	

If paid to individual, enter amount ____________

Name ____________

Address ____________

Social Security Number ____________

Vacation home	
Mortgage line of credit	
Points: ☐ New or ☐ Refinanced # of years of loan ________	

Investment Interest	Amount

Contributions

Cash Contributions

To Whom	Amount
Church	
Red Cross/Scouts	
Salvation Army	
United Fund	
Missions	
Radio broadcast	
College - If located in Indiana or Michigan, enter name ____________	
Other	
Travel: Auto miles	Miles
Fares, Lodging, Meals	$

Noncash Contributions (Totals $500 or less)

Supplies	
FMV clothing & furniture	
Other	

Noncash Contributions (Totals more than $500)

Item #1: Description ____________

Donee Name ____________

Donee Address ____________

Date Contributed	Date Acquired
Cost $	FMV $

Item #2: Description ____________

Donee Name ____________

Donee Address ____________

Date Contributed	Date Acquired
Cost $	FMV $

Note: Items may be individual items or groups of items. If more than two items, attach list.

Itemized Deductions (Continued) - Miscellaneous Deductions

Please list ministry expenses on page 121.

Type of Expense	Amount
Tax Preparation	
Accounting Books	
Union Dues	
Professional Fees	
Professional Publications	
Supplies for Job	
Safety Equipment	
Safety Clothing	
Uniforms	
Cleaning of Uniforms	
Special Shoes/Nylons	
Small Tools	
Equipment	
Telephone/Business	
Employment Agency Fee	
Other Job Expenses	

Investment Expenses	Amount
Publications	
Broker fees	
Safe deposit box	
Escrow fees	
Other	
Job Hunting Expenses	**Amount**
Meals	
Lodging	
Airfare, Auto rental	
Auto travel (miles)	
Postage, typing	
Toll calls	
Other	
Miles Between Two Jobs	**Amount**
Number of days worked two jobs in same day	
Number of miles between the two job sites	

Casualty or Theft

Description of Property	Date Acquired	Date of Casualty or Theft	Cost	FMV Before	FMV After	Insurance Reimbursed

Education Expenses *Hope Scholarship Credit, Lifetime Learning Credit or Job-Related Expenses*

Name of Student				
Name of School				
Date(s) tuition was paid				
Type of Education (College, Vocational, Job related, etc.)				
Was student enrolled at least half-time for at least one academic period in a program leading to a degree, certificate, or other recognized credential? (Hope Credit)	☐ Yes ☐ No	☐ Yes ☐ No	☐ Yes ☐ No	☐ Yes ☐ No
Was student in first or second year of postsecondary education? (Hope Credit)	☐ Yes ☐ No	☐ Yes ☐ No	☐ Yes ☐ No	☐ Yes ☐ No
Tuition and fees	$	$	$	$
Books	$	$	$	$
Supplies	$	$	$	$
Auto Travel (miles)				
Lodging / Room & board	$	$	$	$
Meals (away from home overnight)	$	$	$	$
Scholarship, Grants or Amount Reimbursed	$	$	$	$
If education expense is job related, answer the following questions:				
Are you currently employed	☐ Yes ☐ No	☐ Yes ☐ No	☐ Yes ☐ No	☐ Yes ☐ No
Did your employer require you take courses? .	☐ Yes ☐ No	☐ Yes ☐ No	☐ Yes ☐ No	☐ Yes ☐ No
Were courses directly related to your profession?	☐ Yes ☐ No	☐ Yes ☐ No	☐ Yes ☐ No	☐ Yes ☐ No
Have you already met minimum requirement of your profession?	☐ Yes ☐ No	☐ Yes ☐ No	☐ Yes ☐ No	☐ Yes ☐ No

Minister's Information

Please provide copy of payroll sheet and/or breakdown of your compensation package.

Position ______________________________ Ordained, Licensed, or equivalent *(circle one)*

Yes No

☐ ☐ Are you exempt from paying Social Security? (If yes, send copy of approved Form 4361)

☐ ☐ Have you adequately accounted to your employer and been reimbursed for your professional expenses? (If no, show details on next page.)

☐ ☐ To the best of your knowledge, is your W-2 prepared correctly? If no, what is incorrect?

____

☐ ☐ Did you receive any gifts, bonuses, and allowances (other than parsonage allowance) from your employer that was not included as taxable on your W-2? If yes, what?

______________________________ Amount? ______________________________

$__________ Parsonage allowance officially designated in advance?

$__________ If more than one employer during the year, amount designated with second employer?

$__________ Amount you receive each payday? How often are you paid? ______________________________

$__________ Amount you receive monthly?

Parsonage Information

Parsonage allowance exclusion can apply to only one home at a time, the one that is your personal residence. During a transition or move, you may have incurred parsonage expenses for two homes. Separate the expenses below.

	Home #1	Home #2	Home #3
If employer provided parsonage, what is its rental value?			
If you own, current FMV			
Date occupied			
Location (city & state)			
Type of Expenses Paid By You:	**Amount**	**Amount**	**Amount**

Moving Expenses - Adjustment

Amount Reimbursed or Paid Directly by Employer $____________

Yes No

☐ ☐ *Was any of the amount reimbursed for nonqualifying moving expenses? If yes, how much? . . . . $____________

☐ ☐ Was all or any of the reimbursement included on Form W-2, Box 1? If yes, how much? . . . . $____________

Distance between former residence and new job? ____________ Distance between former residence and former job? ____________

Date of departure? ____/____/____ Date of arrival? ____/____/____

Expenses		Amount
Cost of moving furniture and personal effects		
Transportation of family:	Auto travel	miles
	Fares (air, bus, train, etc.)	
	Cost of lodging enroute	

*** Qualifying expenses include only the cost of moving household goods and personal effects as well as yourself and your family. Cost of meals consumed while traveling, cost of premoving househunting trips, cost of temporary living expenses and the cost of selling or buying a personal residence is no longer deductible as of January 1, 1994.**

Auto Expenses

Amount Reimbursed $__________

If new client, send complete history of business use of auto. Send copies of invoice and complete details of purchase and/or trade for each business auto. Even if you have always used mileage allowance, you may have a taxable gain or deductible loss on the sale of a business auto that must be reported. If leasing, give beginning value.

Auto Information	Auto #1	Auto #2	Auto #3	Auto #4	Auto #5
Year					
Make					
Date of purchase					
Purchase price					
Odometer at purchase					
Total miles for the year					
*Business miles-total for year					
Business miles (1/1/99 - 3/31/99)					
Daily roundtrip commuting					
Commuting miles for the year					
Auto lease					
Garage rent					
Gas, oil, lube					
Repairs					
Tires & batteries					
Insurance & auto club					
Miscellaneous					
Washing & polishing					
License (registration portion)					
**Interest					
**Personal property tax					
***Sales tax					

* If you have used auto for more than one business activity, enter total business miles here and give us extra note stating how may miles were driven for each business activity.

** Employee's auto interest is no longer deductible; Employee's personal property tax is deductible on Sch. A only.

*** Sales tax can be used to increase cost basis.

Yes	No	N/A	
☐	☐		Do you (or your spouse) have another vehicle available for personal purposes?
☐	☐	☐	If your employer provided you with a vehicle, is personal use during off hours permitted?
☐	☐		Do you have evidence to support your deduction?
☐	☐		If yes, is the evidence written?

Travel & Professional Expenses

Amount Reimbursed $__________

Travel - Local	Amount
Parking	
Tolls	
Fares	
Travel - While Away from Home Overnight	
Auto rental, taxi, etc.	
Fares (air, train, bus)	
Parking & tolls	
Laundry & cleaning	
Lodging	
Telephone, postage, fax	
Tips (other than meals)	
Meals and Entertainment	
Meals while away from home overnight	
Number of days away from home	
Entertainment, meals	
Entertainment, other	
Tips for meals	

Professional Expenses	Amount
Education expenses	
Office supplies & postage	
Religious materials	
Seminars & dues	
Subscriptions & paperbacks	
Business telephone	
Gifts	
Other	

Equipment and Library		
Date	Item	Amount

Business Income & Expense: Schedule C

Name of Proprietor ____________________

Principle activity / product or service ____________________

Business name & address ____________________

Employer identification number __ __ - __ __ __ __ __ __ __ *(9 digits)*

Accounting Method: ☐ Cash ☐ Accrual ☐ Other __________

Inventory Method: ☐ Cost ☐ Lower Cost or Market ☐ Other __________

Yes	No	
☐	☐	Was there any change in determining quantities, costs, or valuations between opening and closing inventory?
☐	☐	Did you "materially participate" in operation of business?
☐	☐	Were you a statutory employee with income reported on Form W-2?
☐	☐	Was this business started or acquired this year?
☐	☐	Was this business in operation at the end of the year?

Receipts	Amount
Services	
Sale of Merchandise	
Commissions	
Babysitting, odd jobs	
Honorariums	
Beginning accounts receivable	
Ending accounts receivable	

Cost of Goods Sold	Amount
Beginning inventory	
Purchases	
Less personal use	
Contract labor	
Supplies	
Freight, receiving	
Ending inventory	
Beginning accounts payable	
Ending accounts payable	

*Building & Equipment		
Date	Item	Amount

Business-In-Home	Amount
Total square feet in home	
Square feet used for business	
Date of purchase	/ /
Cost of home	
Cost of improvements	
Rent	
Interest	
Taxes	
Insurance	
Heat & light	
Repairs - entire house	
Repairs - business portion	

Expenses	Amount
Advertising	
Bad debts from sales	
Bank service charges	
**Auto & truck expense	
Commissions	
Depletion	
Employee benefits	
Insurance	
Interest: Mortgage	
Interest: Other	
Legal & professional	
Office expense	
Pension plans	
Rent - Equipment	
Rent - Other business property	
Repairs & maintenance	
Supplies	
Real estate tax	
Personal property tax	
Sales tax	
FICA & unemployment tax	
Travel	
Meals & entertainment	
Utilities	
Telephone	
Wages	
Wages paid spouse	
Wages paid children	
Miscellaneous	

* State details on page 121, Auto Expense

** Bring in last years return so that depreciation can be computed on prior owned items

Sale of Property, Stock: Schedule D

HWJ	Description	# of Shares	Date Acquired	Date Sold	Gross Sales Price	Cost or Basis	Expense of Sale

Installment Sale

If contract began this year, send copies of contract, amortization schedule (list the principal and interest), original purchase closing statement, cost of all improvements. Enter interest on page 3.

Description	Date Acquired	Date Sold	Gross Profit Percentage	Principal Received This Year	Principal Received Prior Years

Sale of Personal Residence *Bring or send copy of purchasing closing statement and selling closing statement.*

Yes No

☐ ☐ Did you own and use the property as your main home for a total of at least 2 years of the 5-year period before the sale?

☐ ☐ If no, did you sell the home because of a change in health or a change in employment?

If yes, enter dates that you did use as main home: From ____/____/____ to ____/____/____

Description	Amount	Description	Amount
Original Cost		Date acquired	/ /
Improvements (list):		Date sold	/ /
		Sales price	
		Expense of sale	
		Energy credits claimed	
		Gain postponed from previous sale	
		Depreciation for previous business use	
		Casualty losses previously allowed	

Child and Dependent Care

Employer-Provided Dependent Care Benefits Received $__________

Persons or Organizations providing the care (nursery & kindergarten school expenses may qualify for the credit):

Name	Address	SSN or EIN	Amount

Qualifying Person(s) for whom expenses were paid (Note: The total of the "Amount" columns above and below should equal).

Name	Age	Relationship	Social Security Number	Amount

Note: You are required to file Sch. H if amounts paid to persons working in your home is $1,100 or more in a calendar year.

Rental Income and Expense: Schedule E

Kind & location of Property
#1
#2
#3
#4
#5

Yes No

☐ ☐ Did you or a member of your family use for personal purposes any of the properties for more than 14 days or 10% of the total days rented at fair rental value? If yes, which property? # ______

☐ ☐ Did you actively participate in the management of your rentals? If no, which property? # ______

Revenues	#1	#2	#3	#4	#5
Gross Rent Income					
Royalties					
Date Rental Activity Began	/ /	/ /	/ /	/ /	/ /
Expenses					
Advertising					
Auto - travel					
Cleaning					
Commissions					
Insurance					
Legal & professional					
Management fees					
Mortgage interest					
Other interest					
Repairs: General					
Plumbing					
Electrical					
Painting					
Supplies					
Taxes & licenses					
Utilities					
Wages & salaries					
Lot Rent					
Other					

Building, Major Improvements, Furniture

Date	Description	Property #	Amount

Farm Income and Expense: Schedule F

Location and size of farm ______________________________

Principle product______________________________

Employer's ID # __ __ - __ __ __ __ __ __ __ *(9 digits)* Accounting Method: ☐ Cash ☐ Accrual

Yes	No	N/A	
☐	☐		Did you make an election in a prior year to include commodity credit loan proceeds as income in that year?
☐	☐		Did you "materially participate" in the operation of this business during this year? If no, and you have a loss, loss will be limited.
☐	☐	☐	Do you elect, or did you previously elect, to currently deduct certain preproductive period expenses?

Income	Amount
Cattle -raised - resale	
Cattle - purchased - resale	
Cost of cattle sold	( )
Dairy or breeding cattle	
Cost of dairy or breeding cattle sold	( )
Sheep - raised - resale	
Sheep - purchased - resale	
Cost of sheep sold	( )
Breeding Sheep	
Cost of breeding sheep sold	( )
Hogs - raised - resale	
Hogs - purchased - resale	
Cost of hogs sold	( )
Breeding hogs sold	
Cost of breeding hogs	( )
Horses	
Poultry	
Dairy products	
Eggs	
Wool	
Cotton	
Tobacco	
Vegetables	
Soybeans	
Corn	
Other grains	
Hay & straw	
Fruits & nuts	
Custom machine hire	
Patronage dividends	
ASCS payments: Cash	
Materials & services	
C.C. loans	
Federal gas tax credit	
State gas tax credit	
Crop insurance proceeds	
Labor	
Other	

* Bring in last year's return so that depreciation can be computed on prior owned items.

** Show details on page 121, Auto Expense

Expenses	Amount
Chemicals	
Conservation expenses	
Custom machine hire	
Employee benefits	
Feed purchased	
Fertilizers & lime	
Freight, trucking	
Gasoline - # of gallons ________	
Other fuel, oil	
Insurance	
Interest: mortgage	
Interest: other	
Labor hired	
Labor, spouse	
Pension plans	
Rent of machinery	
Rent of land, animals	
Repairs & maintenance	
Seeds & plants	
Storage & warehousing	
Supplies	
Real estate taxes	
Personal property taxes	
FICA & unemployment	
Utilities	
Telephone	
Veterinary, medicine, & breeding	
Advertising & accounting	
Dues & subscriptions	
Meals for labor	
Office supplies	
Travel	
Meals & entertainment	
**Truck & auto expense	
Watchdog expense	
Other	

* Building & Equipment		
Date	Item	Amount

IRA, SEP, and Keogh Contributions

HW	Traditional IRA	Roth IRA	Educational IRA	SEP	Keogh

Yes No
☐ ☐ Active participant in employer provided retirement plan?
☐ ☐ Is spouse an active participant in employer provided retirement plan?

Student Loan Interest Paid

$________ Amount of interest paid during the year.
__/__/__ Date interest payments were first required? (Only deductible during first 60 months.)

Yes No
☐ ☐ While a student, were you enrolled at least half-time?

Alimony Paid *Bring or send copy of divorce decree*

To whom ______________ Social Security # __________ Amount $__________

Reside in a Foreign Country During the Year?

Name of Country ______________ Date entered __/__/__ Date left __/__/__

Yes No
☐ ☐ Do you consider yourself a bonafide resident of this country?
☐ ☐ If no, were you (or do you anticipate being) physically present in this country for at least 330 days during a 365 day period?

Presidential Campaign Fund

Yes No
☐ ☐ Do you want $3 to go to this fund?
☐ ☐ If joint return, does spouse want $3 to go to this fund?

Questions *If yes explain below*

Yes No
☐ ☐ Any births, adoptions, marriages, divorces or deaths in your family during the past year?
☐ ☐ Does anyone owe you money that has become a bad debt?
☐ ☐ Have you used bartering to exchange any goods or services?
☐ ☐ Did you or your spouse receive any source of income that is not listed in this checklist?
☐ ☐ Did you sell an auto, equipment or any property? If yes, give details.
☐ ☐ Did you live in more than one state during the year? If yes, give date of move: __/__/__

____

____

____

Nontaxable Income

Child Support . . . . . $________ Veteran's benefits $________ Other *(explain)* . . . . $________
Welfare payments $________ Workman's Comp $________ ________________

Indiana State Information

Amount of rent paid $________ # of months rented ________ School district name ________
Location of principal residence ______________________
Landlord's name ______________ Address ______________
(T) County of residence, Jan. 1? ______________ County of work, Jan. 1? ______________
(S) County of residence, Jan. 1? ______________ County of work, Jan. 1? ______________
Number of Motor Vehicles Owned? ________ Are they registered with Indiana BMV? ☐ Yes ☐ No

Taxpayer's Statement

The information furnished herewith is to enable you to prepare my (our) income tax return for the above year. It is true and complete to the best of my (our) knowledge and belief, and is to be relied upon by you accordingly.

Signature ______________________ Date ______________
Signature ______________________ Date ______________

INDEX

Professional Tax Record Book

- *Business Mileage Diary*
- *Auto Expense*
- *Travel Expense*
- *Professional Expense*
- *Entertainment Expense*
- *Housing Expense*
- *Professional Income*
- *Monthly Summary*

Refill Pages & Tabs without Binder

Quantity	Price
1 to 2	$13.99
3 to 14	$11.90
15 to 99	$11.20
100 or more	$8.40

Vinyl Binder With Pockets
Looseleaf – 160 pages
6 Rings – Tab Dividers
Page Size - 3¾ X 6½

Complete Book with Binder

Quantity	Price
1 to 2	$17.99
3 to 14	$15.30
15 to 99	$14.40
100 or more	$10.80

Auto Log Book

- *Business Mileage Log and Auto Expense Only*
- *Durable Cover – 48 pages*
- *Handy Pocket Size*

Quantity	Price
1 to 2	$3.99
3 to 14	$3.40
15 to 99	$3.20
100 or more	$2.40

Minister's Compensation Package Tax & Financial Planning

WITH B.J. WORTH

ONE HOUR AUDIO PRESENTATION of how to arrange a compensation package that provides good stewardship and teaches how to legally lessen your tax burden and encourages financial planning for retirement .

Minister's Audio Cassette

Quantity	Price
1 to 2	$9.99
3 to 14	$8.50
15 to 99	$8.00
100 or more	$5.99

Worksheet for Form 2106 for Ministers

Worksheet to Compute Auto Basis

Statement of Depreciation and Cost Recovery

Quantity	Price
1 Form	25¢
25 Forms	$3.00
50 Forms	$5.40
100 Forms	$9.00

Payroll Sheets for Employees of Not-For-Profit Organizations

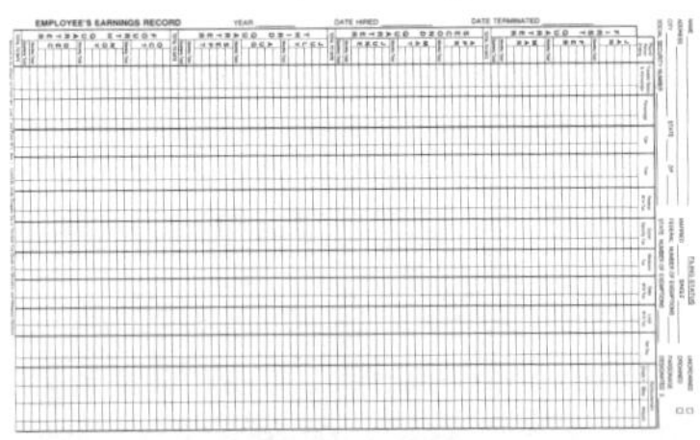

Quantity	Price
1 Sheet	50¢
25 Sheets	$6.00
50 Sheets	$10.80
100 Sheets	$18.00

Income Tax Guide For Ministers and Religious Workers

(Revised annually since 1973)

Quantity	Price
1 to 2	$15.99
3 to 14	$13.60
15 to 99	$12.80
100 to 999	$9.60
1000 or more	call

ORDER FORM

FAX, CALL, MAIL, OR E-MAIL TODAY

Name ____________________

Company or Church Name ____________________

Address ____________________

City, State, Zip ____________________

Send Order To:
Worth Tax & Financial Service
P.O. Box 725
Winona Lake, IN 46590
Fax: (800) 368-0363
Phone: (219) 267-4687
E-Mail: bjworth@worthfinancial.com

METHOD OF PAYMENT:
☐ Check enclosed. Make payable to: Worth Tax & Financial Service
☐ Charge to my credit card. Enter phone number.

Qty	Description	Unit Price	Total
		Total	
		5% Sales Tax (Indiana Only)	
		*Postage & Handling	
		Grand Total	

*** Postage & Handling Schedule**

Order Amount	Charge
$ 0 - $ 5.00	$ 2.00
$ 5.01 - $ 20.00	$ 4.75
$ 20.01 - $ 35.00	$ 6.00
$ 35.01 - $ 50.00	$ 7.00
$ 50.01 - $ 75.00	$ 8.00
$ 75.01 - $100.00	$ 9.00
$100.01 - $150.00	$ 11.00
$150.01 - $200.00	$ 14.00
Over $ 200.00	$ 16.00

☐ Visa ☐ MasterCard ☐ American Express ☐ Discover

Expiration Month Year

Charge this order to my Charge Account as I have indicated to be paid according to the current terms of that Account.

Authorized credit card signature ____________________ Phone ____________________

(Price Subject to Annual Change. Call For Current Prices.)

CONSULTATIONS

We encourage your reading "Income Tax Law For Ministers and Religious Workers" in its entirety. It will answer most of your questions.

We are available for consultation throughout the year and whether you are able to come to our office for an appointment or need to conduct the consultation by phone, or by letter, it is necessary for us to charge for our time. Our fee is $65.00 per hour for consultation.

We prefer phone consultations. Experience has shown us that requests for information and consultation by letter do not provide us with adequate facts. It is often necessary to call and ask for background and facts to give you the correct answer.

Up to 12 minutes -	$13.00
13 to 24 minutes -	$26.00
25 to 36 minutes -	$39.00
37 to 48 minutes -	$52.00
49 to 60 minutes -	$65.00

Please have your charge card number available or be prompt to send amount consultant requests.

For brief informational calls there will be no charge.

PAYROLL SERVICE

We are available for payroll service. It is important to file all government payroll reports and to make deposits on time. Our comprehensive payroll service includes payroll check writing and the preparation of all payday, monthly, quarterly, and annual reports. If you want to write your own checks, then consider using our service for all reporting requirements. Call and ask for more information on how we can help you.

SEMINAR REGISTRATION INFORMATION

Those who attend seminars by Worth Tax & Financial Service are always enthusiastically thankful for the understandable presentation of how they can payless tax legally. Call and ask for details on how you can sponsor a Seminar in your area.

Beverly J Worth will present seminars in person at the locations and times listed on the next page. **Registration** for this seminar is only **$89 per person** when pre-registered ($99.00 at the door.) **$20 off** seminar fee to spouse, or additional persons from same firm or organization. All seminar sessions are from 8:30 a.m. to 4:30 p.m.

* * * *

TAX SEMINARS

For Clergy and Not-For-Profit Organizations

1999-2000 Dates & Locations

Tuesday .... November 23
WARSAW, INDIANA
Ramada Plaza Hotel
2519 E. Center St. (Off US 30)
(219) 269-2323

Tuesday .... November 30
CHATTANOOGA, TENNESSEE
Clarion Hotel
407 Chestnut St. (I-24 exit US 27N to downtown, 1 mile to Exit #1C (4th St.))
(423) 756-5150

Wednesday .... December 1
NASHVILLE, TENNESSEE
Wilson Inn
5566 Franklin Pike Circle (I-65, Exit #74 A)
(615) 221-5001

Thursday .... December 2
LOUISVILLE, KENTUCKY
Signature Inn South
I- 65 & Fern Valley Rd., Exit #128
(502) 968-4100

Tuesday .... December 7
CHICAGO, ILLINOIS
Ramada Inn Chicago South
17040 S. Halsted St. (I-80 & I-294)
(708) 596-1500

Wednesday .... December 8
SPRINGFIELD, ILLINOIS
Signature Inn & Conference Center
I-55 & Stevenson Dr., Exit #94
(217) 529-6611

Thursday .... December 9
TERRE HAUTE, INDIANA
Signature Inn Terre Haute
I-70 & US 41, Exit #7
(812) 238-1461

Monday .... December 13
GRAND RAPIDS, MICHIGAN
Lexington Hotel Suites
5401 28th Street Court, S.E. at I-96
(616) 940-8100

Tuesday .... December 14
DETROIT, MICHIGAN
Ramada Inn - Southfield
17017 West Nine Mile Rd. (5 mi. west of I-75)
(248) 552-7777

Thursday .... December 16
COLUMBUS, OHIO
Signature Inn Columbus
I-270 & Cleveland Ave., Exit #27N
(614) 890-8111

Friday .... December 17
CINCINNATI, OHIO
Signature Inn North
I-275 & I-75/Sharon Rd., Exit #15
(513) 772-7877

Saturday .... December 18
INDIANAPOLIS, INDIANA
Signature Inn Carmel
I-465 & Meridian St., Exit #31
(317) 816-1616

Thursday .... January 20
WARSAW, INDIANA
Ramada Plaza Hotel
2519 E. Center St. (Off US 30)
(219) 269-2323

Friday .... February 25
INDIANAPOLIS, INDIANA
Signature Inn Carmel
I-465 & Meridian St., Exit #31
(317) 816-1616

- **100% MONEY BACK GUARANTEE**
  If you are dissatisfied with this program for any reason, a full-tuition refund will be issued upon written request at the seminar.

$89

See page 130 for details

Recommended for 8 Hours CPE Credits

Worth Tax & Financial Service is registered with the National Association of State Boards of Accountancy as a sponsor of continuing professional education on the National Registry of CPE Sponsors. State boards of accountancy have final authority on the acceptance of individual courses. Complaints regarding sponsors may be addressed to NASBA, 150 Fourth Avenue North, Suite 700, Nashville, TN 37219-2417, (615) 880-4200.

TAX PREPARATION BY MAIL

If you are a typical busy religious worker, you may want to let **Worth Tax & Financial Service** prepare your tax return by mail. We encourage you to take advantage of this special service. Our purpose is to be of service to you in any way possible to prevent a religious worker from being unnecessarily burdened by tax or financial problems.

WHAT YOU SHOULD SEND

1. If you are a minister - **Copy of your employer's PAYROLL RECORD for you**.
2. W-2s showing salaries, 1099s showing interest, dividends, etc., K-1s from partnerships, trusts, etc..
3. **COMPLETED CHECKLIST**. It is very important for you to carefully enter your income and deductions on the CHECKLIST provided in the back of this book. Enter an expense only once. For example, if you enter your home interest under "Parsonage expense," do not enter it again under Schedule A. Keep your receipts and canceled checks.
4. Detailed auto expense for each auto. Send copies of purchase invoices and complete history of auto use. Complete questions on page 12 of CHECKLIST.
5. If you have purchased or sold real estate, send us photocopies of closing statements, contracts and 1099-Bs.
6. We have forms for federal and all states, and you do not need to send your packets. If you want us to prepare city or local tax returns, send us the appropriate forms.
7. Copy of last year's tax return. If you feel your prior year's returns were not correctly prepared, it is possible to file Form 1040X and amend returns for 1996, 1997 and 1998. Corrections can result in substantial refunds, or additional liability.
8. Enter your work, fax and home phone numbers on page 1 of the CHECKLIST and tell us when it is best to reach you. If we feel we need further explanation of your data or that you did not send complete information—**WE WILL CALL. Calls must be at your expense, we will include the phone cost on the invoice for your return.**
9. Your return will be professionally prepared by a tax consultant on the computer and closely checked for accuracy and completeness.

TAX PREP FEES AND PAYMENT

Our fees are very reasonable and are based on the complexity of your return. The cost for a minister's return will average between $90.00 to $225.00. Extra State returns and/or several auto transactions creates a more complex return.

Tax Preparation, Consultation, and orders of books and supplies are all on a **CASH BASIS.** You may pay for our services as follows:

1. **AMERICAN EXPRESS, VISA, MASTERCARD and DISCOVER** convenience is available. Enter your number and expiration date on Page 1 of the Checklist.
2. Ask us to send invoice of fee, and we will hold your return until we receive your check.
3. We can send your completed returns COD. The extra fee for COD in 1999 was $5.00.

SHIPPING INFORMATION

Your finished return will be shipped by U.S Mail-Priority or United Parcel Service. If requesting UPS, be sure and give us a **STREET ADDRESS** as they cannot deliver to a post office box.

WORTH TAX & FINANCIAL SERVICE • P.O. BOX 725 • WINONA LAKE, IN 46590
(219) 267-4687 • (800) 368-0363 (Fax)
E-mail bjworth@worthfinancial.com

Visit our Web home page at http://www.worthfinancial.com